MICROSOFT® CERTIFIED APPLICATION SPECIALIST EXAM REFERENCE FOR MICROSOFT® OFFICE 2007

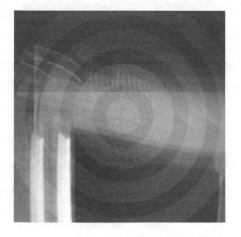

THOMSON
✳
COURSE TECHNOLOGY

Australia • Canada • Mexico • Singapore • Spain • United Kingdom • United States

THOMSON

COURSE TECHNOLOGY
™

Microsoft® Certified Application Specialist Exam Reference for Microsoft® Office 2007 is published by Course Technology.

Senior Acquisitions Editor:
Marjorie Hunt

Senior Product Manager:
Christina Kling Garrett

Product Manager:
Brianna Hawes

Associate Product Manager:
Rebecca Padrick

Editorial Assistant:
Michelle Camisa

Senior Content Project Manager:
Jennifer Goguen McGrail

Contributing Authors:
Rachel Biheller Bunin,
Jennifer T. Campbell,
Barbara Clemens, Pam Conrad,
Lisa Ruffolo

Developmental Editors:
Jeanne Herring, Barbara Waxer

Composition House:
GEX Publishing Services

QA Manuscript Reviewer:
Danielle Shaw

Book Designer:
GEX Publishing Services

ISBN 10: 1-4239-0555-5
ISBN 13: 978-1-4239-0555-4

BRIEF TABLE OF CONTENTS

TABLE OF CONTENTS

ABOUT THIS BOOK

HOW TO USE THIS BOOK

Microsoft® Certified Application Specialist Exam Reference for Microsoft® Office 2007 is a reference tool designed to prepare you for the Microsoft Certified Application Specialist exams. This book assumes that you already understand the concepts that are the basis for the skills covered in this book, and, therefore, the book can be used as a study companion to brush up on skills before taking the exam, or as a desk reference when using Microsoft Office programs.

The Structure of this Book

There are seven chapters in this book. The first chapter, Exam Tips, provides some background information on the Microsoft Certified Application Specialist program, the general process for taking an exam, and some helpful hints for preparing for and successfully passing the exams.

The remaining six chapters each cover a different Microsoft program: Windows Vista, Word, Excel, Access, PowerPoint, and Outlook. Each program-specific chapter begins by covering program basics in a brief Getting Started section. This section covers the basic skills that are not specifically covered in the Microsoft Certified Application Specialist exams, but that are essential to being able to work in the program. Each Getting Started section is followed by the complete set of objectives tested by the Microsoft Certified Application Specialist exams. These sections are labeled and ordered to exactly match the Objectives tested in the Microsoft Certified Application Specialist Exams. Bulleted steps containing clear instructions are provided for each objective.

Because there are often different ways to complete a task, the book provides multiple methods where appropriate, including Ribbon, Shortcut, Menu, Button, Keyboard, Mouse, Toolbar, and Task Pane methods. The Microsoft Certified Application Specialist exams allow you to use any one of these methods, so you can choose the one with which you are most comfortable to complete the task.

Technical Concerns

This book assumes the following regarding your computer's setup:

- ☐ You have installed Office 2007 using the Typical installation.
- ☐ You have installed Windows Vista Ultimate. (Note: You only need Windows Vista Ultimate for the Windows Vista exam section. For all other applications you can use other versions of Windows Vista and Windows XP.)

☐ You have a document open and ready to use when required to work within a specific application. Also, if the steps instruct you to format an Excel worksheet or a Word document, you can format the open document or worksheet in any way you want, choosing options that are appropriate for your needs.

☐ You have an Internet connection to complete certain steps, and you are familiar with how to connect to the Internet.

☐ Your screen may look different from some of the figures in the book depending on your computer's screen resolution and any additional programs you have installed. These differences will not affect your ability to use the book and complete the steps.

ACKNOWLEDGMENTS

Thank you to all of the people who contributed to the process of this book.   We specifically want to thank the team at Course Technology: Marjorie Hunt, Donna Gridley, Brianna Hawes, Jennifer Goguen McGrail, Marisa Taylor, Shelley Palen and Danielle Shaw. We are also grateful to Barbara Waxer and Jeanne Herring for all of their expertise and wonderful suggestions. Lastly, we would like to thank our families; we couldn't have done it without them!

Rachel Biheller Bunin, Jennifer T. Campbell, Barbara Clemens,
Pam Conrad, and Lisa Ruffolo

EXAM TIPS

What Is Microsoft Certified Application Specialist (MCAS) Certification?

Certification is a growing trend in the Information Technology industry whereby a software or hardware company devises and administers exams for users that enable them to demonstrate their abilities to use the software or hardware effectively. By passing a certification exam, users prove their abilities and knowledge of the software or hardware to prospective employers and colleagues.

The Microsoft Certified Application Specialist (MCAS) program is the only comprehensive, performance-based certification program approved by Microsoft to validate desktop computer skills using the Microsoft Office 2007 programs:

☐ Microsoft Word
☐ Microsoft Excel®
☐ Microsoft Access™
☐ Microsoft PowerPoint®
☐ Microsoft Outlook®
☐ Microsoft Windows Vista®

The MCAS program provides computer program literacy, measures proficiency, and identifies opportunities for skills enhancement. Successful candidates receive an MCAS certificate that sets them apart from their peers in the competitive job market. The certificate is a valuable credential recognized worldwide as proof that an individual has the desktop computing skills needed to work productively and efficiently.

By encouraging individuals to develop advanced skills with Microsoft business desktop software, the MCAS program is helping to fill the demand for qualified, knowledgeable people in the workplace. MCAS also helps satisfy an organization's need for a qualitative assessment of employee skills.

1

Exam Tips

The MCAS exams are developed, marketed, and administered by Certiport, Inc., a company that has an exclusive license from Microsoft. The exams are available in 17 different languages and in more than 100 countries. Exams must be taken at an authorized MCAS Certiport Center, which administers exams in a quiet room with the proper hardware and software and has trained personnel to manage and proctor the exams.

Certification Benefits

Achieving MCAS certification in one or several of the Microsoft Office 2007 programs can be beneficial to you and your current or prospective employer. Earning MCAS certification acknowledges that you have the expertise to work with Microsoft Office programs. MCAS-certified individuals report increased competence and productivity with Microsoft Office programs as well as increased credibility with their employers, co-workers, and clients. MCAS certification sets you apart in today's competitive job market, bringing employment opportunities, greater earning potential and career advancement, in addition to increased job satisfaction.

For example, if you have passed the Microsoft Word 2007 MCAS exam and you are interviewing for a job that requires knowledge and use of Word to complete business-related word processing tasks, MCAS certification in Microsoft Word will indicate to your prospective employer that you have the necessary skills to perform that aspect of the job. It also indicates not only that you have a certain level of skill, but that you also have the initiative to prepare for, sign up for, pay for, and take an exam. MCAS certification can help you increase your productivity within your current job and is a great way to enhance your skills without taking courses to obtain a new degree.

The Microsoft Certified Application Specialist (MCAS) Certification Process

There are six steps to successfully completing MCAS certification, as outlined in Table ET-1 and discussed in the remainder of this introductory chapter.

Table ET-1 Microsoft Certified Application Specialist (MCAS) Certification Process

Action	Description
1. Choose an exam	Choose from one of the following exams, based on your skills and interests: • Microsoft Word 2007 • Microsoft Excel 2007 • Microsoft Access 2007 • Microsoft Outlook 2007 • Microsoft PowerPoint 2007 • Microsoft Windows Vista

Exam Tips

Table ET-1 Microsoft Certified Application Specialist (MCAS) Certification Process (continued)

Action	Description
2. Find a testing center	An authorized test center is called a Certiport Center. Verify that there is a Certiport Center near you using the Certiport Center locator at www.certiport.com/Portal/Pages/LocatorView.aspx.
3. Prepare for the exam	Select the method that is appropriate for you, including taking a class or purchasing self-study materials.
4. Take a Pre-Test	Microsoft offers Microsoft Official Pre-Tests, optional online skills assessments for MCAS tests. Microsoft recommends that MCAS candidates take a Pre-Test before taking any exam. • To take a Pre-Test, go to www.certiport.com/portal/ • Click the Take a Pre-Test Now button • Follow the onscreen instructions for purchasing a voucher and taking the test After completing the Pre-Test, you will receive a recommended study and certification plan customized to your needs.

5. Take the exam	• Contact the Certiport Center and make an appointment for the MCAS exam you want to take. Check their payment and exam policies.
	• Purchase an exam voucher
	  1. Go to www.certiport.com/portal/
	  2. Create an account using the username and password of your choice
	  3. At the My Certiport screen, click the Purchase Exam Voucher button and follow the onscreen instructions to purchase a voucher
	• When you go to the Certiport Center to take the test, you *must* bring the following:
	  ✓ A printout of the voucher you purchased online
	  ✓ Your Certiport username and password
	  ✓ A valid picture ID (driver's license or valid passport)
	• Take the exam
	  1. Log in to the exam
	  2. Read the exam directions
	  3. Start the exam

6. Receive exam results	You will find out your results immediately. If you pass, you will receive your certificate two to three weeks after the exam.

1. Choose an Exam

The MCAS certification program offers exams for the five main applications of Microsoft Office 2007: Word, Excel, Access, PowerPoint, and Outlook. You can also take an MCAS exam for Microsoft Windows Vista. Certiport offers one exam for each application. Choose an application that will help you in your current position or job search, or one that tests skills that match your abilities and interests. You can find the list of skills covered in each exam on the MCAS exam Web site. Go to www.microsoft.com/learning/mcpexams/prepare/findexam.mspx, click the appropriate exam link, then click the Requirements link. You can also find more information on the exams at www.certiport.com/microsoftbusiness.

Microsoft Certified Application Professional (MCAP) Certification

The level above MCAS certification is now called the Microsoft Certified Application Professional (MCAP) level. Candidates must successfully complete one job-related skill exam in one of the following areas: Managing Budgets, Managing Presentations, Managing Team Collaboration, and Supporting Organizations. In these exams, candidates must demonstrate that they can use three or more Office applications together to accomplish specific job requirements. It is intended for people working in an office setting who use the Office software programs at least 50% of their day to do their jobs. This book only helps you review for the MCAS exam, not the MCAP exam.

Comparing MCAS and the Microsoft Office Specialist (MOS) Program

The MCAS certification program is similar to the Microsoft Office Specialist (MOS) program, which certifies users in Office 2003 skills. In the MOS program, you can take two levels of exams, called Core and Expert, for Word and Excel. Only one MOS exam level is available for Access and PowerPoint.

MOS and MCAS certification are distinct: If you passed a MOS exam (either Core or Expert) for Office 2003 or an earlier version, that certification is not transferrable to Office 2007 and MCAS certification. You must prepare for and take an MCAS exam, which covers the many new features of Office 2007 applications and Windows Vista.

If you have taken a Microsoft Office Specialist (MOS) exam for an Office 2003 application, you will see similarities: The MOS and MCAS exams are similar in length and question type. However, the MCAS exam objectives are not divided into Core or Expert; there is only one MCAS exam on each application.

2. Find a Testing Center

You must take MCAS certification exams at an authorized testing center, called a Certiport Center. Certiport Centers are located in educational institutions, corporate training centers, and other such locations. Verify that there is a testing center close to you using the Certiport Center locator at www.certiport.com/portal/Pages/LocatorView.aspx, or use the Microsoft Learning test locator at www.microsoft.com/learning/mcp/OfficeSpecialist/OfficeSpecialist_locator.mspx.

Once you locate a Certiport Center near you, you will need to call and schedule a time to take the exam. Some centers may offer walk-in exams, but be sure to call and check the policies of the center you choose. Exams are offered in multiple languages and in several countries, although each site might not offer all languages. If you require a specific language, you should check with the Certiport Center before registering for the exam.

3. Prepare for the Exam

How you prepare for an exam depends on your current skill level, which you can determine by reading through the exam objectives and taking a Pre-Test. (See the "Choose an Exam" section above for information on locating exam objectives. See "Take a Pre-Test" below for more information on Pre-Tests.) If you are new to an Office program, you might want to take an introductory class and learn the program in its entirety. If you are already familiar with the program, you may only need to purchase study materials and learn unfamiliar skills on your own. If you use the program regularly, you might only need to review the skills on the objectives list for the exam you choose and brush up on those few that are problem areas for you or that you don't use regularly.

Take a Class

Taking a class is a good way to help prepare you for a certification exam, especially if you are a beginner. If you are an experienced user and know the basics, consider taking an advanced class. The benefits of taking a class include having an instructor as a resource, having the support of your classmates, and receiving study materials such as a lab book. Some classes are even geared specifically towards taking and passing a certification exam, and are taught by instructors who have passed the exam themselves. Your local community college, career education center, or community/continuing education programs will most likely offer such courses. You can also check the Certiport Center in your area. Classes range from one day to several weeks in duration. You could also take a distance learning class from an online university or through one of the local options listed above. Distance learning offers the flexibility of learning from home on your own time, while teaching the same skills as a traditional classroom course.

Purchase Materials for Self-Study

You can prepare on your own to take an exam by purchasing materials at your local bookstore or from an online retailer. To ensure that the study materials you are purchasing are well-suited to your goal of passing the

Exam Tips

MCAS certification exam, you should consider the following: favorable reviews (reviews are often available when purchasing online); a table of contents that covers the skills you want to master; and the MCAS seal. The MCAS seal indicates that Microsoft has confirmed that the book accurately covers all of the skills for a particular MCAS exam and that it provides testing material on these skills. The seal certifies that Microsoft recognizes the book as being an adequate tool for certification preparation. (Because this book is designed as a reference guide and does not contain material that tests your knowledge of skills, it does not have the MCAS seal.) Depending on your abilities, you might want to purchase a book that teaches you the skills and concepts step-by-step and then tests your knowledge. If you only require a refresher, this book is all that you need.

Here is a list of suggested products published by Course Technology that you can use for self-study. You can purchase these books online at www.course.com.

- □ **Illustrated Series**: For detailed information on this Course Technology book series, visit www.course.com/illustrated/
  - Microsoft Office Word 2007 – Illustrated Complete (ISBN: 978-1-4239-0527-1)
  - Microsoft Office Excel 2007 – Illustrated Complete (ISBN: 978-1-4239-0522-6)
  - Microsoft Office Access 2007 – Illustrated Complete (ISBN: 978-1-4239-0519-9)
  - Microsoft Office PowerPoint 2007 – Illustrated Introductory (ISBN: 978-1-4239-0524-0)
  - Illustrated Course Guide: Microsoft Office Word 2007 Basic (1 of 3, ISBN: 978-1-4239-0539-4)
  - Illustrated Course Guide: Microsoft Office Word 2007 Intermediate (2 of 3, ISBN: 978-1-4239-0540-0)
  - Illustrated Course Guide: Microsoft Office Word 2007 Advanced (3 of 3, ISBN: 978-1-4239-0541-7)
  - Illustrated Course Guide: Microsoft Office Excel 2007 Basic (1 of 3, ISBN: 978-1-4239-0534-9)
  - Illustrated Course Guide: Microsoft Office Excel 2007 Intermediate (2 of 3, ISBN: 978-1-4239-0535-6)
  - Illustrated Course Guide: Microsoft Office Excel 2007 Advanced (3 of 3, ISBN: 978-1-4239-0536-3)
  - Illustrated Course Guide: Microsoft Office Access 2007 Basic (1 of 3, ISBN: 978-1-4239-0531-8)
  - Illustrated Course Guide: Microsoft Office Access 2007 Intermediate (2 of 3, ISBN: 978-1-4239-0532-5)
  - Illustrated Course Guide: Microsoft Office Access 2007 Advanced (3 of 3, ISBN: 978-1-4239-0533-2)
  - Illustrated Course Guide: Microsoft Office PowerPoint 2007 Basic (1 of 2, ISBN: 978-1-4239-0537-0)
  - Illustrated Course Guide: Microsoft Office PowerPoint 2007 Advanced (2 of 2, ISBN: 978-1-4239-0538-7)
- □ **New Perspectives Series**: For detailed information on this Course Technology book series, visit www.course.com/newperspectives/
  - New Perspectives on Microsoft Office Word 2007, Comprehensive (ISBN: 978-1-4239-0582-0)

- New Perspectives on Microsoft Office Excel 2007, Comprehensive (ISBN: 978-1-4239-0585-1)
- New Perspectives on Microsoft Office Access 2007, Comprehensive (ISBN: 978-1-4239-0589-9)
- New Perspectives on Microsoft Office PowerPoint 2007, Comprehensive (ISBN: 978-1-4239-0593-6)
- New Perspectives on Microsoft Windows Vista, Comprehensive (ISBN: 978-1-4239-0602-5)

☐ **Shelly Cashman Series**: For detailed information on this Course Technology book series, visit www.scseries.com
  - Microsoft Office Word 2007: Comprehensive Concepts and Techniques (ISBN: 978-1-4188-4338-0)
  - Microsoft Office Excel 2007: Comprehensive Concepts and Techniques (ISBN: 978-1-4188-4344-1)
  - Microsoft Office Access 2007: Comprehensive Concepts and Techniques (ISBN: 978-1-4188-4341-0)
  - Microsoft Office PowerPoint 2007: Comprehensive Concepts and Techniques (ISBN: 978-1-4188-4347-2)
  - Microsoft Office 2007: Introductory Concepts and Techniques, Windows Vista Edition (1 of 3, ISBN: 978-1-4239-1228-6)
  - Microsoft Office 2007: Advanced Concepts and Techniques (2 of 3, ISBN: 978-1-4188-4332-8)
  - Microsoft Office 2007: Post-Advanced Concepts and Techniques (3 of 3, ISBN: 978-1-4188-4334-2)

4. Take a Pre-Test

Consider taking an online Pre-Test. A Pre-Test lets you determine the areas you should brush up on before taking the certification exam. It is a self-assessment that tests you on the exam objectives and indicates your level of proficiency. After taking a Pre-Test, you will receive a customized learning plan, which is a report that recommends a course of study, including courseware materials appropriate to your needs. You can register and pay for a Pre-Test voucher at www.certiport.com/portal/.

5. Take the Exam

Make an Appointment

Contact a Certiport Center near you and make an appointment for the MCAS exam you want to take. The Certiport Center staff can answer any questions you may have about scheduling, vouchers, and exam administration. Check the center's policies about payment and about changed or missed appointments, in case something comes up that prevents you from taking the exam at the appointed time. Verify the materials that you should bring with you when you take the exam. While some centers may accept your voucher as proof of payment, other centers may have other fees and may require that you pay them directly for the test itself.

Purchase an Exam Voucher

If your Certiport Center verifies that you need a voucher to take the test, go online and purchase a voucher from Certiport. The voucher is your proof that you registered and paid for the exam in advance. To pay for the exam and obtain a voucher, go to www.certiport.com/portal/. Click the Login link and create a user account with a username and password of your choice. At the My Certiport screen, click the Purchase Exam Voucher button and follow the onscreen instructions to purchase a voucher. You can charge the exam fee on any major credit card.

Take the Exam

The day of the exam, prepare yourself by ensuring you have slept well the previous night, have eaten, and that you are dressed comfortably. Arrive at the test site a half an hour before the scheduled exam time to ensure you have plenty of time to check in with the center, acquaint yourself with your surroundings, and complete the login information.

You must bring the following to the Certiport Center on the day of the test:

- ☐ Your **voucher**, which is a printout of the electronic document you received when you paid for the test online. You will need to enter the voucher number when you log in to the test. If necessary, check with the Certiport Center to see if bringing the voucher number, rather than a printout, is acceptable.
- ☐ Your **Certiport username and password**, which you will also have to enter at test login. You will have created a username and password when you paid for the voucher online.
- ☐ A valid **picture ID** (driver's license or valid passport).

If you forget any of these required items, you may not be permitted to take the exam, and will need to reschedule your test for another time.

You may not bring any study or reference materials into the exam. You may not bring writing implements, calculators, or other materials into the test room. The Certiport Center administrator may give you a small dry-erase board and marker for note-taking during the exam, but these must be returned to the proctor when you are finished.

Depending on the voucher you have purchased, you may be allowed to take the exam one more time without any additional fee (a "free retake") if you do not pass the exam the first time. However, if you need to try a third time, you will need to purchase another voucher. No refunds will be given if you do not pass, and you may also be charged for a missed exam appointment, depending on the Certiport Center's policies.

Each exam is administered within a functional copy of the Microsoft program corresponding to the exam that you are taking. The exam tests your knowledge of the program by requiring you to complete specific tasks in the program.

Exam Specifics

☐ **Proctor**: A proctor will take you to the test room containing one or more computers and make sure you complete the login process and that the test is running correctly. He or she will then leave the room, but will remain available nearby in case you run into technical difficulties. Before the proctor leaves, be sure you know where he or she will be located, so you can find him or her quickly if necessary.

☐ **Logging in**: The first step is to log in to the exam. You will need to complete the candidate information section, which includes your Certiport username and password, and the necessary information for completing and mailing your certificate. Then the proctor will assist you in starting the exam.

☐ **Reading the instructions**: The first screens you see after you log in are directions and test-taking tips. You should read all of these, as this information will help you become familiar with the exam environment. The timed portion of the exam does not include your reading of these start-up directional screens, so take your time and make sure you understand the directions before starting the exam.

☐ **The "live" program environment**: The exam is "live in the program," which means that you will work with an actual document, spreadsheet, presentation, etc. and must perform tasks on that document.

☐ **Completing tasks**: You can use any valid method available in the program to complete a task, including keyboard shortcuts. For example, if asked to center text in a Word document, you can click a button on the Ribbon or press [Ctrl][E] to center the text. If you press [Spacebar] repeatedly to move the text to the center of the document, however, you will lose credit, as this is not an appropriate way to center text.

☐ **Using the Reset button**: If you start a question with incorrect steps and want to correct them, you can use the Reset button to return the document to its original state and redo the question from the beginning. Keep in mind that if you click the Reset button, all of your work on that question will be erased and the clock will not restart.

☐ **Saving questions for later**: If you come upon a difficult question that you can't answer readily, you can click a Skip button so you can come back to it after you complete all the other questions, assuming you have time left. You cannot go back to a previous question unless you have marked it as a question you want to return to later. If you are truly stuck, make your best guess and move on.

☐ **Viewing the exam clock**: There is an exam clock on the screen that starts and stops while each question is loading, so the speed with which each question is loaded does not affect the time you have to complete the questions. (In other words, if you are completing the test on a slow computer you will not be penalized.) The total time you spend taking the exam will vary based on the speed of your computer, but the actual time you have to complete the exam will be consistent with anyone else taking the exam.

- ☐ **No Office Online Help**: You cannot use Office Online Help during the exam. The Help feature is disabled during the exam.
- ☐ **Dealing with problems**: If something happens to the exam environment – for instance, if the program freezes or if there is a power failure – contact the exam proctor. He or she will restart the exam and the exam clock where you were before the exam was interrupted. Such interruptions will not count against you. If there are other test-takers in the same room, it's best not to disturb them with questions.

Exam Tips

- ☐ **Pace yourself**: The overall exam is timed, although there is no time limit for each question. Most exams take 50 minutes or less and cover 30 to 35 questions, but the allotted time depends on the subject and level. If you do not complete all of the exam questions within the given timeframe, you will lose points for any unan-swered questions. Because you have to complete the exam in a des-ignated amount of time, you will want to consider the amount of time you have per question. You will not be graded on your effi-ciency (i.e., the time you take per question), but remember that if you spend a lot of time on one question, that leaves you with less time for other questions. Keep in mind that you can always save a particularly difficult question for the end of the test.

- ☐ **Complete each test item**: Each question is comprised of one or more tasks listed in a pane at the bottom of the screen. You should complete the tasks in the order listed and make sure that you com-plete all of the tasks. *You may need to scroll the pane to read all of the tasks in a question.* It is a good idea to reread the entire ques-tion before advancing to the next question to ensure that you have completed all tasks. You will receive only partial credit for any question that you do not complete in its entirety.

- ☐ **Close dialog boxes**: Be sure you have closed all dialog boxes that you might have opened during the course of completing a task. Making the correct dialog box selections is not sufficient; you must always click OK or a similar button to close the dialog box(es) and fully complete the task.

- ☐ **Avoid additional tasks**: The end result of your actions is scored when you advance to the next question. You will not lose points for any extra mouse clicks or movements as they relate to the task, but you should undo any additional changes that are not part of the task that you might accidentally apply to the document. For exam-ple, if the task has you bold a word and you both bold and italicize it, you should undo the italicizing of the word. If you do start a test item with an incorrect action, remember that you can use the Reset button to begin that question again.

- ☐ **Type carefully**: If the task requires typing, you will lose points for spelling mistakes.

6. Receive Exam Results

- □ Exam results appear on the screen as soon as you complete the exam.

- □ You will receive a printout of your score to take with you. If you need additional copies, go to www.certiport.com/portal, and then log in and go to My Certiport, where you can always access your exam results. If you pass the exam, you will receive an official certificate in the mail in approximately two to three weeks.

- □ The exam results are confidential.

- □ If you do not pass, keep in mind that the exams are challenging. Do not become discouraged. If you purchased a voucher with a free retake, that might be all you need to pass. Study your exam results and note areas you need to work on. You can retake the exam as many times as you want, although you may need to purchase an additional voucher for the retake. In addition, candidates who wish to retake the exam a second or subsequent time may need to wait a specific time period before retaking the exam. Check your Certiport Center's exam retake policies.

Exam Tips

MICROSOFT WINDOWS VISTA
EXAM REFERENCE
Getting Started with Windows Vista

The Windows Vista Microsoft Certified Application Specialist (MCAS) exam assumes a basic level of proficiency in Windows Vista. This section is intended to help you reference these basic skills while you are preparing to take the Windows Vista MCAS exam.

□ Starting and turning off Windows Vista
□ Viewing the Windows Vista desktop
□ Starting a program
□ Navigating to a folder
□ Getting Help

START AND TURN OFF WINDOWS VISTA

Start Windows Vista

Shortcut Method

□ Turn on your computer
□ On the Welcome screen, click an account name and enter the appropriate password, if necessary

Turn Off Windows Vista

Shortcut Method

□ Click the **Start button** 🌐 on the taskbar
□ Click the **arrow button** ▶ next to the Lock button 🔒 , then click **Shut Down**

OR

□ Click the **Start button** 🌐 on the taskbar
□ Click the **Power button** ⏻ to put the computer to sleep

VIEW THE WINDOWS VISTA DESKTOP

Navigate the Desktop

Shortcut Method

☐ Follow the steps in bullets 1-2 of the Start Windows Vista Shortcut Method above

☐ Point to icons and other objects to see their ScreenTips on the desktop

☐ Refer to Table WIN-1 for descriptions of the items shown in Figure WIN-1

Figure WIN-1 Windows Vista Desktop

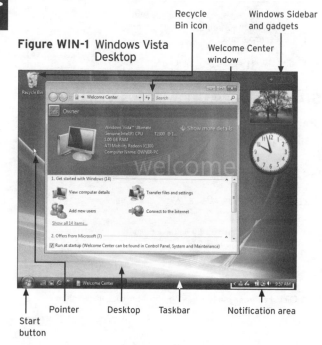

Table WIN-1 Windows Vista Desktop

Element	Description
Desktop	Your workplace on the screen
Icon	Small picture that represents an object available to your computer
Notification area	Area that displays icons corresponding to services running in the background, such as an Internet connection
Pointer	Small object, such as an arrow, that moves on the screen when you move the pointing device
Sidebar and gadgets	Area of the desktop where Windows stores gadgets—small programs such as sticky notes and clocks
Start button	Button that provides access to Windows Vista programs, documents, and information on the Internet
Taskbar	Strip that contains buttons providing quick access to common tools and running programs
Welcome Center window	Window that lists tasks first-time users can perform to quickly set up their computers

Vista

START A PROGRAM

Shortcut Method

☐ Click the **Start button** 🔵 on the taskbar, then click the program name

OR

☐ Click the **Start button** 🔵 on the taskbar, point to **All Programs**, navigate to a program folder, if necessary, then click the program name

OR

☐ Click the **Start button** 🔵 on the taskbar, begin typing the program name in the Start Search text box, then click the program name

NAVIGATE TO A FOLDER

Address Bar Method

☐ If necessary, click the **Start button** 🔵 on the taskbar, then click a folder name

☐ To navigate to a subfolder of the current folder, click the **arrow button** ▶ to the right of the folder name, then click a location

☐ To navigate to the folder containing the current folder, click its name in the Address bar

OR

☐ Click the **chevron button** ≪ , then click a location

☐ To navigate to a folder you opened recently, click the **Address bar arrow**, then click a location

OR

☐ Click the **Recent Pages button** ▾ , then click a location

Shortcut Method

☐ If necessary, click the **Start button** 🏁 on the taskbar, then click a folder name

☐ In the folder window, double-click a folder in the right pane

OR

☐ Click the **Folders bar** to open the Folders list in the Navigation Pane, if necessary, click an **expand icon** ▷ as necessary to find the appropriate folder, then click the appropriate folder icon

GET HELP

Toolbar Method

☐ Click the **Get help button** 💡 in a folder window

Shortcut Method

☐ Click the **Start button** 🏁 on the taskbar, then click **Help and Support**

OR

☐ Press **[F1]**

☐ Use Table WIN-2 as a reference to select the most appropriate way to get help using the Windows Vista Help window

Table WIN-2 Windows Vista Help Window Options

Option	To use
Search Help	Type one or more keywords, then press **[Enter]** or click the **Search Help button** 🔍
Home page	Click the **Home page button** 🏠 to open the Windows Help and Support Home page In the Find an answer section, click a topic category, then click a topic; or click a link in the Ask someone section to get help from another person; or click a link in the Information from Microsoft section to access online information from Microsoft
Table of Contents	Click the **Browse Help button** 📋 to open the Contents page, click a topic category, then click a topic

WINDOWS VISTA EXAM REFERENCE

Objectives:

1. Protecting your computer
2. Managing mobile and remote computing
3. Managing software, disks, and devices
4. Managing files and folders
5. Collaborating with other people
6. Customizing your Windows Vista experience
7. Optimizing and troubleshooting your computer

Note: Depending on the security settings on your computer, as you change Windows settings, a dialog box might open requesting an Administrator password or confirmation. To respond to the dialog box, enter the password or click the **Continue button**.

WINDOWS VISTA OBJECTIVE 1: PROTECTING YOUR COMPUTER

MANAGE WINDOWS FIREWALL

Display Windows Firewall Information

Shortcut Method

☐ Click the **Start button** 🔘 on the taskbar, then click **Control Panel**

☐ If the Control Panel opens in Classic view, double-click **Security Center**
OR
☐ If the Control Panel opens in Category view, click **Security**, then click **Security Center**

☐ In the left pane of the Windows Security Center window, click **Windows Firewall**

Allow Programs Through Windows Firewall

Shortcut Method

☐ Follow the steps in bullets 1–4 of the Display Windows Firewall Information Shortcut Method above

☐ In the left pane of the Windows Security Center window, click **Allow a program through Windows Firewall**

☐ In the Windows Firewall Settings dialog box, click the **Exceptions tab**, if necessary

☐ Click a **check box** for the program you want to allow through Windows Firewall

☐ Click **OK**

MANAGE MALICIOUS SOFTWARE (ALSO CALLED MALWARE) PROTECTION

Display Antivirus Software Status

Shortcut Method

- [ ] Click the **Start button** 🔵 on the taskbar, then click **Control Panel**
- [ ] If the Control Panel opens in Classic view, double-click **Security Center**

  OR
- [ ] If the Control Panel opens in Category view, click **Security**, then click **Security Center**

Display Windows Defender Status

Shortcut Method

- [ ] Click the **Start button** 🔵 on the taskbar, then click **Control Panel**
- [ ] If the Control Panel opens in Classic view, double-click **Security Center**

  OR
- [ ] If the Control Panel opens in Category view, click **Security**, then click **Security Center**
- [ ] In the left pane of the Windows Security Center window, click **Windows Defender**

Remove a Program Blocked by Windows Defender

Shortcut Method

- [ ] Follow the steps in bullets 1–4 of the Display Windows Defender Status Shortcut Method above
- [ ] In the Windows Defender window, click the **Tools button**
- [ ] On the Tools and Settings page, click **Quarantined items**
- [ ] In the Quarantined items list, click a program
- [ ] Click **Remove**

Restore a Program Blocked by Windows Defender

Shortcut Method

- [ ] Follow the steps in bullets 1–4 of the Remove a Program Blocked by Windows Defender Shortcut Method above
- [ ] Click **Restore**

Manage Software with Windows Defender

Shortcut Method

- [ ] Follow the steps in bullets 1–4 of the Display Windows Defender Status Shortcut Method above
- [ ] In the Windows Defender window, click the **Tools button**
- [ ] On the Tools and Settings page, click **Software Explorer**
- [ ] Click the **Category button arrow**, if necessary, to display the software you want to manage
- [ ] Click a program
- [ ] Click **Remove**, **Disable**, or **Enable**

Vista

Use Windows Defender to Monitor Programs

Shortcut Method

- ☐ Log on to Windows Vista as an Administrator
- ☐ Follow the steps in bullets 1-4 of the Display Windows Defender Status Shortcut Method above
- ☐ In the Windows Defender window, click the **Tools button**
- ☐ On the Tools and Settings page, click **Options**
- ☐ On the Options page, scroll down to the Administrator options, then click to select the **Use Windows Defender check box**, if necessary
- ☐ Select other settings to determine how and when you want Windows Defender to monitor programs
- ☐ Click **Save**

Specify that Windows Defender Not Monitor a Program

Shortcut Method

- ☐ When Windows Defender opens the Alert dialog box to alert you about a program, click **Action** on the menu bar, then click **Always Allow**

CONFIGURE WINDOWS UPDATE SETTINGS

Select Windows Update Settings

Shortcut Method

- ☐ Click the **Start button** 🌐 on the taskbar, then click **Control Panel**
- ☐ If the Control Panel opens in Classic view, double-click **Security Center**

  OR
- ☐ If the Control Panel opens in Category view, click **Security**, then click **Security Center**
- ☐ In the left pane of the Windows Security Center window, click **Windows Update**
- ☐ In the left pane of the Windows Update window, click **Change settings**
- ☐ In the Change settings dialog box, select the update options you want to set
- ☐ Click **OK**

Update Windows Manually

Shortcut Method

- ☐ Follow the steps in bullets 1-4 of the Select Windows Update Settings Shortcut Method above
- ☐ In the left pane of the Windows Update window, click **Check for updates**

Display Windows Updates

Shortcut Method

☐ Follow the steps in bullets 1–4 of the Select Windows Update Settings Shortcut Method above
☐ In the left pane of the Windows Update window, click **View update history**

LOCK A COMPUTER

Set the Screen Saver Delay Time

Shortcut Method

☐ Right-click a blank area of the desktop, then click **Personalize**
☐ In the Personalization window, click **Screen Saver**
☐ In the Screen Saver Settings dialog box, change the value in the Wait box
☐ Click **OK**

Lock a Computer Manually

Shortcut Method

☐ Click the **Start button** 🕮 on the taskbar, then click the **Lock button** 🔒

MANAGE WINDOWS INTERNET EXPLORER SECURITY

Select Windows Internet Explorer Security Settings

Shortcut Method

☐ Click the **Start button** 🕮 on the taskbar, then click **Internet Explorer**
☐ Click the **Tools button** on the Internet Explorer toolbar, then click **Internet Options**
☐ In the Internet Options dialog box, select the security options you want to set or change
☐ Click **OK**

Turn on the Phishing Filter

Shortcut Method

☐ Click the **Start button** 🕮 on the taskbar, then click **Internet Explorer**
☐ Click the **Tools button** on the Internet Explorer toolbar, point to **Phishing Filter**, then click **Turn On Automatic Website Checking**, if necessary

Select Phishing Filter Settings

Shortcut Method

☐ Click the **Start button** 🕮 on the taskbar, then click **Internet Explorer**
☐ Click the **Tools button** on the Internet Explorer toolbar, point to **Phishing Filter**, then click **Phishing Filter Settings**

□ Click the **Advanced tab** in the Internet Options dialog box, if necessary, then select the phishing options you want to set or change

Manually Check a Web Site for Phishing Activity

Shortcut Method

□ Click the **Start button** on the taskbar, then click **Internet Explorer**
□ Click the **Tools button** on the Internet Explorer toolbar, point to **Phishing Filter**, then click **Check This Website**

Select Settings for History and Temporary Internet Files

Shortcut Method

□ Click the **Start button** on the taskbar, then click **Internet Explorer**
□ Click the **Tools button** on the Internet Explorer toolbar, then click **Internet Options**
□ Click the **General tab** in the Internet Options dialog box, if necessary
□ In the Browsing history section, click **Settings**
□ In the Temporary Internet Files and History Settings dialog box, set or change options, then click **OK**

Select Privacy Settings

Shortcut Method

□ Click the **Start button** on the taskbar, then click **Internet Explorer**
□ Click the **Tools button** on the Internet Explorer toolbar, then click **Internet Options**
□ Click the **Privacy tab** in the Internet Options dialog box, if necessary
□ Set or change privacy options, then click **OK**

Block or Allow Pop-Up Windows

Shortcut Method

□ Click the **Start button** on the taskbar, then click **Internet Explorer**
□ Click the **Tools button** on the Internet Explorer toolbar, then click **Internet Options**
□ Click the **Privacy tab** in the Internet Options dialog box, if necessary
□ To block most pop-up windows, click the **Turn on Pop-up Blocker check box**, if necessary
□ To allow a pop-up window, click **Settings**, enter the address of the Web site to allow, click **Add**, then click **Close**
□ Click **OK**

CONFIGURE LOCAL USER ACCOUNTS

Create a Standard Account

Shortcut Method

□ Click the **Start button** on the taskbar, then click **Control Panel**
□ If the Control Panel opens in Classic view, double-click **User Accounts**

OR

☐ If the Control Panel opens in Category view, click **User Accounts and Family Safety**, then click **User Accounts**
☐ In the User Accounts window, click **Manage another account**
☐ In the Manage Accounts window, click **Create a new account**
☐ In the Create New Account window, enter the name of the account, click the **Standard user option button**, if necessary, then click **Create Account**
☐ Click **OK**

Create a Password for a Standard Account

Shortcut Method

☐ Log on to Windows Vista using a Standard account
☐ Follow the steps in bullets 1–3 of the Create a Standard Account Shortcut Method above
☐ In the User Accounts window, click **Create a password for your account**
☐ Click in the New password text box, then type your password
☐ Click in the Confirm new password text box, then type your password again
☐ Click in the Type a password hint text box, then type a hint to help you remember your password
☐ Click **Create password**

Require Users to Change Passwords the Next Time They Log on to Windows Vista

Shortcut Method

☐ Click the **Start button** 🅦 on the taskbar, then type **MMC** in the Start Search box
☐ Click **MMC** in the list of programs
☐ If the Local Users and Groups snap-in is not installed, click **File** on the menu bar, click **Add/Remove Snap-in**, click **Local Users and Groups**, click **Add**, make sure the Local computer option button is selected, click **Finish**, then click **OK** to add the snap-in to the Microsoft Management Console (MMC)
☐ In the left pane of the MMC, click the **expand icon** ▷ next to Local Users and Groups, then double-click the **Users folder**
☐ Double-click **New User** in the center pane
☐ Click the **User must change password at next logon check box** to select this option, if necessary
☐ Click **OK**
☐ Close the Microsoft Management Console, then click **Yes**

Disable an Account

Shortcut Method

☐ Follow the steps in bullets 1–4 of the Require Users to Change Passwords the Next Time They Log on to Windows Vista Shortcut Method above
☐ In the User Accounts window, click **Create a password for your account**

☐ Double-click the account name in the center pane
☐ In the account's Properties dialog box, click the **General tab**, if necessary
☐ Click the **Account is disabled check box**
☐ Click **OK**
☐ Close the Microsoft Management Console, then click **Yes**

Vista

Vista

Windows Vista Objective 2: Managing Mobile and Remote Computing

Manage the Computer Power State

Note: The skills described in this section apply to mobile computers, not desktop computers.

Select a Power Plan

Shortcut Method

☐ Click the **Start button** 🔵 on the taskbar, point to **All Programs**, click **Accessories**, then click **Windows Mobility Center**

☐ Click the **Change power settings button**, then click a power plan, referring to Table WIN-3 to select an appropriate power plan

OR

☐ Click the **battery icon** in the notification area of the taskbar

☐ Click a power plan option button, referring to Table WIN-3 to select an appropriate power plan

Table WIN-3 Power Plans

Power Plan	Description
Power saver	Saves power on your computer by reducing system performance and extending battery life
High performance	Provides the highest level of performance on your mobile computer but consumes the most energy
Balanced	Balances energy consumption and system performance by adjusting your computer's processor speed to match your activity

Select Power Settings

Shortcut Method

☐ Click the **Start button** 🔵 on the taskbar, then click **Control Panel**

☐ If the Control Panel opens in Classic view, double-click **Power Options**

OR

☐ If the Control Panel opens in Category view, click **Hardware and Sound**, then click **Power Options**

☐ Click **Change plan settings** for the power plan you want to modify

☐ Click a button for a power setting, then click the amount of time to wait before applying the setting

☐ Click **Change advanced power settings**, if necessary, expand an advanced setting, change the setting, then click **OK**

☐ Click **Save changes**

Put a Mobile Computer to Sleep

Shortcut Method

☐ Press the **power button** on the mobile PC

OR

☐ Close the lid on the mobile PC

OR

☐ Click the **Start button** 🌀 on the taskbar, point to the **arrow button** ▶ next to the Lock button 🔒, then click **Sleep**

Put a Mobile Computer into Hibernation

Shortcut Method

☐ Click the **Start button** 🌀 on the taskbar, point to the **arrow button** ▶ next to the Lock button 🔒, then click **Hibernate**

MANAGE NETWORK CONNECTIONS

Select a Network Connection

Ribbon Method

☐ Click the **Start button** 🌀 on the taskbar, then click **Control Panel**
☐ If the Control Panel opens in Classic view, double-click **Network and Sharing Center**

OR

☐ If the Control Panel opens in Category view, click **Network and Internet**, then click **Network and Sharing Center**
☐ In the left pane of the Network and Sharing Center window, click **Connect to a network** in the Network and Sharing Center window
☐ In the Connect to a network window, click a network, then click **Connect**

Detect and Connect to a Wireless Network

Shortcut Method

☐ Click the **Start button** 🌀 on the taskbar, then click **Connect to**
☐ In the Show list, click **Wireless**
☐ Click a wireless network, then click **Connect**
☐ Enter your password, if necessary, then click **Close**

Check the Wireless Network Connection

Shortcut Method

☐ Click the **network icon** 🖳 in the notification area of the taskbar; a small notification window shows the status of your network connection

Connected to a Wired Network Remotely

Ribbon Method

□ Click the **Start button** 🔵 on the taskbar, then click **Control Panel**
□ If the Control Panel opens in Classic view, double-click **Network and Sharing Center**

OR

□ If the Control Panel opens in Category view, click **Network and Internet**, then click **Network and Sharing Center**
□ In the left pane of the Network and Sharing Center window, click **Set up a connection or network**
□ Click **Connect to a workplace**, then click **Next**
□ To connect to the VPN using the Internet, click **Use my Internet connection (VPN)**
□ Enter the Internet address of the VPN server
□ Enter the Destination name of the VPN server, then click **Next**
□ Enter your user name and password, then click **Create**
□ After the wizard creates the connection, click **Connect now**, if necessary, to connect to the network

---

MANAGE REMOTE ACCESS TO YOUR COMPUTER

Allow Remote Desktop Connections

□ Click the **Start button** 🔵 on the taskbar, then click **Control Panel**
□ If the Control Panel opens in Classic view, double-click **System**

OR

□ If the Control Panel opens in Category view, click **System and Maintenance**, then click **System**
□ In the left pane of the System window, click **Remote settings**
□ Click the **Allow Remote Assistance connections to this computer check box**, if necessary, to insert a check mark
□ Click **OK**

Specify Who Can Connect Remotely

Shortcut Method

□ Click the **Start button** 🔵 on the taskbar, then click **Control Panel**
□ If the Control Panel opens in Classic view, double-click **System**

OR

□ If the Control Panel opens in Category view, click **System and Maintenance**, then click **System**
□ In the left pane of the System window, click **Remote settings**
□ Click the **Allow connections only from computers running Remote Desktop with Network Level Authentication (more secure) option button**
□ Click **Select Users**
□ In the Remote Desktop Users dialog box, click **Add**, if necessary, select a user account, then click **OK**
□ Click **OK** to close the Remote Desktop Users dialog box
□ Click **OK** to close the System Properties dialog box

Disable Remote Desktop Connections

Shortcut Method

- ☐ Click the **Start button** 🔵 on the taskbar, then click **Control Panel**
- ☐ If the Control Panel opens in Classic view, double-click **System**

  OR

- ☐ If the Control Panel opens in Category view, click **System and Maintenance**, then click **System**
- ☐ In the left pane of the System window, click **Remote settings**
- ☐ Click the **Allow Remote Assistance connections to this computer check box**, if necessary, to remove the check mark
- ☐ Click **OK** to close the Remote Desktop Users dialog box
- ☐ Click **OK** to close the System Properties dialog box

CONNECT TO ANOTHER COMPUTER

Use Remote Desktop Connection to Connect to Another Computer

Ribbon Method

- ☐ Click the **Start button** 🔵 on the taskbar, point to **All Programs**, click **Accessories**, then click **Remote Desktop Connection**
- ☐ In the Computer text box, type the name of the computer to which you want to connect
- ☐ Click **Connect**
- ☐ Enter your user name and password, then click **OK**
- ☐ Click **Close**

Map a Drive to Connect to Another Computer

Ribbon Method

- ☐ Click the **Start button** 🔵 on the taskbar, then click **Computer**
- ☐ Press **[Alt]** to open the menu bar
- ☐ Click **Tools** on the menu bar, then click **Map Network Drive**
- ☐ Click **Browse**
- ☐ Navigate to, then click the folder to which you want to map a drive
- ☐ Click the **Reconnect at logon check box**, if appropriate
- ☐ Click **OK**
- ☐ Click **Finish**

Browse a Network to Connect to Another Computer

Shortcut Method

- ☐ Click the **Start button** 🔵 on the taskbar, then click **Network**
- ☐ In the Network window, double-click a computer icon

Access Shared Folders

Shortcut Method

□ Click the **Start button** 🌐 on the taskbar, then click **Control Panel**
□ If the Control Panel opens in Classic view, double-click **Network and Sharing Center**

OR

□ If the Control Panel opens in Category view, click **Network and Internet**, then click **Network and Sharing Center**
□ In the Sharing and Discovery section, click the **expand icon** ⊗ to the right of Public folder sharing, then click the **Turn on sharing so anyone with network access can open, change, and create files option button**
□ Click **Apply**

ACCESS FILES STORED IN SHARED NETWORK FOLDERS WHEN YOUR COMPUTER IS OFFLINE

Use Offline Files

Shortcut Method

□ Click the **Start button** 🌐 on the taskbar, then click **Control Panel**
□ If the Control Panel opens in Classic view, double-click **Offline Files**

OR

□ If the Control Panel opens in Category view, click **Network and Internet**, then click **Offline Files**
□ If offline files are disabled on your computer, click **Enable Offline Files**
□ Click **OK**

Make a Folder Available Offline

Ribbon Method

□ Click the **Start button** 🌐 on the taskbar, then click **Control Panel**
□ If the Control Panel opens in Classic view, double-click **Network and Sharing Center**

OR

□ If the Control Panel opens in Category view, click **Network and Internet**, then click **Network and Sharing Center**
□ In the left pane of the Network and Sharing Center window, click **View network computers and devices**
□ In the Network window, double-click a computer to display the users and resources on the computer, then navigate to the folder you want to make available offline
□ Right-click the folder, then click **Always Available Offline**, if not checked

Synchronize Files and Respond to Synchronization Conflicts

Shortcut Method

- [ ] Click the **Start button** 🔵 on the taskbar, point to **All Programs**, click **Accessories**, then click **Windows Mobility Center**
- [ ] Click **Sync settings** in the Sync Center tile
- [ ] In the Sync Center window, click the **Offline Files** sync partnership, then click **Sync** on the toolbar, if necessary
- [ ] When the sync is finished, click **View sync results** in the left pane of the Sync Center window to display the results
- [ ] If Sync Center detects a conflict, and indicates that some items are in conflict and did not sync, click **Resolve**
- [ ] In the Resolve dialog box, click **Keep this version of the file and copy it to the other location**, or click **Delete both copies**
- [ ] Click **OK**

Vista

WINDOWS VISTA OBJECTIVE 3: MANAGING SOFTWARE, DISKS, AND DEVICES

MANAGE SOFTWARE

Create a System Restore Point

Shortcut Method

- [ ] Click the **Start button** 🔵 on the taskbar, point to **All Programs**, click **Accessories**, click **System Tools**, then click **System Restore**
- [ ] In the System Restore dialog box, click the **Open System Protection link settings button**
- [ ] Click the **System Protection tab**, if necessary, then click **Create**
- [ ] Enter a description to help you identify the restore point, then click **Create**
- [ ] Click **OK**

Install a Program

Shortcut Method

- [ ] To install a program from a CD or DVD, insert the disc into the appropriate drive, then follow the instructions on the screen

  OR

- [ ] To install a program from a Web site, click the link to the program on the Web page, click **Open** or **Run** to install the program immediately, or click **Save** to download the installation file to your computer, double-click the file, click **Yes** or **OK** if security warning dialog boxes open and you trust the source of the program, then follow the instructions on the screen

  OR

- [ ] To install a program from a network, click the **Start button** 🔵 on the taskbar, click **Control Panel**; in Category view, click **Programs**, then click **Get Programs**; in Classic view, double-click **Get Programs**
- [ ] Select a program in the list, then click **Install**
- [ ] Follow the instructions on the screen

Uninstall a Program

Shortcut Method

- [ ] Click the **Start button** 🔵 on the taskbar, then click **Control Panel**
- [ ] If the Control Panel opens in Classic view, double-click **Programs and Features**

  OR

- [ ] If the Control Panel opens in Category view, click **Programs**, then click **Programs and Features**
- [ ] Select a program in the list, then click **Uninstall**
- [ ] Follow the instructions on the screen

Install a Program Update

Shortcut Method

- ☐ Click the **Start button** 🌐 on the taskbar, point to **All Programs**, then click **Windows Update**
- ☐ In the left pane of the Windows Update window, click **Check for updates**, then wait while Windows looks for the latest updates for your computer
- ☐ If Windows finds updates, click **View available updates**
- ☐ Select the updates you want to install, then click **Install updates**
- ☐ Restart your computer, if necessary

Set Up a Program for Compatibility

Shortcut Method

- ☐ Click the **Start button** 🌐 on the taskbar, then click **Control Panel**
- ☐ If the Control Panel opens in Classic view, double-click **Programs and Features**

  OR

- ☐ If the Control Panel opens in Category view, click **Programs**, then click **Programs and Features**
- ☐ In the left pane, click **Use an older program with this version of Windows**
- ☐ In the first Program Compatibility Wizard dialog box, click **Next**
- ☐ Choose whether you want to select an older program from a list of programs, use a program in the CD-ROM drive, or locate the program manually, then click **Next**
- ☐ Select compatibility settings as necessary, then click **Next**
- ☐ Click **Next** to test the program with the new compatibility settings
- ☐ Click the **No, I am finished trying compatibility settings**, then click **Next**
- ☐ In the wizard dialog box that asks if you want to send information about the compatibility problems to Microsoft, click **Yes** or **No**
- ☐ Click **Finish**

MANAGE DISKS

Check the Amount of Available Space on a Hard Disk

Shortcut Method

- ☐ Click the **Start button** 🌐 on the taskbar, then click **Computer**
- ☐ Right-click a hard disk in the Computer window, then click **Properties**

Determine Whether a Hard Disk is Partitioned

Shortcut Method

- ☐ Click the **Start button** 🌐 on the taskbar, then click **Control Panel**
- ☐ If the Control Panel opens in Classic view, double-click **System**

OR

☐ If the Control Panel opens in Category view, click **System and Maintenance**
☐ Scroll the Administrative Tools category, then click **Create and format hard disk partitions** to open the Disk Management window

Check for Problems on a Hard Disk

Shortcut Method

☐ Click the **Start button** 🔵 on the taskbar, then click **Computer**
☐ Right-click a hard disk in the Computer window, then click **Properties**
☐ In the Local Disk (C:) Properties dialog box, click the **Tools tab**
☐ Click **Check Now**
☐ Click **Start**
☐ If a dialog box opens indicating that Windows can't check the disk for errors while the disk is in use, and asks if you want to check for hard disk errors the next time you start your computer, click **OK**

MANAGE DEVICES AND DRIVES

Enable or Disable a Device

Shortcut Method

☐ Click the **Start button** 🔵 on the taskbar, then click **Control Panel**
☐ If the Control Panel opens in Classic view, double-click **System**
  OR
☐ If the Control Panel opens in Category view, click **System and Maintenance**
☐ Click **Device Manager**
☐ Expand the list of devices as necessary, then click a device
☐ If the device is disabled, click the **Enable button** on the toolbar to enable it; if the device is enabled, click the **Disable button** on the toolbar to disable it

Install or Update a Device Driver

Shortcut Method

☐ Click the **Start button** 🔵 on the taskbar, then click **Control Panel**
☐ If the Control Panel opens in Classic view, double-click **System**
  OR
☐ If the Control Panel opens in Category view, click **System and Maintenance**
☐ Click **Device Manager**
☐ In the Device Manager window, double-click the device for which you want to install or update a driver
☐ In the device's Properties dialog box, click the **Driver tab**
☐ Click **Update Driver**
☐ Click **Search automatically for updated driver software**
☐ Click **Close**

Vista

Roll Back a Device Driver

Shortcut Method

☐ Click the **Start button** 🌐 on the taskbar, then click **Control Panel**
☐ If the Control Panel opens in Classic view, double-click **System**

OR

☐ If the Control Panel opens in Category view, click **System and Maintenance**
☐ Click **Device Manager**
☐ In the Device Manager window, double-click the device for which you want to roll back a driver
☐ In the device's Properties dialog box, click the **Driver tab**
☐ Click **Roll Back Driver**
☐ Click **Yes** to confirm you want to roll back the driver to a previous version
☐ Click **Close**

Remove PC Cards and USB Devices Safely

Shortcut Method

☐ Click the **Safely Remove Hardware icon** 📇 in the notification area of the taskbar to display a list of devices you can remove
☐ Click **Safely remove USB Device** or **Safely remove PC Card** (the wording of your notification might differ)
☐ In the Safe To Remove Hardware dialog box, click **OK**
☐ Remove the PC card or USB device

MANAGE DISPLAY SETTINGS

Change Display Resolution

Shortcut Method

☐ Right-click a blank area of the desktop, then click **Personalize**
☐ In the Personalization window, click **Display Settings**
☐ In the Display Settings dialog box, drag the **Resolution slider** to a new resolution setting
☐ Click **OK**

Change the Display Refresh Rate

Shortcut Method

☐ Right-click a blank area of the desktop, then click **Personalize**
☐ In the Personalization window, click **Display Settings**
☐ In the Display Settings dialog box, click **Advanced Settings**
☐ In the Properties dialog box for your monitor, click the **Monitor tab**
☐ Click the **Screen refresh rate list arrow**, then click a refresh rate
☐ Click **OK**

Vista

Change the Display Color Depth Setting

Shortcut Method

- ☐ Right-click a blank area of the desktop, then click **Personalize**
- ☐ In the Personalization window, click **Display Settings**
- ☐ In the Display Settings dialog box, click the **Colors button**, then click a color depth
- ☐ Click **OK**

Change the Icon Size

Shortcut Method

- ☐ Right-click a blank area of the desktop, then click **Personalize**
- ☐ In the left pane of the Personalization window, click **Adjust font size (DPI)**
- ☐ In the DPI Scaling dialog box, click the **Larger scale (120 DPI) - make text more readable option button**, or click the **Default scale (96 DPI) - fit more information option button**
- ☐ Click **OK**
- ☐ Click **Restart Now** or click **Restart Later**

CONFIGURE MULTIPLE MONITORS

Change the Resolution of a Secondary Monitor

Shortcut Method

- ☐ Right-click a blank area of the desktop, then click **Personalize**
- ☐ In the Personalization window, click **Display Settings**
- ☐ Click a monitor, then click the **This is my main monitor check box**
- ☐ Drag the **Resolution slider** to change the resolution
- ☐ Click **OK**

Extend the Desktop to Another Monitor

Shortcut Method

- ☐ Physically connect the additional monitor to your computer
- ☐ In the New Display Detected dialog box, click the **Show different parts of my desktop on each display (extended) option button**
- ☐ Click the **Left option button** or the **Right option button**
- ☐ Click **OK**

Specify the Primary Monitor

Shortcut Method

- ☐ Right-click a blank area of the desktop, then click **Personalize**
- ☐ In the Personalization window, click **Display Settings**
- ☐ Click a monitor, then click the **This is my main monitor check box**
- ☐ Click **OK**

INSTALL AND CONFIGURE A PRINTER

Set Up a Local Printer

Shortcut Method

☐ Follow the printer manufacturer's instructions to connect the printer to
   your computer
☐ If Windows does not automatically detect the printer and install its dri-
   vers, click the **Start button** 🌀 on the taskbar, then click **Control
   Panel**; in Classic view, double-click **Printers**; in Category view, click
   Hardware and Sound, then click **Printers**
☐ Click the **Add a printer button** on the toolbar
☐ In the Add Printer Wizard, click **Add a local printer**
☐ Click **Next** to accept the existing printer port
☐ Select the printer manufacturer and the printer name, then click **Next**
☐ Enter a printer name, then click **Next**
☐ Click **Finish**

Specify a Printer as the Default

Shortcut Method

☐ Click the **Start button** 🌀 on the taskbar, then click **Control Panel**
☐ If the Control Panel opens in Classic view, double-click **Printers**

   OR

☐ If the Control Panel opens in Category view, click **Hardware and
   Sound**, then click **Printers**
☐ Right-click the printer you want to set as the default, then click **Set as
   Default Printer**

Find and Install a Network Printer

Shortcut Method

☐ Click the **Start button** 🌀 on the taskbar, then click **Control Panel**
☐ If the Control Panel opens in Classic view, double-click **Printers**

   OR

☐ If the Control Panel opens in Category view, click **Hardware and
   Sound**, then click **Printers**
☐ In the Printers window, click the **Add a printer button** on the toolbar
☐ Click **Add a Network, Wireless, or Bluetooth printer**
☐ After the wizard scans your network and displays available printers,
   click the network printer in the list of printers, then click **Next** to start a
   wizard that installs the network printer

Share a Printer

Shortcut Method

☐ Click the **Start button** 🌀 on the taskbar, then click **Network**
☐ In the Network window, click the **Network and Sharing Center button**
   on the toolbar

Vista

□ In the Sharing and Discovery section, click the **expand icon** ⊙ to the right of Printer Sharing, then click **Turn on printer sharing**

□ Click **Apply**

Provide Printer Drivers for Network Computers Running Other Versions of Windows

Shortcut Method

□ To download compatible drivers from a printer manufacturer's Web site, verify which version of Windows you're running

□ Click the **Start button** 🕹 on the taskbar, point to **All Programs**, click **Accessories**, click **System Tools**, then click **System Information**

□ Click **System Summary**, then review the **OS Name** and **System Type** to find out which version of Windows you're running

□ Go to the printer manufacturer's Web site and search for a printer driver that is compatible with your version of Windows

□ Follow the instructions on the Web site to download and install the driver

WINDOWS VISTA OBJECTIVE 4: MANAGING FILES AND FOLDERS

MANAGE WINDOWS EXPLORER SETTINGS

Show or Hide Filename Extensions

Shortcut Method

☐ Click the **Start button** 🔘 on the taskbar, then click **Control Panel**
☐ If the Control Panel opens in Classic view, double-click **Folder Options**

OR

☐ If the Control Panel opens in Category view, click **Appearance and Personalization**, then click **Folder Options**
☐ Click the **View tab**
☐ To hide file extensions, click the **Hide extensions for known file types check box** to insert a check mark

OR

☐ To display file extensions, click the **Hide extensions for known file types check box** to remove the check mark
☐ Click **OK**

Show or Hide System Files

Shortcut Method

☐ Click the **Start button** 🔘 on the taskbar, then click **Control Panel**
☐ If the Control Panel opens in Classic view, double-click **Folder Options**

OR

☐ If the Control Panel opens in Category view, click **Appearance and Personalization**, then click **Folder Options**
☐ Click the **View tab**
☐ To hide system files, click the **Hide protected operating system files (recommended) check box** to insert a check mark

OR

☐ To display system files, click the **Hide protected operating system files (recommended) check box** to remove the check mark
☐ Click **OK**

Show or Hide Hidden Files

Shortcut Method

☐ Click the **Start button** 🔘 on the taskbar, then click **Control Panel**
☐ If the Control Panel opens in Classic view, double-click **Folder Options**

OR

☐ If the Control Panel opens in Category view, click **Appearance and Personalization**, then click **Folder Options**
☐ Click the **View tab**

Vista

☐ To show hidden system files and folders, click the **Show hidden files and folders option button**

OR

☐ To hide system files and folders, click the **Do not show hidden files and folders option button**

☐ Click **OK**

Select a Layout for the Windows Explorer Window

Shortcut Method

☐ Open a folder window

☐ Click **Organize** on the toolbar, point to **Layout**, then click **Menu Bar** to display the menu bar

☐ Click **Organize** on the toolbar, point to **Layout**, then click a pane you want to display or close in the window

---

MANAGE AND SECURE FOLDERS

Create a New Folder

Shortcut Method

☐ Open a folder window

☐ If necessary, click the **Folders bar** in the Navigation Pane to open the Folders list

☐ Click the drive or folder in which you want to create a folder

☐ Click **Organize** on the toolbar, then click **New Folder**

OR

☐ Right-click a folder in the Folders list or right-click a blank area in the folder window, point to **New**, then click **Folder**

☐ Type a name for the folder, then press **[Enter]**

Rename a Folder

Shortcut Method

☐ Right-click the folder you want to rename, then click **Rename**

☐ Type a new name for the folder, then press **[Enter]**

Add a Shortcut to a Folder to the Start Menu

Shortcut Method

☐ Drag the folder from a window to the **Start button** 🔵 on the taskbar

Add a Folder to the Favorite Links List in the Navigation Pane

Shortcut Method

☐ Open a folder window

☐ If necessary, click the **Folders bar** in the Navigation Pane to open the Folders list

☐ Drag a folder to the Favorite Links list in the Navigation Pane

Set Up NTFS Permissions on a Folder

Shortcut Method

☐ In a folder window, click the folder for which you want to set up permissions, then click the **Share button** on the toolbar

☐ In the File Sharing dialog box, click the **arrow** to the right of the top (empty) list box, then click a user name

☐ Click **Add** to add the user name to the list of users permitted to access the folder

☐ Click a **permission level** (such as Reader) for the selected user

☐ Click **Share**

☐ Click **Done**

Specify the Folder Type

Shortcut Method

☐ Right-click a folder, then click **Properties**

☐ In the folder's Properties dialog box, click the **Customize tab**

☐ Click the **Use this folder type as a template list box arrow**, then click a folder type

☐ To apply the same folder type to all existing and future subfolders of the folder, click the **Also apply this template to all subfolders check box**

☐ Click **OK**

SHARE FOLDERS

Share a Folder Using the Public Folder

Shortcut Method

☐ Open a folder window that displays the folder you want to share

☐ If necessary, click the **Folders bar** in the Navigation Pane to open the Folders list

☐ Display the Public folder in the Navigation Pane

☐ Move or copy the folder to the Public folder

Share a Folder by Specifying Permissions

Shortcut Method

☐ Open a folder window that displays the folder you want to share

☐ Click the folder you want to share, then click the **Share button** on the toolbar

☐ In the File Sharing dialog box, enter the name of the person with whom you want to share the folder, then click **Add**

OR

☐ If your computer is on a domain, click the **arrow** to the right of the text box, click **Everyone**, then click **Add**; or click **Find**, enter the name of the person with whom you want to share the folder, click **Check Names**, then click **OK**

Vista

OR

☐ If your computer is on a workgroup, click the **arrow** to the right of the text box, click the person's name in the list, then click **Add**

☐ In the Permission Level section, click the **arrow** next to each person or group and select sharing permissions as described in Table WIN-4

Table WIN-4 Sharing Permissions

Permission	Description
Reader	Can view shared files, but not add, change, or delete them
Contributor	Can view or add shared files, but can only change or delete files the user has contributed
Co-owner	Can view, add, change, or delete any shared file

SEARCH FOR FILES AND FOLDERS

Include or Remove a Folder from the Index

Shortcut Method

☐ Click the **Start button** 🏵 on the taskbar, then click **Control Panel**

☐ If the Control Panel opens in Classic view, double-click **Indexing Options**

OR

☐ If the Control Panel opens in Category view, click **System and Maintenance**, then click **Indexing Options**

☐ Click **Modify**

☐ To add a folder to the list of indexed locations, click the folder's check box in the Change selected locations list to insert a check mark

OR

☐ To remove a folder from the list of indexed locations, click the folder's check box in the Change selected locations list to remove the check mark

☐ Click **OK**

Search for Files or Programs

Shortcut Method

☐ Choose a search tool as described in Table WIN-5

Table WIN-5 Search Tools

Search tool	Use when	Windows searches
Search box in a folder window	You know where to start looking for a file and want to search by filename or contents	The current folder and all of its subfolders
Search pane in a folder window	You want to use criteria other than text in the filename or contents, or you want to combine search criteria	Any single folder and its subfolders
Search box on the Start menu	You want to find a program, a Web site included in your browser's history, or a file or folder stored in your personal folder	Your personal folder, including Documents, Pictures, Music, Desktop, and other common locations
Search folder	You don't know where a file or folder is located or are looking for files from several folders	One, some, or all of the folders on your computer

Vista

Use a Virtual Folder to Search for Files

Shortcut Method

☐ Click the **Start button** 🔵 on the taskbar, then click **Search**
☐ Click a search filter button to show only certain kinds of files

OR

☐ Click the **Advanced Search button** to show additional filters, select criteria, then click **Search**

OR

☐ Click an item in the Location list to select a different location for the search
☐ When the search is complete, click the **Save Search button** on the toolbar
☐ In the File name box, type a name for the search, then click **Save**
☐ To search using the virtual folder you created, click the **Searches link** in the Navigation Pane

Use Keywords to Search for Files

Shortcut Method

☐ Open the folder you want to search
☐ Click in the Search box, then type a word or phrase associated with the files you want to find
☐ If Windows does not find the files you want, click **Search in File Contents** in the Search Results window

OR
□ Click **Advanced Search** in the Search Results window, select additional criteria using the options in the expanded Search pane, then click **Search**

Use Wildcards to Search for Files

Shortcut Method

□ Open the folder you want to search
□ Click in the Search box, then type the search text using an asterisk (*) to stand for one or more characters
□ Follow the steps in bullets 3–4 of the Use Keywords to Search for Files Shortcut Method above

Save a Search

Shortcut Method

□ Follow the steps in bullets 1–4 of the Use Keywords to Search for Files Shortcut Method above
□ In the search results window, click the **Save Search button** on the toolbar
□ In the Save As dialog box, enter a name, if necessary, then click **Save**

Show the Results of a Previous Search

Shortcut Method

□ Open a folder window
□ If necessary, click the **Folders bar** in the Navigation Pane to open the Folders list
□ If you've conducted a search recently, click the appropriate search results in the Folders list
   OR
□ To search using a saved search, click the **Searches folder** in the Navigation Pane, then double-click the search you want to redisplay

Filter the Search Results

Shortcut Method

□ Open the folder you want to search
□ In the Search box, enter search criteria
□ To filter the search results, enter additional criteria
   OR
□ Click **Advanced Search** in the Search Results window, then select additional criteria
□ Click the **Search button**

ORGANIZE FILES WITHIN FOLDERS

Change How Files Are Displayed

Shortcut Method

□ Open a folder window
□ Click the **Views button arrow** on the toolbar, then click a view

OR

- [ ] To cycle through the views listed on the Views menu, click the **Views button** more than once

    OR

- [ ] Click the **Views button arrow** on the toolbar, then drag the **slider**

Show or Hide File and Folder Details

Shortcut Method

- [ ] Open a folder window
- [ ] If the Details Pane is not open, click the **Organize button** on the toolbar, point to **Layout**, then click **Details Pane** to open the Details pane and show details for the selected file or folder

Group Files

Shortcut Method

- [ ] Open a folder window
- [ ] Click the **column heading arrow** of the detail you want to group by, then click **Group**

Sort Files

Shortcut Method

- [ ] Open a folder window
- [ ] Click the **column heading arrow** of the detail you want to sort by to sort the files in ascending or descending order
- [ ] To sort the files in the opposite order, click the **column heading arrow** of the same detail again

Stack Files

Shortcut Method

- [ ] Open a folder window
- [ ] Click the **column heading arrow** of the detail you want to stack by, then click **Stack by *detail***, where *detail* is the detail you want to use for stacking, such as Type

MANAGE FILES

Add Tags to a File

Shortcut Method

- [ ] Open a folder window, then click the file to which you want to add a tag
- [ ] Click the **Tags text box** in the Details pane, then type a tag; to enter another tag, type a semicolon (;) followed by the next tag
- [ ] Click **Save** in the Details pane

Vista

Add Properties to a File

Shortcut Method

- ☐ Open a folder window
- ☐ Right-click the file to which you want to add properties, then click **Properties**
- ☐ In the file's Properties dialog box, click the **Details tab**
- ☐ Enter properties in the appropriate text boxes
- ☐ Click **OK**

Remove Personal Information from a File

Shortcut Method

- ☐ Open a folder window
- ☐ Right-click the file from which you want to remove properties, then click **Properties**
- ☐ In the file's Properties dialog box, click the **Details tab**
- ☐ Click **Remove Properties and Personal Information**
- ☐ In the Remove Properties dialog box, delete the appropriate properties
- ☐ Click **OK** to close the Remove Properties dialog box
- ☐ Click **OK** to close the file's Properties dialog box

Create a File

Shortcut Method

- ☐ Start a program, then use the program's tools to add content to a new file
- ☐ Use the program's tools to save the file
- ☐ In the Save As dialog box, enter a name for the file, select a file type, and select a location for the file
- ☐ Click **Save**

Move a File

Shortcut Method

- ☐ Open a folder window containing the file you want to move, and another folder window displaying the destination folder
- ☐ Right-click and drag the file you want to move to the destination folder, then click **Move Here**

  OR

- ☐ If you want to move a file from one folder to another on the same drive, drag the file to the destination folder

  OR

- ☐ Right-click the file you want to move, click **Cut**, navigate to and right-click the destination folder, then click **Paste**

Rename a File

Shortcut Method

- ☐ Right-click the file you want to rename, then click **Rename**
- ☐ Enter a new name for the file, then press **[Enter]**

Delete a File

Shortcut Method

- ☐ Right-click the file you want to delete, then click **Delete** or press **[Delete]**
- ☐ Click **Yes** when asked to confirm the deletion

Copy Data Files to an Optical Disc

Shortcut Method

- ☐ Open a folder window displaying the files you want to copy
- ☐ Click the **Burn button** on the toolbar, then click **Data**
- ☐ Insert a blank CD or DVD into the appropriate drive
- ☐ Drag files from the file list to the List pane
- ☐ Click **Start Burn**

BACK UP FILES AND FOLDERS

Back Up Files

Shortcut Method

- ☐ Click the **Start button** 🔵 on the taskbar, then click **Control Panel**
- ☐ If the Control Panel opens in Classic view, double-click **Backup and Restore Center**

  OR

- ☐ If the Control Panel opens in Category view, click **System and Maintenance**, then click **Backup and Restore Center**
- ☐ Click **Back up files**
- ☐ Follow the steps in the Back Up Files Wizard
- ☐ In the final dialog box in the wizard, click **Save settings and start backup**

Set a Schedule for Automatic Backups

Shortcut Method

- ☐ Follow the steps in bullets 1-5 of the Back Up Folders and Files Shortcut Method above
- ☐ In the final dialog box in the wizard, click the **What time button**, then click a time to schedule an automatic backup
- ☐ Click **Save settings and start backup**

Restore Files

Shortcut Method

- ☐ Click the **Start button** 🔵 on the taskbar, then click **Control Panel**
- ☐ If the Control Panel opens in Classic view, double-click **Backup and Restore Center**

  OR

- ☐ If the Control Panel opens in Category view, click **System and Maintenance**, then click **Backup and Restore Center**
- ☐ Click **Restore files**

□ In the Restore Files Wizard, click the **Files from the latest backup option button**, if necessary, then click **Next**
□ Click the **Add folders button**, navigate to and click the folder you want to restore, click **Add**, then click **Next**
□ Select a location for the restored files, then click **Start restore**
□ If Windows needs to restore a file with the same name as a file in the destination folder, select an option in the Copy File dialog box
□ Click **Finish**

Restore an Earlier Version of a File

Shortcut Method

□ Open the folder window containing the appropriate file
□ Right-click the file, then click **Restore previous versions**
   OR
□ Right-click the file, click **Properties**, then click the **Previous Versions tab**
□ In the file's Properties dialog box, click **Restore**
□ In the Previous Versions dialog box, click **Restore**
□ When Windows displays a message indicating the file was successfully restored, click **OK**
□ Click **OK** to close the file's Properties dialog box

WINDOWS VISTA OBJECTIVE 5: COLLABORATING WITH OTHER PEOPLE

COLLABORATE IN REAL TIME

Sign in to a Collaboration Network

Shortcut Method

- ☐ Make sure you are connected to a network, and that you and the people with whom you want to meet are on the same network and using Windows Vista
- ☐ Click the **Start button** 🔵 on the taskbar, point to **All Programs**, then click **Windows Meeting Space**
- ☐ If this is the first time you are using Windows Meeting Space, click **Yes, continue setting up Windows Meeting Space**, type your display name, then click **OK**
- ☐ Click the **People Near Me** icon in the notification area of the taskbar, then click **Join a meeting near me**

Start a Meeting and Invite Participants

Shortcut Method

- ☐ Click the **Start button** 🔵 on the taskbar, point to **All Programs**, then click **Windows Meeting Space**
- ☐ Click **Start a new meeting**
- ☐ Provide a meeting name, if necessary, and a password
- ☐ Click **Create a meeting**
- ☐ Click **Invite people**
- ☐ Click the check boxes for the people you want to invite, then click **Send Invitations**

Join a Meeting

Shortcut Method

- ☐ Click the **Start button** 🔵 on the taskbar, point to **All Programs**, then click **Windows Meeting Space**
- ☐ Click **Join a meeting near me**
- ☐ Select the meeting you want to join
- ☐ Enter the password for the meeting, then click the **Next button** 🔵

PRESENT INFORMATION TO AN AUDIENCE

Set Up Your Computer for a Presentation

Shortcut Method

- ☐ Click the **Start button** 🔵 on the taskbar, point to **All Programs**, click **Accessories**, then click **Windows Mobility Center**
- ☐ In the Presentation Settings tile, click the **Change presentation settings icon**

Vista

☐ Click the **Turn off the screen saver check box**
☐ Click the **Set the volume to: check box**, then drag the slider to increase the volume, if necessary
☐ Click the **Show this background** check box, then click **(None)**
☐ Click **OK**

Present Information on an External Display Device

Shortcut Method

☐ Connect your computer to an external display device, such as a projector or secondary monitor
☐ If Windows does not automatically detect the external display and open the New Display Detected dialog box, click the **Start button** 🌀 on the taskbar, point to **All Programs**, click **Accessories**, click **Windows Mobility Center**, then click the **Connect display button** in the External Display tile
☐ Click the appropriate option button to mirror (the default), extend, or show your desktop on the external display only
☐ If you are extending your desktop, click the **Left option button** or **Right option button** to extend your desktop in one of these directions
☐ Click **OK**

Use a Network Projector

Shortcut Method

☐ Click the **Start button** 🌀 on the taskbar, point to **All Programs**, click **Accessories**, then click **Connect to a Network Projector**
☐ If you are asked for permission to connect, click **Yes**
☐ Search for a projector on the network or enter the projector's network address
☐ Click an available projector in the list and enter the projector password, if necessary, then click **Connect**

WINDOWS VISTA OBJECTIVE 6: CUSTOMIZING YOUR WINDOWS VISTA EXPERIENCE

CUSTOMIZE AND MODIFY THE START MENU

Change the User Picture on the Start Menu

Shortcut Method

☐ Click the **Start button** 🌀 on the taskbar, then click the **user picture** at the top of the right pane

☐ In the User Accounts window, click **Change your picture**

☐ In the Change Your Picture window, click a new image, then click **Change Picture**

Change the Size of the Icons on the Start Menu

Shortcut Method

☐ Right-click the **Start button** 🌀 on the taskbar, then click **Properties**

☐ In the Taskbar and Start Menu Properties dialog box, click **Customize**

☐ In the Customize Start Menu dialog box, scroll to the bottom of the list of items you can customize, then click the **Use large icons check box** to remove the check mark to use small icons, or click the **Use large icons check box** to insert a check mark to use large icons

☐ Click **OK** to close the Customize Start Menu dialog box

☐ Click **OK** to close the Taskbar and Start Menu Properties dialog box

Customize Other Start Menu Settings

Shortcut Method

☐ Right-click the **Start button** 🌀 on the taskbar, then click **Properties**

☐ In the Taskbar and Start Menu Properties dialog box, click **Customize**

☐ In the Customize Start Menu dialog box, select options you want to set for the Start menu

☐ Click **OK** to close the Customize Start Menu dialog box

☐ Click **OK** to close the Taskbar and Start Menu Properties dialog box

Pin and Unpin an Item on the Start Menu

Shortcut Method

☐ Click the **Start button** 🌀 on the taskbar, right-click the program you want to pin, then click **Pin to Start Menu**

☐ To unpin an item, click the **Start button** 🌀 on the taskbar, right-click the item on the Start menu, then click **Unpin from Start Menu**

Set a Program to Start Automatically

Shortcut Method

☐ Click the **Start button** 🌀 on the taskbar, point to **All Programs**, right-click the **Startup folder**, then click **Open**

☐ Click the **Start button** 🌀 on the taskbar, then navigate to and drag a program icon to the Startup folder window

Vista

Include a Program on the Start Menu

Shortcut Method

☐ Display the appropriate program file
☐ Right-click, then drag the program file to the **Start button** 🌀 on the taskbar

CUSTOMIZE THE TASKBAR

Include the Quick Launch Toolbar on the Taskbar

Shortcut Method

☐ If the taskbar does not display the Quick Launch toolbar (which it does by default), right-click a blank area of the taskbar, point to **Toolbars**, then click **Quick Launch**

Include a Toolbar on the Taskbar

Shortcut Method

☐ Right-click a blank area of the taskbar, point to **Toolbars**, then click the toolbar you want to display; see Table WIN-6 for a description of taskbar toolbars

Table WIN-6 Taskbar Toolbars

Taskbar toolbar	Description
Address	Use to open any Web page you specify
Desktop	Use to access items on your desktop, such as the Recycle Bin and Computer, from the taskbar
Links	Use to access links to product information on the Web and add Web links by dragging them to the toolbar
New Toolbar	Create a custom taskbar toolbar to store shortcuts to folders, documents, or other objects you use often
Quick Launch	Use to access icons you can click to quickly open programs, show the desktop, or perform other tasks
Tablet PC Input Panel	Use to access the Tablet PC Input Panel, which lets you enter text without a standard keyboard
Windows Media Player	Use to display controls for playing music and other media, including Play, Stop, and Pause buttons

Move the Taskbar

Shortcut Method

☐ Right-click a blank spot on the taskbar, then click **Lock the Taskbar** to remove the check mark, if necessary, to unlock the taskbar
☐ Drag the taskbar to a new location (the top, bottom, left, or right edge of the desktop)

Vista

Automatically Hide the Taskbar

Shortcut Method

☐ Right-click a blank spot on the taskbar, then click **Properties**
☐ In the Taskbar and Start Menu Properties dialog box, click the **Taskbar tab**, if necessary, then click the **Auto-hide the taskbar check box** to insert a check mark
☐ Click **OK**

Customize the Notification Area of the Taskbar

Shortcut Method

☐ Right-click the **Start button** 🪟 on the taskbar, then click **Properties**
☐ Click the **Notification Area tab**
☐ Select the options you want to set
☐ Click **OK**

PERSONALIZE THE APPEARANCE AND SOUND OF A COMPUTER

Change the Desktop Background

Shortcut Method

☐ Right-click a blank area of the desktop, then click **Personalize**
☐ In the Personalization window, click **Desktop Background**
☐ Select an image in the Desktop Background window or click the **Picture Location arrow** or the **Browse button** to select images stored in a different location
☐ Select a positioning option, if necessary
☐ Click **OK**

Rearrange Desktop Icons

Shortcut Method

☐ Right-click a blank area of the desktop, point to **View**, then click **Auto Arrange** to remove the check mark
☐ If necessary, right-click a blank area of the desktop, point to **View**, then click **Align to Grid** to remove the check mark
☐ Drag desktop icons to new locations on the desktop

Change the Sound Scheme

Shortcut Method

☐ Click the **Start button** 🪟 on the taskbar, then click **Control Panel**
☐ If the Control Panel opens in Classic view, double-click **Sound**
   OR
☐ If the Control Panel opens in Category view, click **Hardware and Sound**, then click **Sound**
☐ Click the **Sounds tab** to display the sound schemes
☐ Click a program event, click the **Sounds arrow button**, then click a sound

Vista

☐ Click **Save As**, then enter a name for the sound scheme
☐ Click **OK**

Activate a Screen Saver

Shortcut Method

☐ Right-click a blank area of the desktop, then click **Personalize**
☐ In the Personalization window, click **Screen Saver**
☐ In the Screen Saver Settings dialog box, click the **Screen saver arrow** to display the screen savers installed on your computer
☐ Click a screen saver
☐ Click **Save**
☐ Click **OK**

Customize Mouse Settings

Shortcut Method

☐ Click the **Start button** 🏵 on the taskbar, then click **Control Panel**
☐ If the Control Panel opens in Classic view, double-click **Mouse**
   OR
☐ If the Control Panel opens in Category view, click **Hardware and Sound**, then click **Mouse**
☐ In the Mouse Properties dialog box, click the **Buttons tab**, if necessary, then click to select the **Switch primary and secondary buttons check box** if you are left-handed
☐ To change the double-click speed, drag the **Double-click speed slider** to the left or right
☐ Click **OK**

MANAGE THE WINDOWS SIDEBAR

Open the Windows Sidebar

Shortcut Method

☐ Click the **Start button** 🏵 on the taskbar, point to **All Programs**, click **Accessories**, then click **Windows Sidebar**

Customize the Windows Sidebar

Shortcut Method

☐ If necessary, open the Windows Sidebar by following the steps in bullet 1 of the Open the Windows Sidebar Shortcut Method above
☐ Right-click a blank spot on the Sidebar, then click **Properties**
☐ In the Windows Sidebar Properties dialog box, select options
☐ Click **OK**

Add a Gadget to the Windows Sidebar

Shortcut Method

☐ If necessary, open the Windows Sidebar by following the steps in bullet 1 of the Open the Windows Sidebar Shortcut Method above

☐ Click the **Add Gadgets button** at the top of the Sidebar
☐ In the gadget gallery, double-click a gadget

Download a Gadget for the Windows Sidebar

Shortcut Method

☐ If necessary, open the Windows Sidebar by following the steps in bullet 1 of the Open the Windows Sidebar Shortcut Method above
☐ Click the **Add Gadgets button** at the top of the Sidebar
☐ In the gadget gallery, click **Get more gadgets online**
☐ On the Personalize Windows Vista Sidebar Web page, select a gadget, then follow the instructions on the Web page to download the gadget to your computer

Vista

WINDOWS VISTA OBJECTIVE 7: OPTIMIZING AND TROUBLESHOOTING YOUR COMPUTER

INCREASE PROCESSING SPEED

Increase Memory with Windows ReadyBoost

Shortcut Method

☐ Plug a USB flash drive into an available USB port on your computer
☐ In the AutoPlay dialog box, click **Speed up my system**

OR

☐ If the AutoPlay dialog box does not open, click the **Start button** 🔵 on the taskbar, click **Computer**, right-click the USB flash drive, click **Open Autoplay**, then click **Speed up my system**
☐ In the Properties dialog box for the USB flash drive, click the **ReadyBoost tab**, if necessary
☐ Click the **Use this device option button**
☐ Drag the **slider** as necessary to select the amount of space on your USB flash drive you want to reserve for boosting your system speed
☐ Click **OK**

Defragment Your Hard Disk

Shortcut Method

☐ Click the **Start button** 🔵 on the taskbar, click **Computer**, right-click the hard disk you want to defragment, then click **Properties**
☐ In the hard disk's Properties dialog box, click the **Tools tab**
☐ Close all open programs, then click **Defragment Now**

Adjust Power Options

Shortcut Method

☐ Click the **Start button** 🔵 on the taskbar, then click **Control Panel**
☐ If the Control Panel opens in Classic view, double-click **Power Options**

OR

☐ If the Control Panel opens in Category view, click **Hardware and Sound**, then click **Power Options**
☐ Click **Change plan settings** for the power plan you want to modify
☐ Click a button for a power setting, then click the amount of time to wait before applying the setting
☐ Click **Change advanced power settings**
☐ Expand an advanced setting, change the setting, then click **OK**
☐ Click **Save changes**

LOCATE TROUBLESHOOTING INFORMATION

Find Troubleshooting Information in Windows Help and Support

Shortcut Method

- ☐ Click the **Start button** 🔵 on the taskbar, then click **Help and Support**
- ☐ In the Windows Help and Support window, click **Troubleshooting**
- ☐ In the Troubleshooting in Windows page, click a link that describes the problem you want to troubleshoot
- ☐ Read the Help article, clicking the **Show all link** or **Show Content link** as necessary to display steps for all the actions you can try when troubleshooting

Find Troubleshooting Information in the Microsoft Knowledge Base

Shortcut Method

- ☐ Click the **Start button** 🔵 on the taskbar, then click **Help and Support**
- ☐ In the Windows Help and Support window, click the **Ask button** on the Windows Help and Support toolbar
- ☐ In the Get customer support or other types of help window, click the **Knowledge Base link**
- ☐ In the Search the Support Knowledge Base (KB) Web page, click in the For text box, type a word or phrase describing what you want to troubleshoot, then click **Search**
- ☐ Click an article title

LOCATE SYSTEM INFORMATION

Determine Your Computer's CPU and Page File Usage

Shortcut Method

- ☐ Right-click a blank spot on the taskbar, then click **Task Manager**
- ☐ In the Windows Task Manager dialog box, click the **Performance tab**

Track Your Computer's Page File Usage

Shortcut Method

- ☐ Click the **Start button** 🔵 on the taskbar, then click **Control Panel**
- ☐ If the Control Panel opens in Classic view, double-click **Performance Information and Tools**

  OR

- ☐ If the Control Panel opens in Category view, click **System and Maintenance**, then click **Performance Information and Tools**
- ☐ In the left pane of the Performance Information and Tools window, click **Advanced tools**
- ☐ In the Advanced Tools window, click **Open Reliability and Performance Monitor**

□ In the left pane of the Reliability and Performance Monitor window, click **Performance Monitor**
□ Click the **Add button** 🔹 on the Performance Monitor toolbar
□ In the Add Counters dialog box, scroll the Available counters list, then double-click **Paging File**
□ Click **% Usage**, then click **Add**
□ Click **OK**, then close the Reliability and Performance Monitor window

Determine the Amount of RAM Installed and the Speed of Your Processor

Shortcut Method

□ Follow the steps in bullets 1–4 of the Track Your Computer's Page File Usage Shortcut Method above
□ In the Advanced Tools window, click **View advanced system details in System Information**, then click **System Summary**, if necessary
□ In the System Information window, look for Processor and Total Physical Memory

Determine the Hardware Devices on Your Computer

Shortcut Method

□ Follow the steps in bullets 1–2 of the Determine the Amount of RAM Installed and the Speed of Your Processor Shortcut Method above
□ In the System Information window, click the **expand icon** ⊞ next to Components to display a list of the types of devices installed on your computer
□ Click a device to view details about it in the right pane of the System Information window

Find the System Performance Rating

Shortcut Method

□ Click the **Start button** 💿 on the taskbar, then click **Control Panel**
□ If the Control Panel opens in Classic view, double-click **Performance Information and Tools**

OR

□ If the Control Panel opens in Category view, click **System and Maintenance**, then click **Performance Information and Tools**
□ View the Windows Experience Index base score and subscores for your computer using Table WIN-7 as a reference; if these scores are not displayed, click **Score this computer**
□ To find out if your score has changed, click **Update my score**

Table WIN-7 System Performance Ratings

Base score	What the computer can do
1–1.9	Complete general computing tasks, such as running office productivity programs and searching the Internet, but not use Windows Aero or the advanced multimedia features of Windows Vista
2–2.9	Respond more quickly than computers in the 1.0 range while running the same types of programs; some computers in this range can run Windows Aero, though performance might decline
3–3.9	Run Windows Aero and other new Windows Vista features at a level adequate for most computer users; for example, the computer can display a desktop theme at a high resolution, but not on multiple monitors
4 or higher	Use all the new features of Windows Vista, including advanced, graphics-intensive experiences, such as multiplayer and 3-D gaming

REPAIR A NETWORK CONNECTION

Determine the IP Address of Your Computer

Shortcut Method

☐ Click the **network icon** 🖳 in the notification area of the taskbar, then click **Network and Sharing Center**

☐ In the Network and Sharing Center window, click **View status** in the column next to the connection name

☐ In the Status dialog box for that connection, click **Details**

   OR

☐ Click the **Start button** 🌀 on the taskbar, point to **All Programs**, click **Accessories**, then click **Command Prompt**

☐ In the Command Prompt window, type **ipconfig** then press **[Enter]**

Ping Another Computer

Shortcut Method

☐ Click the **Start button** 🌀 on the taskbar, point to **All Programs**, click **Accessories**, then click **Command Prompt**

☐ In the Command Prompt window, type **ping *address***, where *address* is the IP address or host name of the computer you want to ping

☐ Press **[Enter]**; if your computer is connected and the site is working correctly, you will receive a few responses from the site

Vista

Enable or Disable a Network Connection

Shortcut Method

☐ Follow the steps in bullets 1–2 of the Determine the IP Address of Your Computer Shortcut Method above

☐ In the Network Connection Status dialog box, click **Disable** to disable the network connection

OR

☐ In the Network Connection Status dialog box, click **Enable** to enable the network connection

RECOVER FROM SOFTWARE ERRORS

Handle Unresponsive Programs

Shortcut Method

☐ Right-click a blank spot on the taskbar, then click **Task Manager**

☐ In the Task Manager dialog box, click the **Applications tab**, if necessary

☐ If a program has a Not Responding status, you can close the program by clicking it, then clicking **End Task**

Repair a Program

Shortcut Method

☐ Click the **Start button** 🔘 on the taskbar, then click **Control Panel**

☐ If the Control Panel opens in Classic view, double-click **Programs and Features**

OR

☐ If the Control Panel opens in Category view, click **Programs**, then click **Programs and Features**

☐ Click the troublesome program, then click **Repair**

TROUBLESHOOT PRINTING ERRORS

Display the Status of a Printer

Shortcut Method

☐ Click the **Start button** 🔘 on the taskbar, then click **Control Panel**

☐ If the Control Panel opens in Classic view, double-click **Printers**

OR

☐ If the Control Panel opens in Category view, click **Hardware and Sound**, then click **Printers**

☐ If necessary, click the **Views arrow button**, then click **Details** to display the printer details, including the status

Work with Print Job and Queues

Shortcut Method

☐ Follow the steps in bullets 1–3 of the Display the Status of a Printer Shortcut Method above

- [ ] To open a printer's print queue, double-click the **printer icon**
- [ ] To pause a print job in the queue, right-click the **print job**, then click **Pause**
- [ ] To delete a print job from the queue, right-click the **print job**, then click **Cancel**
- [ ] To restart the printer after pausing or deleting a print job, right-click the **print job**, then click **Resume**

RECOVER THE OPERATING SYSTEM FROM A PROBLEM

Select Advanced Startup Options

Shortcut Method

- [ ] Restart your computer
- [ ] Press and hold **[F8]** before the Windows logo appears
- [ ] On the Advanced Boot Options screen, select an advanced startup option

Restore Your Computer

Shortcut Method

- [ ] Click the **Start button** 🏵 on the taskbar, then click **Control Panel**
- [ ] If the Control Panel opens in Classic view, double-click **System**

  OR

- [ ] If the Control Panel opens in Category view, click **System and Maintenance**, then click **System**
- [ ] In the left pane of the System window, click **System protection**
- [ ] In the System Properties dialog box, click **System Restore**
- [ ] In the first dialog box of the System Restore Wizard, accept the most recent restore point or choose a different one, then click **Next**
- [ ] If necessary, select a restore point, then click **Next**
- [ ] Click **Finish**

Repair Windows Vista

Shortcut Method

- [ ] Insert the Windows installation disc
- [ ] Restart your computer
- [ ] Select your language settings, then click **Next**
- [ ] Click **Repair your computer**
- [ ] Select the operating system to repair, then click **Next**
- [ ] On the System Recovery Options menu, click **Startup Repair**

REQUEST AND MANAGE REMOTE ASSISTANCE

Enable Remote Assistance

Shortcut Method

- [ ] Click the **Start button** 🏵 on the taskbar, then click **Control Panel**
- [ ] If the Control Panel opens in Classic view, double-click **System**

Vista

OR

- ☐ If the Control Panel opens in Category view, click **System and Maintenance**, then click **System**
- ☐ In the left pane of the System window, click **Remote settings**
- ☐ In the System Properties dialog box, click the **Remote tab**, if necessary
- ☐ If necessary, click the **Allow Remote Assistance connections to this computer check box** to insert a check mark
- ☐ Click **OK**

Limit a Remote Assistance Invitation

Shortcut Method

- ☐ Follow the steps in bullets 1–5 in the Enable Remote Assistance Shortcut Method above
- ☐ On the Remote tab of the System Properties dialog box, click **Advanced**
- ☐ In the Remote Assistance Settings dialog box, click in the Set the maximum amount of time invitations can remain open box, then change the amount of time a Remote Assistance invitation is available
- ☐ Click **OK** to close the Remote Assistance Settings dialog box
- ☐ Click **OK** to close the System Properties dialog box

Request Remote Assistance

Shortcut Method

- ☐ Click the **Start button** 🔘 on the taskbar, then click **Help and Support**
- ☐ In the Ask someone section of the Windows Help and Support window, click **Windows Remote Assistance**
- ☐ In the Windows Remote Assistance Wizard, click **Invite someone you trust to help you**
- ☐ Click **Use e-mail to send an invitation**
- ☐ Enter a password, retype it in the Retype the password box, then click **Next**
- ☐ After Remote Assistance opens an invitation e-mail in your default e-mail program, send an invitation to someone you trust

Turn Off Remote Assistance Invitations

Shortcut Method

- ☐ Follow the steps in bullets 1–5 of the Enable Remote Assistance Shortcut Method above
- ☐ Click the **Allow Remote Assistance connections to this computer check box** to remove the check mark
- ☐ Click **OK**

MICROSOFT OFFICE WORD 2007
EXAM REFERENCE
Getting Started with Word 2007

The Word Microsoft Certified Application Specialist (MCAS) exam assumes a basic level of proficiency in Word. This section is intended to help you reference these basic skills while you are preparing to take the Word exam.

- ☐ Starting and exiting Word
- ☐ Viewing the Word window
- ☐ Using the Ribbon
- ☐ Opening, saving, and closing documents
- ☐ Navigating in the document window
- ☐ Using views
- ☐ Using keyboard KeyTips
- ☐ Getting Help

START AND EXIT WORD

Start Word

Shortcut Method

- ☐ Click the **Start button** 🏶 on the Windows taskbar, then point to **All Programs**
- ☐ Click **Microsoft Office**, then click **Microsoft Office Word 2007**

  OR
- ☐ Double-click the **Microsoft Word program icon** 🔲 on the desktop

  OR
- ☐ Click the **Microsoft Office Word 2007 icon** on the Quick Launch toolbar

Exit Word

Ribbon Method

- ☐ Click the **Office button** 🔵, then click **Exit Word**

  OR
- ☐ Click the **Close button** ☒ on the Word program window title bar

Shortcut Method

- ☐ Press **[Alt][F4]**

VIEW THE WORD WINDOW

Figure WD-1 Word program window

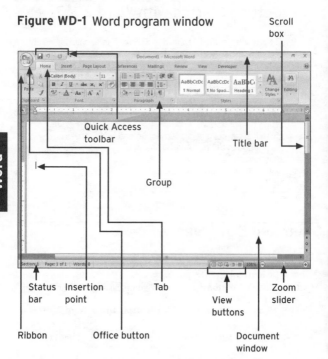

Scroll box

Quick Access toolbar

Title bar

Group

Status bar

Insertion point

Tab

View buttons

Zoom slider

Ribbon

Office button

Document window

Word

USE THE RIBBON

Display Tabs on the Ribbon

Ribbon Method

☐ Open a document, then click any tab

Hide the Ribbon

Ribbon Method

☐ Double-click the active tab to show only the tabs

Shortcut Method

☐ Right-click any tab, then click **Minimize the Ribbon** to select it

Work with the Ribbon

Ribbon Method

- ☐ Click a **button**, a **button list arrow**, or the **More button** ⬇ (when available) in any group, then click a command or gallery option, if necessary

  OR

- ☐ Click a **dialog box launcher** ▣ to open a dialog box or a pane offering more options

Customize the Quick Access Toolbar

Ribbon Method

- ☐ Right-click any button on the Quick Access toolbar
- ☐ To hide that button, click **Remove from Quick Access Toolbar**
- ☐ To add or remove a button, click **Customize Quick Access Toolbar**, click a command in the left or right column, then click **Add** or **Remove**

Reposition the Quick Access Toolbar

Ribbon Method

- ☐ Right-click any button on the Quick Access toolbar
- ☐ Click **Show Quick Access Toolbar Below the Ribbon**

OPEN, SAVE, AND CLOSE DOCUMENTS

Open a New Document

Ribbon Method

- ☐ Click the **Office button** 🏛, then click **New**
- ☐ Click **Blank document** under Blank and recent, then click **Create**

Shortcut Method

- ☐ Press **[Ctrl][N]**

Open an Existing Document

Ribbon Method

- ☐ Click the **Office button** 🏛, then click **Open**
- ☐ In the Open dialog box, navigate to the drive and folder where you stored your file
- ☐ Click the file, then click **Open**

Shortcut Method

- ☐ Press **[Ctrl][O]**
- ☐ Follow the steps in bullets 2–3 of the Open an Existing Document Ribbon Method above

Use Save As

Ribbon Method
☐ Click the **Office button** 🔵, then click **Save As**
☐ In the Save As dialog box, navigate to the appropriate drive and folder, if necessary
☐ Type an appropriate filename in the File name text box, then click **Save**

Shortcut Method
☐ Press **[F12]**
☐ Follow the steps in bullets 2–3 of the Use Save As Ribbon Method above

Save an Existing Document

Ribbon Method
☐ Click the **Office button** 🔵, then click **Save**

Shortcut Method
☐ Press **[Ctrl][S]**
   OR
☐ Click the **Save button** 💾 on the Quick Access toolbar

Close a Document

Ribbon Method
☐ Click the **Office button** 🔵, then click **Close**
☐ If prompted to save the file, click **Yes** or **No**, as appropriate

Shortcut Method
☐ Click the **Close Window button** ✖ on the title bar
☐ If prompted to save the file, click **Yes** or **No**, as appropriate
   OR
☐ Press **[Ctrl][W]** or **[Alt][F4]**
☐ If prompted to save the file, click **Yes** or **No**, as appropriate

NAVIGATE IN THE DOCUMENT WINDOW

Ribbon Method
☐ Click the **Home tab**, click the **Find button** in the Editing group, then click the **Go To tab**
☐ In the Find and Replace dialog box, select an option in the Go to what list; in the related text box, type the go to identifier, then click **OK**

Shortcut Method
☐ Press **[Ctrl][G]**
☐ Follow the step in bullet 2 of the Navigate in the Document Window Ribbon Method above
   OR
☐ Use Table WD-1 as a reference to navigate through the document using keyboard shortcuts

Table WD-1 Navigation Keyboard Shortcuts

Key	Moves the insertion point
[Ctrl][Home]	To the beginning of the document
[Ctrl][End]	To the end of the document
[Home]	To the beginning of the current line
[End]	To the end of the current line
[Page Up]	One screen up
[Page Down]	One screen down
[→], [←]	To the right or left one character at a time
[Ctrl][→] [Ctrl][←]	To the right or left one word at a time
[↓], [↑]	Down or up one line at a time

Mouse Method

To change the view without moving the insertion point, do one of the following:

- ☐ Drag the **scroll box** in a scroll bar to move within the document
- ☐ Click above the scroll box in the vertical scroll bar to move up a screen without moving the insertion point
- ☐ Click below the scroll box in the vertical scroll bar to move down a screen without moving the insertion point
- ☐ Click the up scroll arrow in the vertical scroll bar to move up one line
- ☐ Click the down scroll arrow in the vertical scroll bar to move down one line
- ☐ Repeat bullets 2–5 above using the horizontal scroll bar and replacing up and down with left and right
- ☐ Click the **Next Page button** or the **Previous Page button** on the vertical scroll bar to move to the next or previous page

Word

USE VIEWS

Refer to Table WD-2 to change document views.

Table WD-2 Document Views

View	What you see	Ribbon Method - View tab	Shortcut Method - status bar
Print Layout view	Displays a document as it will look on a printed page	Click the **Print Layout button**	Click the **Print Layout view button**
Full Screen Reading view	Displays document text so it is easy to read and annotate	Click the **Full Screen Reading button**	Click the **Full Screen Reading view button**
Web Layout view	Displays a document as it will appear when viewed in a Web browser	Click the **Web Layout button**	Click the **Web Layout view button**
Outline view	Displays the headings and their related subtext in hierarchical order	Click the **Outline button**	Click the **Outline view button**
Draft view	Displays a simplified layout of a document, without margins, etc.	Click the **Draft button**	Click the **Draft view button**

USE KEYBOARD KEYTIPS

Display KeyTips

Shortcut Method

- [ ] Press **[Alt]** to display the KeyTips for any active tab on the Ribbon and on the Quick Access toolbar
- [ ] Press the letter or number for the specific command for the active tab on the Ribbon
- [ ] Press additional letters or numbers as needed to complete the command sequence
- [ ] If two letters appear, press each one in order; for some commands you will find that you have to click an option from a gallery or menu to complete the command sequence
- [ ] The KeyTips turn off automatically at the end of the command sequence

Hide KeyTips

Shortcut Method

☐ Press **[Alt]** to hide the KeyTips for each Ribbon command

GET HELP

Ribbon Method

☐ Click the **Microsoft Office Word Help button** 🔘 on the Ribbon
☐ Use Table WD-3 as a reference to select the most appropriate way to search for help using the Microsoft Word Help task pane

OR

☐ Point to any button on the Ribbon, then read the ScreenTip text
☐ If you see "Press F1 for more help." at the bottom of the ScreenTip, continue pointing to the button, then press **[F1]** to see targeted help on that button from Word Help

Shortcut Method

☐ Press **[F1]**
☐ Use Table WD-3 as a reference to select the most appropriate way to search for help using the Microsoft Word Help window

Table WD-3 Microsoft Help Window Options

Option	To use
Browse Word Help	Click a link representing a topic you want to read about; click subtopics that appear until you see help text for the topic
Back button	Click to return to the previously displayed information
Forward button	Click to go forward in the sequence of previously displayed information
Stop button	Click to stop searching on a topic
Refresh button	Click to refresh the Help window content
Home button	Click to return to the Word Help and How-to window
Print button	Click to print the current page
Change Font Size button	Click to enlarge or shrink the help text
Show Table of Contents	Click to show the Table of Contents pane, showing topic links you can click
Keep on Top	Click to keep the Help window on top as you work; button becomes the Not On Top button, which you click to let the Help window go behind the current window as you work
Type words to search for box	Type a word, then click the Search button
Search button list arrow	Click the list arrow, then click the area, such as Content from Office Online, All Word, or Word help

Word

WORD EXAM REFERENCE

Objectives:

1. Creating and customizing documents
2. Formatting content
3. Working with visual content
4. Organizing content
5. Reviewing documents
6. Sharing and securing content

WORD OBJECTIVE 1: CREATING AND CUSTOMIZING DOCUMENTS

WORK WITH TEMPLATES

Create Documents Using Templates

Ribbon Method

- [ ] Click the **Office button** , click **New**, click **Installed Templates**, click a category in the left pane, click an appropriate template in the preview window, then click **Create** to create a template based on a Microsoft template
- [ ] Click the **Office button** , click **New**, click **My Templates**, click a category in the left pane, click an appropriate template in the preview window, then click **Create** to create a template based on a user-created template

Create Templates Based on Documents

Ribbon Method

- [ ] Open or create a document, click the **Office button** , click **Save As**, click **Word Template**, type a meaningful name in the File name text box, navigate to an appropriate location, then click **Save**

Apply Quick Styles to Documents

Ribbon Method

- [ ] Select the text, click the **More button** in the Styles group on the Home tab, then click an appropriate style

FORMAT DOCUMENTS USING THEMES

Preview and Change the Theme Applied to a Document

Ribbon Method

☐ Click the **Page Layout tab**, click the **Themes button** in the Themes group, then move the pointer over each theme in the gallery to preview the theme

☐ Click an appropriate theme

Change the Theme Set as the Default

Ribbon Method

☐ Click the **Office button** 🗔, click **New**, click **Blank document**, then click **Create**

☐ Click the **Page Layout tab**, click the **Themes button** in the Themes group, then click an appropriate theme

☐ Click the Home tab, click the **Change Styles button** in the Styles group, then click **Set as Default**

Shortcut Method

☐ Press **[Ctrl][N]** to open a new blank document

☐ Follow the steps in bullets 2–3 of the Change the Theme Set as the Default Ribbon Method above

Reset Template to Its Default Theme

Ribbon Method

☐ Click the **Page Layout tab**, click the **Themes button** in the Themes group, then click **Reset to Theme from Template**

CUSTOMIZE THEMES

Customize Theme Effects

Ribbon Method

☐ Click the **Page Layout tab**, then click the **Theme Effects button** in the Themes group

☐ Click an appropriate option

Customize Theme Fonts

Ribbon Method

☐ Click the **Page Layout tab**, then click the **Theme Fonts button** 🄰 in the Themes group

☐ Click an appropriate **option**

OR

☐ Click **Create New Theme Fonts**, select a Heading font and a Body font, type a name in the **Name text box**, then click **Save**

Customize Theme Colors

Ribbon Method

- [ ] Click the **Page Layout tab**, then click the **Theme Colors button** in the Themes group
- [ ] Click an appropriate option

  OR

- [ ] Click **Create New Theme Colors**, select appropriate options, type a name in the **Name text box**, then click **Save**

FORMAT DOCUMENT BACKGROUNDS

Apply Watermarks

Ribbon Method

- [ ] Click the **Page Layout tab**, then click **Watermark** in the Page Background group
- [ ] Scroll to see the preset watermarks available, then click an appropriate watermark

  OR

- [ ] Click the **Page Layout tab**, click **Watermark** in the Page Background group, click **Custom Watermark**, then click the **Picture watermark option button** in the Printed Watermark dialog box
- [ ] Click **Select Picture**, navigate to an appropriate drive and folder, double-click the picture, click **Apply**, then click **Close**

Change Page Background Color

Ribbon Method

- [ ] Click the **Page Layout tab**, click **Page Color** in the Page Background group, then click an appropriate color

Apply Page Borders

Ribbon Method

- [ ] Click the **Page Layout tab**, click **Page Borders** in the Page Background group, then click an appropriate border

Insert a Blank Page

Ribbon Method

- [ ] Click the **Insert tab**, then click **Blank Page** to add a blank page at the location of the insertion point

Insert a Cover Page

- [ ] Click the **Insert tab**, click **Cover Page**, scroll through the gallery of choices, then click an appropriate cover page
- [ ] Replace the placeholder text with your content

FORMAT PAGES

Set Page Orientation

Ribbon Method

☐ Click the **Page Layout tab**, click the **Orientation button**, then click **Portrait** or **Landscape**

OR

☐ Click the **Page Layout tab**, click the **launcher** 🔲 in the Page Setup group to open the Page Setup dialog box, click the **Margins tab** if necessary, then click **Portrait** or **Landscape**

Set Paper Size

Ribbon Method

☐ Click the **Page Layout tab**, click the **launcher** 🔲 in the Page Setup group to open the Page Setup dialog box, click the **Paper tab** if necessary, click the **Paper Size list arrow**, then select a paper size

OR

☐ Click the **Page Layout tab**, click the **launcher** 🔲 in the Page Setup group to open the Page Setup dialog box, click the **Paper tab** if necessary, then enter values in the Width and Height text boxes

Set Margins

Ribbon Method

☐ Click the **Page Layout tab**, then click the **Margins button** in the Page Setup group

☐ Click a **preset margin option** or click **Custom Margins**, enter values in the Top, Bottom, Left, and Right text boxes, then click **OK**

OR

☐ Click the **Page Layout tab**, click the **launcher** 🔲 in the Page Setup group, then click the **Margins tab** in the Page Setup dialog box, if necessary

☐ Enter values in the Top, Bottom, Left, and Right text boxes, then click **OK**

Mouse Method

☐ Click the **View Ruler button** 🔲 at the top of the vertical scroll bar to display the rulers if necessary, then select appropriate text to apply new margins
(*Note*: Press **[Ctrl][A]** to select the entire document or drag the mouse over text you want to select)

☐ Drag the **Left Indent marker** 🔲 to an appropriate location on the horizontal ruler

☐ Drag the **Right Indent marker** 🔺 to an appropriate location on the horizontal ruler

Insert Page Numbers

Ribbon Method

□ Click the **Insert tab**
□ Click the **Page Number button** in the Header & Footer group
□ Point to a location where you want the page number to appear, then click an appropriate option

OR

□ Click the **Insert tab**, click **Header**, click one of the built-in headers or click **Edit Header** to open the Header area, then follow the steps in bullets 2–3 of the Insert Page Numbers Ribbon Method above

OR

□ Click the **Insert tab**, click **Footer**, click one of the built-in footers or click **Edit Footer** to open the Footer area, then follow the steps in bullets 2–3 of the Insert Page Numbers Ribbon Method above

CREATE AND MODIFY HEADERS AND FOOTERS (NOT USING QUICK PARTS)

Add Automatic Date and Time Stamps

Ribbon Method

□ Click the **Insert tab**, then click the **Date & Time button** in the Text group
□ In the Date and Time dialog box, select an appropriate format in the Available formats list
□ Check the **Update automatically** check box to automatically update the date and time stamp each time the document is opened

Modify Automatic Date and Time Stamps

Ribbon Method

□ Select the date and time stamp you want to modify, then follow the steps in bullets 1–3 of the Add Automatic Date and Time Stamps Ribbon Method above

Shortcut Method

□ Right-click the date and time stamp, click **Edit Field** on the shortcut menu, then select a new date format in the Field properties list in the Field dialog box

OR

□ Right-click the date and time stamp, then click **Update Field** on the shortcut menu

OR

□ Click the date and time stamp, then click **Update** on the content control title bar

OR

□ Select the date and time stamp, then press **[F9]** to update the field

Create Different First Pages

Ribbon Method

☐ Press **[Ctrl][Home]** to move to the beginning of the document, click the **Insert tab**, click the **Header button**, then click one of the built-in headers or click **Edit Header** to open the Header area or click the **Footer button**, then click one of the built-in footers or click **Edit Footer** to open the Footer area

☐ Click the **Different First Page check box** in the Options group to select it

☐ Type the text or insert the content you want to appear in the first page header, if any

☐ Click the **Next Section button**, then type the text or insert the content you want to appear in the header for the remaining pages in the section

Add or Modify Page Numbers in Headers and Footers

Ribbon Method

☐ Press **[Ctrl][Home]** to move to the beginning of the document, click the **Insert tab**, click the **Header button**, then click one of the built-in headers or click **Edit Header** to open the Header area or click the **Footer button**, then click one of the built-in footers or click **Edit Footer** to open the Footer area

☐ To add a page number, click the **Page Number button** in the Header and Footer group on the Header and Footer Tools Design tab

☐ Point to the **location** (Top of Page, Bottom of Page, Page Margins, or Current Position) where you want the page number to appear, view the options in the gallery that opens, then click the option you want

OR

☐ To modify a page number, select a page number in a header or footer area, point to the location where you want the page number to appear, then click the option you want to replace the current option

OR

☐ To format a page number, select a page number in a header or footer area, then select formatting options in the Font group and in the Paragraph group

Shortcut Method

☐ To format a page number, select a **page number** in a header or footer area, then select **formatting options** on the Mini toolbar

CREATE AND FORMAT COLUMNS

Set Columns

Ribbon Method

☐ Select the text you want to format as columns
(*Note*: To format a section of a document in columns, position the insertion point at the beginning of the section)

☐ Click the **Page Layout tab**, then click the **Columns button** in the Page Setup Group

☐ Select one of the **predefined options** in the menu that opens

OR

☐ Click **More Columns** to open the Columns dialog box, select the desired settings, then click **OK**

Change Column Width and Spacing

Ribbon Method

☐ Position the insertion point in the text you want to change
☐ Click the **Page Layout tab**, click the **Columns button** in the Page Setup group, then click **More Columns** to open the Columns dialog box
☐ Enter the desired settings in the width and spacing text boxes, then click **OK**

Mouse Method

☐ Position the insertion point in the text you want to change
☐ Drag the column markers on the horizontal ruler to the new location(s)

CREATE, MODIFY, AND UPDATE TABLES OF CONTENTS

Update Tables of Contents

Ribbon Method

☐ Make changes to the document (such as changing page numbers or deleting heads and their subtext)
☐ Click an entry in the table of contents to select the table of contents, click the **References tab**, then click the **Update Table button** in the Table of Contents group
☐ Select an appropriate **option**, then click **OK**
☐ Click the Table of Contents head (or anywhere in the document) to deselect the table of contents

Shortcut Method

☐ Make changes to the document (such as changing page numbers, deleting heads and their subtext)
☐ Right-click the **table of contents**, then click **Update Field** on the shortcut menu that opens
☐ Follow the steps in bullets 2–3 of the Update Tables of Contents Ribbon Method above

Modify Tables of Contents by Adding or Deleting Text

Ribbon Method

☐ Select the text you want to add to the table of contents
☐ Click the **References tab**, click the **Add Text list arrow** in the Table of Contents group, then select the level (1, 2, or 3) you want to associate with the selected text
☐ Click **Update Table** in the Table of Contents group to add the text to the table of contents

OR

□ Follow the steps in the Update Tables of Contents Ribbon Method above to add or delete text from a table of contents

□ To delete an entry but not the content associated with an entry, position the selection pointer ⩗ to the left of the table of contents entry you want to delete, click to select the entry (the entire table of contents is shaded gray and the entry is shaded blue indicating it is selected), then press **[Delete]** to delete the entry

Apply a Different Format to the Tables of Contents

Ribbon Method

□ Click the **References tab**, then click the **Table of Contents button** in the Table of Contents group to open the Table of Contents dialog box

□ Click the **Formats list arrow** in the General section, scroll as needed to select a new format, click the format you want to apply, then click **OK**

□ Click **Yes** if a warning box opens asking to replace the current table of contents

CREATE, MODIFY, AND UPDATE INDEXES

Mark Text as an Entry for Indexing

Ribbon Method

□ Select the text you want to mark as an index entry, click the **Reference tab**, then click the **Mark Entry button** in the Index group to open the Mark Index Entry dialog box

□ Verify the text you selected appears in the Main Entry text box in the Index section, or adjust the Mark Index Entry dialog box as needed to create an appropriate type of index entry (such as subentry, cross-reference)

□ Click **Mark** to mark only the selected text as the index entry or click **Mark All** to include all instances of the selected text in the index

Modify an Index

Ribbon Method

□ Scroll to the index, click the **References tab**, then click the **Insert Index button** in the Index group

□ In the Index dialog box, select a new format and make other changes as appropriate, then click **OK**

□ Click **Yes** to replace the current index

Update an Index

Ribbon Method

□ Mark more entries or change marked entries

□ Click an entry in the Index to select the index, click the **References tab**, then click the **Update Index button** in the Index group

□ Click the Index head (or anywhere in the document) to deselect the index

Shortcut Method
- [ ] Mark more entries or change marked entries
- [ ] Right-click the index, then click **Update Field** on the shortcut menu that opens
- [ ] Click the Index head (or anywhere in the document) to deselect the index

MODIFY DOCUMENT PROPERTIES

Enter Keywords Associated with the Document

Ribbon Method
- [ ] Click the **Office button** 🔘, point to **Prepare**, then click **Properties** to open the Document Information panel
- [ ] Click in the **Keywords text box**, then type words or phrases you want associated with the document

Properties from View Tab

Ribbon Method
- [ ] Click the **View tab**, then click a view in the Document Views group

INSERT DOCUMENT NAVIGATION TOOLS

Add Bookmarks

Ribbon Method
- [ ] Select the text you want to mark as a bookmark (or place the insertion point where you want to add a bookmark), click the **Insert tab**, click the **Bookmark button** in the Links group, type the text you want to use as the bookmark under the Bookmark name, then click **Add** (*Note*: Bookmark names must begin with a letter, can contain numbers, cannot include spaces, and can include an underscore to separate words)

Add Hyperlinks

Ribbon Method
- [ ] Select the text or picture you want to create as a hyperlink, click the **Insert tab**, then click the **Hyperlink button** in the Links group
- [ ] In the Insert Hyperlinks dialog box, click the option you want to link to in the Links to list, complete the rest of the Insert Hyperlinks dialog box based on the Links to option you selected, then click **OK**

Shortcut Method
- [ ] Right-click the text or picture you want to create as a hyperlink, then click **Hyperlink** on the shortcut menu that opens
- [ ] Follow the steps in bullet 2 of the Add Hyperlinks Ribbon Method above

CUSTOMIZE WORD OPTIONS

Set Custom AutoCorrect Options

Ribbon Method

- ☐ Click the **Office button** 🔵, click **Word Options** on the Office menu, click **Proofing** in the Word Options dialog box, then click the **AutoCorrect Options button**
- ☐ Click the **AutoCorrect tab** in the AutoCorrect dialog box, if necessary
- ☐ Type the text you want to correct automatically in the Replace text box
- ☐ Type the text you want to insert automatically in the Replace with text box
- ☐ Click **Add**, click **OK**, then click **OK** in the Word Options dialog box

Set Custom Options for the Quick Access Toolbar

Ribbon Method

- ☐ Click the **Customize Quick Access toolbar button** ▼ in the title bar, then click the command you want to add from the list of options or click **More Options** to open the Customize tab of the Options dialog box
- ☐ On the Customize tab in the Options dialog box, click the **Choose commands list arrow**, then click a category
- ☐ Select a command in the list under the category, click **Add**, then click **OK**
- ☐ To move the Quick Access toolbar below the Ribbon, click the **Customize Quick Access toolbar button** ▼ in the title bar, then click **Show Below the Ribbon**
- ☐ To minimize the Quick Access toolbar below the Ribbon, click the **Customize Quick Access toolbar button** ▼ in the title bar, then click **Minimize the Ribbon**

Change the Default Save Location

Ribbon Method

- ☐ Click the **Office button** 🔵, click the **Word Options button**, click **Save** in the left pane, then write down the contents of the Default file location text box
- ☐ Click **Browse** next to the Default file location text box, navigate to the folder where you want to save your files, select the folder, click **OK** to select the location, then click **OK** as needed to exit the Word Options dialog box
- ☐ Start a new blank document, click the **Save button** 💾 on the Quick Access toolbar, then verify that the default file location you specified appears as the location where the document should be saved

Set the Open E-mail Attachments Feature in Reading Mode to Disabled

Ribbon Method

- ☐ Click the **View tab**, then click the **Full Screen Reading button**
- ☐ Click the **View Options button** on the title bar, then click **Don't Open Attachments in Full Screen**

Shortcut Method
☐ Click the **Full Screen Reading button** 🖼 on the status bar
☐ Click the **View Options button** on the title bar, then click **Don't Open Attachments in Full Screen**

Change Username and Initials

Ribbon Method
☐ Click the **Office button** 🗔, click **Word Options**, then click the **Popular tab**, if necessary
☐ Select the **contents** of User Name text box, type a new user name, press **[Tab]**, type new initials in the Initial text boxes, then click **OK**

OR

☐ Click the **Review tab**, click the **Track Changes list arrow**, then click **Change User Name**
☐ Select the contents of User Name text box, type a new user name, press **[Tab]**, type new initials in the Initial text boxes, then click **OK**

Change Research Options

Ribbon Method
☐ Click the **Review tab**, then click the **Research button** in the Proofing group to open the Research task pane
☐ Click the **Research options link** at the bottom of the task pane to open the Research Options dialog box
☐ Check or uncheck options to select or deselect services, click the **Add Services button** to add services available, click the **Update/Remove button** to update or remove services already listed, or click the **Parental Control button** to set restrictions

OR

☐ Click the **Review tab**, click the **Thesaurus button** in the Proofing group to open the Research task pane, then follow the steps in bullets 2–3 of the Change Research Options Ribbon Method above

OR

☐ Click the **Review tab**, click the **Translate button** in the Proofing group to open the Research task pane, then follow the steps in bullets 2–3 of the Change Research Options Ribbon Method above

WORD OBJECTIVE 2: FORMATTING CONTENT

APPLY STYLES

Change from One Style to Another

Ribbon Method

- ☐ Click the **Home tab**, click the **Change Styles button** in the styles group, click **Style Set**, then click an appropriate style set

  OR

- ☐ Select the text, click the **Home tab**, click the **More button** ⬇ in the Styles group, then click an appropriate Quick Style

  OR

- ☐ Select the text, click the **Home tab**, then click the **launcher** ⬜ in the Styles group to open the **Styles task pane**
- ☐ Scroll the list of available styles, then click an appropriate style

Shortcut Method

- ☐ Select the text, right-click, then click the **Styles button** 🔼 on the Mini toolbar
- ☐ Click a Quick Style in the gallery that opens or click **Apply Styles** at the bottom of the gallery to open the Apply Styles dialog box, click the **Style Name list arrow**, select a style, then close the dialog box

Copy Formats Using the Format Painter

Ribbon Method

- ☐ Select the text that has the formatting you want to copy, then click the **Home tab**
- ☐ Click the **Format Painter button** 🖌 in the Clipboard group one time, then select the text you want to format

  OR

- ☐ Click the **Format Painter button** 🖌 in the Clipboard group two times, select the text you want to format and apply the same formatting to multiple places in the document, then click 🖌 to turn off the Format Painter

Shortcut Method

- ☐ Select the text that has the formatting you want to copy, then press **[Ctrl][Shift][C]** to copy the formatting
- ☐ Select the text you want to format, then press **[Ctrl][Shift][V]** to apply the formatting
- ☐ Repeat for each instance

Apply Heading Styles

Ribbon Method

- ☐ Select the text you want to apply a Heading style to, click the **Home tab**, click the **More button** ⬇ in the Styles group, then click the Quick Style heading you want to apply

Word

OR

☐ Select the text you want to apply a style to, click the **Home tab**, then click the **launcher** 🖺 in the Styles group to open the Styles task pane

☐ Scroll the list of available styles, then click the heading style you want to apply

Shortcut Method

☐ Select the text to which you want to apply a style, right-click, then click the **Styles button** 🔼 on the Mini toolbar

☐ Click a Quick Style heading in the gallery that opens or click **Apply Styles** at the bottom of the gallery to open the Apply Styles dialog box, click the **Style Name list arrow**, select a heading style, then close the dialog box

Format Text as Body Text

Ribbon Method

☐ Click the **View tab**, then click the **Outline button** in the Document Views group

☐ Select the text you want formatted as body text, then click the **Demote to Body Text button** 🢖 in the Outline Tools group

OR

☐ Select the text you want to format as body text, click the **Home tab**, then click the **Normal style button** in the Styles group to return the text to the Normal style (body text) or click the **No Spacing button** in the Styles group to clear all formatting and return the text to Normal style with no formatting

OR

☐ Select the text you want to format as body text, click the **Home tab**, then click the **Clear Formatting button** 🔲 in the Font group to return the text to the Normal style (body text)

Shortcut Method

☐ Select the text you want to format as body text, right-click, then click the **Styles button** 🔼 on the Mini toolbar

☐ Click **Normal style** in the gallery that opens or click **Apply Styles** at the bottom of the gallery to open the Apply Styles dialog box, click the **Style Name list arrow**, select **Normal**, then close the dialog box

CREATE AND MODIFY STYLES

Format Text and Create a New Style

Ribbon Method

☐ Apply the formatting you want associated with a new style to text

☐ Click the **Home tab**, then click the **More button** 🔽 in the Styles group

☐ Click **Save Selection as a New Quick Style**, then in the Create New Style from Formatting dialog box, type a name for the new style

☐ Click **Modify** to make any changes to the style, select the font and paragraph formatting you want, then click **OK**

Shortcut Method
- ☐ Apply the formatting you want associated with a new style to text, then click the **Styles button** 🔽 on the Mini toolbar
- ☐ Follow the steps in bullets 2–3 of the Format Text and Create a New Style Ribbon Method above

Change Fonts Associated with a Style or Theme

Ribbon Method
- ☐ Click the **Home tab**, click the **Change Styles button** 🔽, then point to the **Fonts button**
- ☐ Scroll the list of built-in fonts, then click the font you want to apply

OR

- ☐ Click the **Home tab**, click the **Change Styles button**, point to the **Fonts button**, or click the **Page Layout tab**, then click the **Theme Fonts button** 🔽 in the Themes group
- ☐ Click **Create New Theme Fonts**
- ☐ In the Create New Theme Fonts dialog box, click the **Heading font list arrow**, select a heading font, click the **Body font list arrow**, select a body text font, type a name in the Name text box, then click **Save**
- ☐ Repeat the steps in bullets 1–2 of the Change Fonts Associated with a Style or Theme Ribbon Method above to apply the font

Create a New Style Based on an Existing Style

Ribbon Method
- ☐ Click the **Home tab**, click the **launcher** 🔲 in the Styles group, then click the **New Style button** 🔳
- ☐ In the Create New Style from Formatting dialog box, type a name for the new style, click the **Style type list arrow**, select a style type, click the **Style based on list arrow**, select an appropriate style, font, and paragraph formatting options, then click **OK**

Reveal Style Formatting

Ribbon Method
- ☐ Click the **Home tab**, then click the **launcher** 🔲 in the Styles group to open the Styles task pane
- ☐ Select the word in the document for which you want to reveal formatting, click the **Style Inspector button** 🔳 at the bottom of the Styles task pane, then click the **Reveal Formatting button** 🔳 in the Style Inspector to open the Reveal Formatting task pane
- ☐ Click appropriate format expand buttons, then review the formatting settings for the selected word

Shortcut Method
- ☐ Select the text in the document for which you want to reveal formatting, then press **[Shift][F1]**
- ☐ In the Reveal Formatting task pane, click appropriate format expand buttons, then review the formatting settings for the selected word

Word

FORMAT CHARACTERS

Apply and Modify Character Formats

☐ Select the text to which you want to apply a character format, then use Table WD-3 as a reference to apply the character formatting you want

Table WD-3 Applying and Modifying Character Formats

Format to apply or modify	Ribbon Method: Home tab/Font group	Shortcut Method: Mini toolbar	Shortcut Method: Keyboard	Launcher in the Font group: Font dialog box
Apply a new font	Click the **Font list arrow**, then click a font	Click the **Font list arrow**, then click a font	Press **[Ctrl][Shift][F]**	Click a font
Apply a new font size	Click the **Font Size list arrow**, then click a font size, or type a value in the Font Size text box	Click the **Font Size list arrow**, then click a font size, or type a value in the Font Size text box	Press **[Ctrl][Shift][P]**, then click a font size; or type the value in the Font Size text box	Click a font size; or type the value in the Font Size text box
Increase the font size one point	Click the **Grow Font button** A⁺	Click the **Grow Font button** A⁺	Press **[Ctrl][>]**	
Decrease the font size one point	Click the **Shrink Font button** A˅	Click the **Shrink Font button** A˅	Press **[Ctrl][<]**	
Clear formatting	Click the **Clear Formatting button**	Click the **Styles button** A˅ on the Mini Toolbar, then click **Clear Formatting**	Right-click, click the **Styles button** A˅ on the Mini Toolbar, then click **Clear Formatting**	
Apply bold	Click the **Bold button** B	Click the **Bold button** B	Press **[Ctrl][B]**	Click **Bold** in the Font style list
Apply italic	Click the **Italic button** I	Click the **Italic button** I	Press **[Ctrl][I]**	Click **Italic** in the Font style list

(continued)

Table WD-3 Applying and Modifying Character Formats (continued)

Format to apply or modify	Ribbon Method: Home tab/Font group	Shortcut Method: Mini toolbar	Shortcut Method: Keyboard	Launcher in the Font group: Font dialog box
Apply underlining	Click the **Underline button** $\boxed{\text{U}}$; or click the **Underline list arrow** $\boxed{\text{U} \; \cdot}$, select a preformatted underline or click More Underlines to open the Font dialog box, then refer to the directions in the last column		Press **[Ctrl][U]**	Click the **Underline style list arrow** and select a style, click the **Underline color list arrow**, select a color, then click **OK**
Apply strikethrough	Click the **Strikethrough button** $\boxed{\text{abc}}$			Click the **Strikethrough check box** in the Effects section
Apply subscript	Click the **Subscript button** $\boxed{\text{x}_2}$		Press **[Ctrl][=]**	Click the **Subscript check box** in the Effects section
Apply superscript	Click the **Superscript** $\boxed{\text{x}^2}$		Press **[Ctrl][Shift][+]**	Click the **Superscript check box** in the Effects section
Apply highlighting to text	Click the **Text Highlight Color button** $\boxed{\text{aby}}$ to apply the active highlight color or click the **Text Highlight Color list arrow** $\boxed{\text{aby} \cdot}$, then select a new color	Click the **Text Highlight Color button** $\boxed{\text{aby}}$ to apply the active highlight color or click the **Text Highlight Color list arrow** $\boxed{\text{aby} \cdot}$, then select a new color		

(continued)

Table WD-3 Applying and Modifying Character Formats (continued)

Format to apply or modify	Ribbon Method: Home tab/Font group	Shortcut Method: Mini toolbar	Shortcut Method: Keyboard	Launcher in the Font group: Font dialog box
Apply a new font color	Click the **Font Color button** A to apply the active font color; click the **Font Color list arrow** A ·, then select a color from a palette of available colors; or click **More Colors**, then create a custom color	Click the **Font Color button** A to apply the active font color or click the **Font Color list arrow** A · to select a color from a palette of available colors; or click **More Colors**, then create a custom color		Click the **Font Color list arrow** to select a color from a palette of available colors; or click **More Colors** to create a custom color

Apply Character Spacing

Ribbon Method

☐ Select the text, click the **launcher** in the Font group to open the Font dialog box, then click the **Character Spacing tab**

☐ On the Character Spacing tab, specify the **Scale**, **Spacing**, **Position**, and **Kerning** for the selected text, then click **OK**

FORMAT PARAGRAPHS

Apply Line Spacing

Ribbon Method

☐ Click anywhere in the paragraph you want to format

☐ Click the **Line Spacing list arrow** , then click a preset line spacing option or click **Line Spacing Options**

☐ On the Indents and Spacing tab in the Paragraph dialog box, click the appropriate line spacing option, then click **OK**

OR

☐ Click the **launcher** in the Paragraph group, click the **Indents and Spacing tab** if necessary, select the appropriate line spacing option, then click **OK**

Apply Paragraph Spacing

Ribbon Method

☐ Click the **Page Layout tab**

☐ Click the **Spacing Before arrows** in the paragraph group to increase or decrease the amount of space before a paragraph or type the value in the Before text box

☐ Click the **Spacing After arrows** in the paragraph group to increase or decrease the amount of space after a paragraph or type the value in the After text box

OR

☐ Click the **launcher** 🔲 in the Paragraph group on the Page Layout tab or the Home tab to open the Paragraph dialog box

☐ Click the **Indents and Spacing tab** if necessary, select the appropriate Before and After options, then click **OK**
(*Note*: Click the Don't add spacing between paragraphs of the same style check box, if you do not want to change paragraph spacing between paragraphs with the same style)

Apply Alignment

☐ Click anywhere in the paragraph you want to align, then use Table WD-4 as a reference to apply the alignment formatting you want

Table WD-4 Applying Alignment

Alignment to apply or modify	Ribbon Method: Home tab/ Paragraph group	Shortcut Method: Mini toolbar	Shortcut Method: Keyboard	Paragraph dialog box/ Indents and Spacing tab*
Left	Click the **Align Text Left button** 📄		Press **[Ctrl][L]**	In the General section, click the **Alignment list arrow**, then click **Left**
Center	Click the **Center button** 📄	Click the **Center button** 📄	Press **[Ctrl][E]**	In the General section, click the **Alignment list arrow**, then click **Center**

* Click the launcher 🔲 in the Paragraph group on the Home tab or on the Page Layout tab to open the Paragraph dialog box.

(continued)

Table WD-4 Applying Alignment (continued)

Alignment to apply or modify	Ribbon Method: Home tab/ Paragraph group	Shortcut Method: Mini toolbar	Shortcut Method: Keyboard	Paragraph dialog box/ Indents and Spacing tab*
Right	Click the **Align Text Right** button ▤		Press **[Ctrl][R]**	In the General section, click the **Alignment list arrow**, then click **Right**
Justify	Click the **Justify** button ▤		Press **[Ctrl][J]**	In the General section, click the **Alignment list arrow**, then click **Justify**

* Click the launcher ▣ in the Paragraph group on the Home tab or on the Page Layout tab to open the Paragraph dialog box.

Set Paragraph Indentation

☐ Click anywhere in the paragraph you want to indent, then use Table WD-5 as a reference to apply the indent formatting you want

Table WD-5 Applying Indentation Formatting

Indent formatting to apply	Ribbon Method	Shortcut Method: Mini toolbar	Shortcut Method: Ruler	Paragraph dialog box/ Indents and Spacing tab*
Increase indent by preset .5"	Click the **Home tab**, click the **Increase indent button** ▤ in the Paragraph group	Click the **Increase indent button** ▤		

* Click the launcher ▣ in the Paragraph group on the Home tab or on the Page Layout tab to open the Paragraph dialog box.

(continued)

Word

Table WD-5 Applying Indentation Formatting (continued)

Indent formatting to apply	Ribbon Method	Shortcut Method: Mini toolbar	Shortcut Method: Ruler	Paragraph dialog box/ Indents and Spacing tab*
Decrease indent by preset .5"	Click the **Home tab**, click the **Decrease Indent button** 📃 in the Paragraph group	Click the **Decrease Indent button** 📃		
Left indent	Click the **Page Layout tab**, then use the arrows or enter a value in the Indent Left text box		Drag the **Left Indent marker** ▢ to the desired position	Use the arrows or enter a value in the Left text box in the Indentation section
Right indent	Click the **Page Layout tab**, then use the arrows or enter a value in the Indent Right text box		Drag the **Right Indent marker** △ to the desired position	Use the arrows or enter a value in the Right text box in the Indentation section
First Line Indent			Drag the First **Line Indent marker** ▽ to the desired position OR Scroll to the **First Line Indent marker** ▽ in the tab indicator, click ▽ to select it, then click the ruler at the desired position	

* Click the launcher 📧 in the Paragraph group on the Home tab or on the Page Layout tab to open the Paragraph dialog box.

(continued)

Table WD-5 Applying Indentation Formatting (continued)

Indent formatting to apply	Ribbon Method	Shortcut Method: Mini toolbar	Shortcut Method: Ruler	Paragraph dialog box/ Indents and Spacing tab*
Hanging Indent			Drag the **Hanging Indent marker** 🔲 to the desired position on the ruler OR Scroll to the **Hanging Indent marker** 🏠 in the tab indicator, click 🏠 to select it, then click the ruler at the desired position	
Negative Indent (Outdent)	Click the **Page Layout tab**, then use the arrows or enter a negative value in the Indent Left text box		Drag the **Left Indent marker** 🔲 to the desired position on the ruler (the position is to the left of the current paragraph)	Use the arrows or enter a negative value in the Left text box in the Indentation section

* Click the launcher 🔲 in the Paragraph group on the Home tab or on the Page Layout tab to open the Paragraph dialog box.

Format Quoted Material

Ribbon Method

☐ Click the **Home tab**, position the insertion point in the quotation, click the **More button** 🔽 in the Styles group, then click **Intense Quote**

OR

☐ Click the **Home tab**, position the insertion point in the quotation, then refer to Table WD-5 and use one of the methods listed in the table to indent the left margin and right margin of the quoted material

SET AND CLEAR TABS

Set Tabs

Use Table WD-6 as a reference on how to set tabs.

Table WD-6 Setting Tabs

Tab setting to apply	Ribbon Method	Shortcut Method: Ruler
	To open the Tabs dialog box: Click the **launcher** 🔲 in the Paragraph group on the Home tab or the Page Layout tab to open the Paragraph dialog box, then click the **Tabs button** OR Double-click a tab stop on the horizontal ruler	To use the tab indicators: Click **View Ruler button** 🔲 at the top of the vertical scroll bar to display the rulers if necessary, then click the tab indicator at the left end of the horizontal ruler until the desired tab indicator is active
🔲 Left tab	Type the value in the Tab stop position text box, then click **OK**	With the Left tab indicator active, click the horizontal ruler
🔲 Center tab	Type the value in the Tab stop position text box, then click **OK**	With the Center tab indicator active, click the horizontal ruler
🔲 Right tab	Type the value in the Tab stop position text box, then click **OK**	With the Right tab indicator active, click the horizontal ruler
🔲 Decimal tab	Type the value in the Tab stop position text box, then click **OK**	With the Decimal tab indicator active, click the horizontal ruler
🔲 Bar tab	Type the value in the Tab stop position text box, then click **OK**	With the Bar tab indicator active, click the horizontal ruler

Set Tabs with Leaders

Ribbon Method

☐ Open the **Tabs dialog box** (refer to Table WD-6 as needed), select the tab stop in the Tab stop position list box that you want to modify, click the **leader style option button** for an appropriate leader style, then click **OK**

Remove One Tab

Ribbon Method

☐ Open the **Tabs dialog box** (refer to Table WD-6 as needed), select the tab stop in the Tab stop position list box that you want to modify, click the **Clear button**, then click **OK**

Mouse Method

☐ Position the pointer over the tab stop you want to remove
☐ Use the ▷ pointer to drag the tab stop off the horizontal ruler

Remove All Tabs

Ribbon Method

☐ Open the **Tabs dialog box** (refer to Table WD-6 as needed), click the **Clear All button**, then click **OK**

CUT, COPY, AND PASTE TEXT

Cut and Paste

Ribbon Method

☐ Select the text you want to cut, click the **Home tab**, then click the **Cut button** 🔏
☐ Position the insertion point where you want to paste the text, then click the **Paste button** 📋

Shortcut Method

☐ Select the text you want to cut, right-click, then click **Cut** on the shortcut menu
☐ Position the insertion point where you want to paste the text, right-click, then click **Paste** on the shortcut menu

OR

☐ Select the text you want to cut, then press **[Ctrl][X]**
☐ Position the insertion point where you want to paste the text, then press **[Ctrl][V]**

Copy and Paste

Ribbon Method

☐ Select the text you want to copy, click the **Home tab**, then click the **Copy button** 📄
☐ Position the insertion point where you want to paste the text, then click the **Paste button**

Shortcut Method

☐ Select the text you want to copy, right-click, then click **Copy** on the shortcut menu
☐ Position the insertion point where you want to paste the text, right-click, then click **Paste** on the shortcut menu

OR

□ Select the text you want to copy, then press **[Ctrl][C]**
□ Position the insertion point where you want to paste the text, then press **[Ctrl][V]**

Use the Clipboard to Paste Text

Ribbon Method

□ Click the **Home tab**, then click the **launcher** 🖫 in the Clipboard group
□ Use the **Cut button** ✂ and the **Copy button** 🗈 in the Clipboard group on the Home tab to cut and copy text to the Clipboard
□ Position the insertion point where you want to paste the text
□ Move the pointer over the text in the Clipboard you want to paste, click the arrow that appears, then click **Paste**

Use the Mouse to Move Text

Mouse Method

□ Select the text you want to move, position the pointer over the selected text, then press and hold the mouse pointer until the pointer changes to ▷
□ Drag the pointer's vertical line to where you want to move the text, then release the mouse button

Use Paste Special

Ribbon Method

□ Select the text or object you want to paste, click the **Home tab**, then click the **Paste list arrow** to open the Paste Special dialog box
□ Click the **Paste option button** to create an embedded object OR click the **Paste link option button** to create a linked object
□ Click the format in the As list box, then click **OK**

Use Paste All

Ribbon Method

□ Follow the steps in bullets 1–3 of the Use the Clipboard to Paste Text Ribbon Method above
□ Click the **Paste All button** to paste all items on the Clipboard into the document at the location of the insertion point

Paste One

Ribbon Method

□ Follow the steps in bullets 1–3 of the Use the Clipboard to Paste Text Ribbon Method above
□ Move the pointer over the text in the Clipboard you want to paste in the document, then **click**

FIND AND REPLACE TEXT

Find Text

Ribbon Method

- ☐ Click the **Home tab**, then click the **Find button** in the Editing group to open the Find and Replace dialog box with the Find tab active
- ☐ Type the text you want to find in the Find what text box
- ☐ Click the **More button** to view and select additional search options
- ☐ Click the **Find Next button** to view each instance of the text in the Find what text box
- ☐ Click **Cancel** to close the Find and Replace dialog box

Shortcut Method

- ☐ Press **[Ctrl][F]** to open the Find and Replace dialog box with the Find tab active
- ☐ Follow the steps in bullets 2–5 of the Find Text Ribbon Method above

Find and Replace Text

Ribbon Method

- ☐ Click the **Home tab**, then click the **Replace button** in the Editing group to open the Find and Replace dialog box with the Replace tab active
- ☐ Type the text you want to find and replace in the Find what text box
- ☐ Type the replacement text in the Replace with text box
- ☐ Click the **More button** to view additional search options, then select the appropriate search options
- ☐ Click the **Find Next button** to view the next instance of the text in the Find what text box, review the selected text, then click **Replace** to replace the selected text or click **Find Next** to leave the selected text as is and move to the next instance
- ☐ Click **Cancel** to close the Find and Replace dialog box

Shortcut Method

- ☐ Press **[Ctrl][H]** to open the Find and Replace dialog box with the Replace tab active
- ☐ Follow the steps in bullets 2–6 of the Find and Replace Text Ribbon Method above

Use Replace All

Ribbon Method

- ☐ Follow the steps in bullets 1–4 of the Find and Replace Text Ribbon Method above
- ☐ Click **Replace All** to replace all instances without preview
- ☐ Click **Cancel** to close the Find and Replace dialog box

Search for and Highlight Specific Text

Ribbon Method

☐ Follow the steps in bullets 1–3 of the Find Text Ribbon Method above
☐ Click **Reading Highlight**, then click **Highlight All** to highlight all instances of the text in the Find what text box
☐ Click **Cancel** to close the Find and Replace dialog box

CONTROL PAGINATION

Insert Page Breaks

Ribbon Method

☐ Position the insertion point where you want the page break to occur
☐ Click the **Page Layout tab**, click the **Breaks button** in the Page Setup Group, then click **Page** in the Page Breaks section

Shortcut Method

☐ Position the insertion point where you want the page break to occur, then press **[Ctrl][Enter]**

Delete Page Breaks

Shortcut Method

☐ Click the **Home tab**, click the **Show/Hide button** ¶ in the Paragraph group to display formatting marks
☐ Click to the left of the page break you want to delete to select it, then press **[Delete]**
OR
☐ Double-click a page break to select it, then press **[Delete]**

CREATE AND MODIFY SECTIONS

Create Section Breaks

Ribbon Method

☐ Position the insertion point where you want the section break to occur
☐ Click the **Page Layout tab**, click the **Breaks button**, then click the type of break you want to insert in the Section Breaks area

Remove Section Breaks

Ribbon Method

☐ Click the **Home tab**, then click the **Show/Hide button** ¶ in the Paragraph group to display formatting marks
☐ Position the insertion point to the left of the section break, then press **[Delete]**

Word

Change the Header and Footer for a Section

Ribbon Method

☐ Follow the steps in the Create Section Breaks Ribbon Method above
☐ Click the **Insert tab**, click the **Header button** (or the **Footer button**) in the Header & Footer group, then click **Edit Header** (or **Edit Footer**) to open the Header (or Footer) area
☐ Click the **Next Section button** (or **Previous Section button**) in the Navigation group on the Header and Footer Tools Design tab until you are in the section that you want to modify
☐ Click the **Link to Previous button** to deselect it, then type the text or insert the Quick Parts you want in the header (or footer) for this section (*Note*: You must deselect the Link to Previous button in both the header and the footer area to differentiate the header and footer in a section from the preceding section)
☐ Click the **Close Header and Footer button** in the Close group

WORD OBJECTIVE 3: WORKING WITH VISUAL CONTENT

INSERT ILLUSTRATIONS

Select and Insert SmartArt Graphics

Ribbon Method

- ☐ Position the insertion point where you want the SmartArt graphic to be inserted in the document
- ☐ Click the **Insert tab**, then click the **SmartArt button** in the Illustrations group
- ☐ In the Choose a SmartArt Graphic dialog box, click the category of diagram in the left pane, select a specific diagram layout and design in the middle pane, then preview your selection in the right pane
- ☐ Click **OK**
- ☐ Replace the placeholder text and use the SmartArt Tools Design and Format tabs as needed to format and customize the SmartArt graphic

Select and Insert Pictures from Files

Ribbon Method

- ☐ Position the insertion point in the desired location
- ☐ Click the **Insert tab**, then click the **Picture button** in the Illustrations group
- ☐ In the Insert Picture dialog box, navigate to the appropriate drive and folder, then select an appropriate picture
- ☐ Click **Insert**

Shortcut Method

- ☐ Follow the steps in bullets 1–3 of the Select and Insert Pictures from Files Ribbon Method above
- ☐ Double-click an appropriate picture

Find and Insert Clip Art

Ribbon Method

- ☐ Position the insertion point in the desired location
- ☐ Click the **Insert tab**, then click the **Clip Art button** in the Illustrations group
- ☐ In the Clip Art task pane, type the search criteria in the Search for text box, use the **Search in list arrow** to identify where to search, use the **Results should be in list arrow** to identify the format to find, then click **Go**
- ☐ Position the ☐ pointer over the image you want to insert
- ☐ Click the list arrow that appears, then click **Insert**

Shortcut Method

- ☐ Follow the steps in bullets 1–4 of the Select and Insert Pictures from Files Ribbon Method above
- ☐ Double-click an appropriate image

Word

Insert Shapes

Ribbon Method

- [ ] Position the insertion point in the desired location
- [ ] Click the **Insert tab**, then click the **Shapes button** in the Illustrations group
- [ ] In the gallery of shapes that opens, click an appropriate shape, then use the $+$ pointer to draw the shape

FORMAT ILLUSTRATIONS

Apply Text Wrapping

Ribbon Method

- [ ] Click the graphic, then click the **Picture Tools Format tab** or **Drawing Tools Format tab** depending on the graphic type selected
- [ ] On the Picture Tools Format (or Drawing Tools Format) tab, click the **Text Wrapping button** in the Arrange group, then click an appropriate text wrapping option or click **More Layout options** to open the Advanced Layout dialog box
- [ ] In the Advanced Layout dialog box, click the **Text Wrapping tab**, then select the appropriate text wrapping options including the wrapping style, how the text should wrap, and values to set the precise distance from text, then click **OK**

OR

- [ ] Click the graphic, then click the **Picture Tools Format tab** or **Drawing Tools Format tab** depending on the graphic type selected
- [ ] On the Picture Tools Format (or Drawing Tools Format) tab, click the **Position button** in the Arrange group, then click a **With Text Wrapping option** to position the graphic and apply text wrapping at the same time
- [ ] Click **More Layout options** to apply advanced text wrapping

Size a Graphic

Ribbon Method

- [ ] Click the graphic to select it, then click the **Picture Tools Format tab** or **Drawing Tools Format tab** depending on the graphic type selected
- [ ] On the Picture Tools Format (or Drawing Tools Format) tab, type values in the Shape Height and Shape Width text boxes in the Size group

OR

- [ ] On the Picture Tools Format (or Drawing Tools Format) tab, click the **launcher** 🔲 in the Size group, open the Size (or Format Autoshape) dialog box, enter appropriate values in the Size and Rotate section on the Size tab, then click **OK** to resize the graphic precisely

Mouse Method

- [ ] Click a graphic to select it, move the mouse over a corner sizing handle, then drag the ⬉ pointer or the ⬈ pointer to resize the graphic proportionally

OR

- ☐ Move the mouse over a corner sizing handle, then press **[Shift]** and drag the 🖰 pointer or the 🖰 pointer to resize the graphic proportionally

    OR

- ☐ Move the mouse over a side, top, or bottom sizing handle, then press **[Ctrl]** and drag the ⟷ pointer or the ↕ pointer to resize the graphic vertically or horizontally while keeping the center position fixed

    OR

- ☐ Move the mouse over a corner sizing handle, then press **[Ctrl]** and drag the 🖰 pointer or the 🖰 pointer to resize the graphic diagonally while keeping the center position fixed

    OR

- ☐ Move the mouse over a corner sizing handle, then press **[Shift][Ctrl]** and drag the 🖰 pointer or the 🖰 pointer to resize the graphic proportionally while keeping the center position fixed

Crop a Graphic
Ribbon Method
- ☐ Click the graphic to select it, then click the **Picture Tools Format tab** or **Drawing Tools Format tab** depending on the graphic type selected
- ☐ On the Picture Tools Format (or Drawing Tools Format) tab, click the **Crop button** in the Size group
- ☐ Position the 🖰 pointer over a cropping handle (solid black line), then drag the cropping handle inward

    OR

- ☐ On the Picture Tools Format (or Drawing Tools Format) tab, click the **launcher** 🔲 in the Size group to open the Size (or Format Autoshape) dialog box, enter appropriate values in the Crop from section on the Size tab, then click **OK** to crop the graphic precisely

Scale a Graphic
Ribbon Method
- ☐ Click the graphic to select it, then click the **Picture Tools Format tab** or **Drawing Tools Format tab** depending on the graphic type selected
- ☐ On the Picture Tools Format (or Drawing Tools Format) tab, click the **launcher** 🔲 in the Size group to open the Size (or Format Autoshape) dialog box, enter appropriate values in the Scale section on the Size tab, then click **OK** to scale the graphic precisely

Rotate a Graphic
Ribbon Method
- ☐ Click the graphic to select it, then click the **Picture Tools Format tab** or **Drawing Tools Format tab** depending on the graphic type selected
- ☐ On the Picture Tools Format (or Drawing Tools Format) tab, click the **launcher** 🔲 in the Size group to open the Size (or Format Autoshape) dialog box, enter appropriate values in the Size and Rotate section on the Size tab, then click **OK** to rotate the graphic precisely

Word

OR

☐ Click the **Rotate button** 🔄 ▾ in the Arrange group, click the appropriate option or click **More Rotation Options** to open the Size (or Format AutoShape) dialog box, then enter the rotation value

Mouse Method

☐ Click the graphic, position the pointer over the green rotation handle, then use the 🔄 pointer to drag the green rotation handle

OR

☐ Press **[Shift]**, then use the 🔄 pointer to drag the green rotation handle in 15-degree increments

Format Using Quick Styles

Ribbon Method

☐ Click the picture to select it, then click the **Picture Tools Format tab**
☐ Click the **More button** ▾ in the Picture Styles group on the Picture Tools Format tab, then select a **Quick Style**

OR

☐ Click the graphic to select it
☐ On the Drawing Tools Format tab, click the **More button** ▾ in the Shapes Styles group, then select a **Quick Style**

Apply Contrast, Brightness, and Coloration

Ribbon Method

☐ Click the picture to select it, then click the **Picture Tools Format tab**
☐ Click the **Contrast button** in the Adjust group on the Picture Tools Format tab, then click the percentage you want to apply

OR

☐ Click the **Brightness button** in the Adjust group, then click the percentage you want to apply

OR

☐ Click the **Recolor button** in the Adjust group, then click an appropriate option

OR

☐ Click the **launcher** 🔲 in the Picture Styles group to open the Format Picture dialog box, click **Picture** in the left pane if necessary, then select the appropriate options for contrast, brightness, and recoloring

Insert Text in SmartArt Graphics

Shortcut Method

☐ Click the placeholder box, then type appropriate text
☐ Press **[Shift][Enter]** to move to a new line in a placeholder box

OR

☐ Click the **text pane arrow** to expand the text pane, then type appropriate text
☐ Press **[↓]** or **[↑]** to move between placeholder boxes or click the placeholder box
☐ Press **[Shift][Enter]** to move to a new line in a placeholder box

Add Text to Shapes

Shortcut Method

☐ Right-click the shape, then click **Add Text** on the shortcut menu
☐ Type the text

Compress Pictures

Ribbon Method

☐ Click the desired picture to compress, then click the **Picture Tools Format tab**
☐ Click **Compress Pictures** in the Adjust group, then click the **Apply to selected pictures only check box** to select it
☐ Click the **Options button** to specify the resolution, click **OK**, then click **OK**

FORMAT TEXT GRAPHICALLY

Insert WordArt

Ribbon Method

☐ Position the insertion point in the location where you want to insert the WordArt, click the **Insert tab**, then click the **WordArt button** in the Text group
☐ Select a **WordArt style**, type the text in the Edit WordArt text box, then click **OK**

Modify WordArt

Ribbon Method

☐ Click the **WordArt object**, click the **WordArt Format tab**, if necessary
☐ Use the buttons in the Text group to edit the text, change the spacing, set the letter height as even, or change the text direction
☐ Use the buttons in the WordArt Styles group to change the style, the fill color, the outline color, or the shape
☐ Use the buttons in the Shadow Effects group to add or nudge shadows
☐ Use the 3-D button to add a 3-D effect to the WordArt
☐ Use the buttons in the Arrange group to position and add text wrapping
☐ Use the buttons in the Size group to resize the WordArt object

Insert Pull Quotes

Ribbon Method

☐ Position the insertion point in the location where you want the pull quote to appear, click the **Insert tab**, then click the **Text Box button** in the Text group
☐ Scroll through the list of options, then click an appropriate pull quote style
☐ Replace the placeholder text with appropriate text

Word

Insert Drop Caps

Ribbon Method

☐ Position the insertion point in the paragraph where you want the drop cap to appear, click the **Insert tab**, then click the **Drop Cap button** in the Text group
☐ Preview and select one of the options on the menu, or click **Drop Cap Options**
☐ In the Drop Cap dialog box, select the position, font, number of lines to drop, and distance you want the drop cap to be from the paragraph text, then click **OK**

Modify Drop Caps

☐ Select the drop cap, click the **Drop Cap button** in the Text group, then click **Drop Cap Options**
☐ In the Drop Cap dialog box, select appropriate options, then click **OK**
   OR
☐ Select the drop cap, click the **launcher** 🔲 in the Font group on the Home tab to open the Font dialog box or click the **Borders and Shading list arrow** and click **Borders and Shading** to open the Borders and Shading dialog box, then apply formatting options

INSERT AND MODIFY TEXT BOXES

Insert a Text Box

Ribbon Method

☐ Position the insertion point where you want the text box to appear, click the **Insert tab**, then click the **Text Box button** in the Text group or click the **Shapes button** in the Illustrations group, then click the **Text Box icon**
☐ Select a preformatted text box from the gallery
   OR
☐ Click **Draw Text Box**, use the $+$ pointer to draw a text box, then type text

Format a Text Box

Ribbon Method

☐ Click the text box to select it, then use buttons on the Text Box Tools Format tab to format the text box, including changing its size, position, text wrapping, and style
☐ Select the text in the text box, then use buttons in the Font group and the Paragraph group on the Home tab or on the Mini toolbar to format the text

Link a Text Box to Another Text Box

Ribbon Method

☐ Create a text box and fill it with text, then create a second empty text box
☐ Select the first text box, be sure the Text Box Tools Format tab is the active tab, then click the **Create Link button** in the Text group to activate the 🖐 pointer
☐ Use the 🖐 pointer to click the second text box to link it to the first text box

WORD OBJECTIVE 4: ORGANIZING CONTENT

INSERT BUILDING BLOCKS IN DOCUMENTS

Use the Building Blocks Organizer to Insert Sidebars

Ribbon Method

- ☐ Position the insertion point where you want the sidebar to appear, then click the **Insert tab**
- ☐ Click the **Quick Parts button** in the Text group, then click **Building Blocks Organizer**
- ☐ In the Building Blocks Organizer dialog box, click **Gallery** in the title bar, scroll to **Text Boxes** in the Gallery list, click the sidebar you want to insert, preview the **sidebar**, then click **Insert**

Use the Building Blocks Organizer to Edit the Properties of Building Block Elements

Ribbon Method

- ☐ Click the **Insert tab**, click the **Quick Parts button** in the Text group, then click **Building Blocks Organizer**
- ☐ In the Building Blocks Organizer dialog box, click the **Edit Properties button**, then make appropriate changes in the Edit Properties dialog box to the Name, Gallery, Category, Description, Save In, and Options
- ☐ Click **OK**, then click **Yes** if asked to confirm

Use the Building Blocks Organizer to Sort Building Blocks by Name, Gallery, or Category

Ribbon Method

- ☐ Click the **Insert tab**, click the **Quick Parts button** in the Text group, then click **Building Blocks Organizer**
- ☐ In the Building Blocks Organizer dialog box, click **Name** in the title bar to sort the building blocks by name

  OR

- ☐ Click **Gallery** in the title bar to sort the building blocks by gallery

  OR

- ☐ Click **Category** in the title bar to sort the building blocks by category

SAVE FREQUENTLY USED DATA AS BUILDING BLOCKS

Save Frequently Used Data as a Building Block

Ribbon Method

- ☐ Create the frequently used data, then select it
- ☐ Click the **Quick Parts button** in the Text group on the Insert tab, then click **Save Selection to Quick Part Gallery**

☐ In the Create New Building Block dialog box, type a unique name, make appropriate changes in the Edit Properties dialog box, then click **OK**

Save Company Contact Data as a Building Block

Ribbon Method

☐ Create the company contact information, then select all components of the contact information
☐ Click the **Quick Parts button** in the Text group on the Insert tab, then click **Save Selection to Quick Part Gallery**
☐ In the Create New Building Block dialog box, type a unique name, make appropriate changes in the Edit Properties dialog box, then click **OK**

Modify a Building Block and Save It with the Same Name

Ribbon Method

☐ Insert the building block you want to modify in a document, then edit the content
☐ Click the **Quick Parts button** in the Text group on the Insert tab, then click **Save Selection to Quick Part Gallery**
☐ In the Create New Building Block dialog box, be sure the Name and the Gallery are the same as the Building Block you want to replace, then click **OK**

INSERT FORMATTED HEADERS AND FOOTERS FROM QUICK PARTS

Insert a Header from Quick Parts and Edit the Document Title

Ribbon Method

☐ Press **[Ctrl][Home]**, click the **Insert tab**, then click the Header button in the Header & Footer group
☐ Scroll the Header gallery, click the **built-in Header Quick Part** you want to insert
☐ Click **Type the document title** to select the Title property control, then type the title
☐ Click the **Close Header and Footer button**

Insert Fields from Quick Parts

Ribbon Method

☐ Position the insertion point in the desired location, click the **Insert tab**, click the **Quick Parts button** in the Text group, then click **Field**
☐ In the Field dialog box, scroll the Field names list box as needed, click the name of the appropriate field, select additional properties associated with the field in the Field Properties list box as needed, then click **OK**

CREATE TABLES AND LISTS

Create a Table

Ribbon Method

☐ Click the **Insert tab**, click the **Table button** in the Tables group, then click **Insert table**
☐ Type a number in the Number of columns text box, then type a number in the Number of rows text box
☐ Set other options as appropriate, then click **OK**

OR

☐ Click the **Insert tab**, click the **Table button** in the Tables group, drag over the grid to select the number of columns and rows, then click the mouse

Create a List

Ribbon Method

☐ Position the insertion point where you want the list to begin
☐ Click the **Home tab**, then click the **Bullets button** 📋 in the Paragraph group to apply the current bullet style
☐ To add a bullet to a new bulleted list, type the text, then press **[Enter]**
☐ To add a bullet to an existing list, click at the end of any item in the list, press **[Enter]**, then type the text for the next item

OR

☐ Click the **Home tab**, then click the **Numbering button** 📋 in the Paragraph group to apply the current numbering style
☐ To add a new item to a numbered list, type the text, then press **[Enter]**
☐ To add a new item to an existing numbered list, click at the end of any item in the list, press **[Enter]**, then type the **text** for the next item

OR

☐ Click the **Home tab**, then click the **Multilevel List button** 📋 in the Paragraph group to apply the current style
☐ To add a new item to a multilevel list, type the **text**, then press **[Enter]**
☐ To add a new item to an existing multilevel list, click at the end of any item in the list, press **[Enter]**, then type the text for the next item
☐ Follow the steps in the Demote and Promote List Items section under Modify List Formats below to change the level of an item in a list

Shortcut Method

☐ Right-click where you want to create the bulleted list, then click the **Bullets button** 📋 on the Mini toolbar

Create a Table from Text

Ribbon Method

☐ Select the desired text, then click the **Insert tab**
☐ Click the **Insert tab**, click the **Table button** in the Tables group, then click **Convert Text to Table**
☐ Enter the appropriate options in the Convert Text to Table dialog box, then click **OK**

Create a List Using Existing Text

Ribbon Method

☐ Select the text you want to convert to a list, then follow the steps in bullets 2–5 of the Create a List Ribbon Method above depending on the type of list desired

Shortcut Method

☐ Select the text you want to convert to a bulleted list, then click the **Bullets button** 🔢 on the Mini toolbar

Create Text from a Table

Ribbon Method

☐ Click anywhere in the table you want to convert to text, then click the **Table Tools Layout tab**
☐ Click the **Convert to Text button** in the Data group, enter the appropriate options in the Convert Table to Text dialog box, then click **OK**

SORT CONTENT

Sort Table Data

Ribbon Method

☐ Click anywhere in the table you want to sort, click the **Table Tools Layout tab**, then click the **Sort button** in the Data group
☐ In the Sort dialog box, choose appropriate options to identify primary, secondary, and tertiary criteria, then click **OK**

Sort List Items

Ribbon Method

☐ Select the appropriate items to sort, click the **Home tab**, then click the **Sort button** 🔢 in the Paragraph group
☐ In the Sort dialog box, choose appropriate options to identify primary, secondary, and tertiary criteria, then click **OK**

MODIFY LIST FORMATS

Modify the Numbering Style

Ribbon Method

☐ Click anywhere in the list, click the **Home tab**, then click the **Numbering list arrow** 🔢 ▾ in the Paragraph group
☐ Click a new numbering style or click **Define New Number Format**
☐ In the Define New Number Format dialog box, choose appropriate options for the new numbering style, then click **OK**

Word

Shortcut Method

☐ Select the numbered list you want to modify, right-click, point to **Numbering** on the menu, in the Define New Number Format dialog box, choose appropriate options for the new numbering style, then click **OK**

Modify the Bullet Style

Ribbon Method

☐ Click anywhere in the list, click the **Home tab**, then click the **Bullets list arrow** ☰▾ in the Paragraph group
☐ Click a new bullet style or click **Define New Bullet**
☐ In the Define New Bullet dialog box, choose appropriate options for the new bullet style, then click **OK**

Shortcut Method

☐ Select the bulleted list, right-click, point to **Bullets** on the menu, in the Define New Bullet dialog box, choose appropriate options for the new bullet style, then click **OK**

Demote and Promote List Items

Ribbon Method

☐ To demote a list item, click anywhere in the item you want to demote, click the **Home tab**, then click the **Increase Indent button** ☷ in the Paragraph group
☐ To promote a list item, click anywhere in the item you want to promote, click the **Home tab**, then click the **Decrease Indent button** ☷ in the Paragraph group

Shortcut Method

☐ Select the item you want to demote or promote, then click the **Increase Indent button** ☷ or the **Decrease Indent button** ☷ on the Mini toolbar

OR

☐ Select the item you want to demote or promote, right-click, then click **Increase Indent** or **Decrease Indent** on the menu

OR

☐ Place the insertion point in front of the item you want to demote or promote, then press **[Tab]** to demote the item or press **[Shift][Tab]** to promote the item

MODIFY TABLES

Apply Quick Styles to Tables

Ribbon Method

☐ Create the table, click anywhere in the table, click the **Table Tools Design tab**, then click the **More button** ▾ in the Table Styles group

☐ In the Table Styles gallery, click the Quick Style you want to apply or click **Modify Table Style**
☐ In the Modify Style dialog box, select appropriate options, then click **OK**

Modify Table Properties and Options

Ribbon Method

☐ Create the table, click anywhere in the table, click the **Table Tools Layout tab**, then click the **Properties button** in the Table group
☐ In the Table Properties dialog box, select appropriate options on the Table, Row, Column, and Cell tabs, then click **OK**

Insert or Delete a Row

Ribbon Method

☐ Create a table, then click in a row
☐ To insert a row, click the **Table Tools Layout tab**, then click the **Insert Above button** or **Insert Below button** in the Rows & Columns group
☐ To delete the row, click the **Delete button** in the Rows & Columns group, then click **Delete Rows**

Shortcut Method

☐ To delete a row or rows, select the row(s), right-click, then click **Delete Rows**

OR

☐ To delete row(s), select the row(s), then press **[Shift][Delete]**

Insert or Delete a Column

Ribbon Method

☐ Create a table, then click in a column
☐ To insert a column, click the **Table Tools Layout tab**, then click the **Insert Left button** or **Insert Right button** in the Rows & Columns group
☐ To delete a column, click the **Table Tools Layout tab**, click the **Delete button** in the Rows & Columns group, then click **Delete Columns**

Shortcut Method

☐ To delete one or more columns, select the column(s), right-click, then click **Delete Columns**

OR

☐ To delete one or more columns, select the column(s), then press **[Shift][Delete]**

Apply Borders

Ribbon Method

☐ Create the table, click anywhere in the table to select it, then click the **Table Tools Design tab**
☐ Click the **Borders button** in the Table Styles group
☐ In the Borders and Shading dialog box, select the appropriate options on the Borders tab, then click **OK**

OR

☐ Click anywhere in the table, click the **Home tab**, click the **Border list arrow** in the Paragraph group, then select a border or click **Borders and Shading**

☐ In the Borders and Shading dialog box, select the appropriate options on the Borders tab, then click **OK**

Shortcut Method

☐ Right-click the table, then click **Borders and Shading** on the menu that opens

☐ In the Borders and Shading dialog box, select the appropriate options on the Borders tab, then click **OK**

Apply Shading

Ribbon Method

☐ Create the table, click anywhere in the table to select it, then click the **Table Tools Design tab**

☐ Click the **Shading button** in the Table Styles group

☐ Select a color in the gallery or click **More colors**, select the appropriate options on the Custom tab in the Colors dialog box, then click **OK**

OR

☐ Click anywhere in the table, click the **Home tab**, then click the **Shading list arrow** in the Paragraph group

☐ Select a color in the gallery or click **More colors**, select the appropriate options on the Custom tab in the Colors dialog box, then click **OK**

Shortcut Method

☐ Right-click the table, then click the **Borders and Shading button** on the menu that opens

☐ In the Borders and Shading dialog box, select the appropriate options on the Shading tab, then click **OK**

Merge Table Cells

Ribbon Method

☐ Select the cells you want to merge into one cell, click the **Table Tools Layout tab**, then click the **Merge Cells button** in the Merge group

Shortcut Method

☐ Select the cells you want to merge into one cell, right-click, then click **Merge Cells** on the menu

Split Table Cells

Ribbon Method

☐ Click the cell you want to split, click the **Table Tools Layout tab**, then click the **Split Cells button** in the Merge group

☐ In the Split Cells dialog box, enter the appropriate options, then click **OK**

Shortcut Method

☐ Select the cell you want to split, right-click, then click **Split Cell** on the menu
☐ In the Split Cells dialog box, enter the appropriate options, then click **OK**

Use Calculations in Tables

Ribbon Method

☐ Create the table, click the cell, click the **Table Tools Layout tab**, then click the **Formula button** in the Data group
☐ In the Formula dialog box, enter the appropriate options, then click **OK**

Change the Direction of Cell Contents

Ribbon Method

☐ Select the text, then click the **Table Tools Layout tab**
☐ Click the **Text Direction button** in the Alignment group one time to rotate the text 90 degrees or click the **Text Direction button** two times to rotate the text 270 degrees

Shortcut Method

☐ Select the text you want to apply a different orientation to, right-click, then click **Text Direction** on the menu
☐ In the Text Direction – Table Cell dialog box, enter the appropriate options, then click **OK**

Change the Alignment of Cell Contents

Ribbon Method

☐ Select the text you want to align, click the **Table Tools Layout tab**, then click **Properties** in the Table group
☐ In the Table Properties dialog box, click the **Cell tab**, enter the appropriate options, then click **OK**

Shortcut Method

☐ Select the text you want to align, right-click, then click **Table Properties** on the menu
☐ In the Table Properties dialog box, click the **Cell tab**, enter the appropriate options, then click **OK**

INSERT AND FORMAT REFERENCES AND CAPTIONS

Create Sources

Ribbon Method

☐ Click the **References tab**, click the **Insert Citation list arrow** in the Citations & Bibliography group, then click **Add New Source**
☐ In the Create Source dialog box, enter the appropriate information, then click **OK**

Modify Sources

Ribbon Method

☐ Click the **References tab**, then click the **Manage Sources button** in the Citations & Bibliography group
☐ In the Source Manager dialog box, select the **source** you want to edit, then click the **Edit button**
☐ Enter the appropriate information in the Edit Source dialog box, click **OK**, answer **Yes/No** if prompted, then click **Close**

OR

☐ Click a citation, click the **content control list arrow**, click **Edit Citation**, then follow bullet 3 in the Modify Sources Ribbon Method above

Insert and Modify Citations

Ribbon Method

☐ Position the insertion point next to the text you want to cite, click the **References tab**, then click the **Insert Citation button** in the Citations & Bibliography group
☐ If the source for the citation has not been created, click **Add New Source**, enter the appropriate information in the Create New Source dialog box, then click **OK**
☐ If the source for the citation has already been created, then click the source in the menu that opens
☐ To create the source at a later time, click **Add Placeholder**, type a name for the placeholder, then click **OK**

OR

☐ To modify a citation, click the citation, click the **content control list arrow**, click **Edit Citation**, enter the appropriate information in the Edit Citation dialog box, then click **OK**

Insert and Modify Captions

Ribbon Method

☐ Position the insertion point where you want the caption to appear
☐ Click the **References tab**, then click the **Insert Caption button** in the Captions group
☐ In the Caption dialog box, enter the appropriate options, then click **OK**

OR

☐ Select the item you want to caption, then follow the steps in bullets 2–3 of the Insert and Modify Captions Ribbon Method above

OR

☐ To modify a caption, select the caption, then follow the steps in bullets 2–3 of the Insert and Modify Captions Ribbon Method above

Insert Bibliographies

Ribbon Method

☐ Press **[Ctrl][End]** to move to the end of the document, then press **[Ctrl][Enter]** to create a new blank page
☐ Click the **References tab**, then click the **Bibliography button** in the Citations & Bibliography group
☐ To insert a built-in Bibliography content control, click **Bibliography** in the Built-in section
☐ To insert a built-in Works cited content control, click **Works Cited** in the Built-in section
☐ To insert a bibliography, click **Insert Bibliography**

Modify Bibliographies

Ribbon Method

☐ Add sources and citations as needed, select the **Bibliography**, right-click, then click **Update Field**
☐ For a content control, follow the steps in bullets 3-4 of the Insert Bibliographies Ribbon Method above, then click **Update Citations and Bibliography** in the title bar of the content control

Shortcut Method

☐ Add sources and citations as needed, then select the **Bibliography**
☐ Right-click, then click **Update Field**

SELECT REFERENCE STYLES

Set Reference Style as MLA, APA, or Chicago Manual of Style

Ribbon Method

☐ Open a document with references, click the **References tab**, click the **Style list arrow** in the Citations & Bibliography group, then click an appropriate style

Create, Modify, and Update Tables of Figures

Ribbon Method

☐ Follow the steps in the Insert and Modify Captions section above, then position the insertion point where you want the Table of Figures to appear
☐ Click the **References tab**, then click the **Insert Table of Figures button** in the Captions group
☐ On the Table of Figures tab in the Table of Figures dialog box, enter appropriate options, then click **OK**

Word

OR
- ☐ To modify the Table of Figures, click the **Insert Table of Figures button** in the Captions group
- ☐ Click the **Modify button** on the Table of Figures tab in the Table of Figures dialog box, enter appropriate options, then click **OK**

OR
- ☐ To update a Table of Figures, click the **Update Table button** in the Captions group

Shortcut Method
- ☐ To update the Table of Figures, right-click the **Table of Figures**, then click **Update Field**

Create, Modify, and Update Tables of Authorities

Ribbon Method
- ☐ Select all or part of the text you want to include as a reference in the Table of Authorities, click the **References tab**, then click the **Mark Citation button** in the Table of Authorities group
- ☐ In the Mark Citation dialog box, enter the appropriate information, then click **Mark**
- ☐ Continue to follow the steps in bullets 1–2 above to mark references to include in the Table of Authorities
- ☐ Position the insertion point where you want the Table of Authorities to be placed, click the **Insert Table of Authorities button** 🔳 in the Table of Authorities group, enter appropriate information on the Table of Authorities tab in the Table of Authorities dialog box, then click **OK**

OR
- ☐ To modify a Table of Authorities, click the **Insert Table of Authorities button** 🔳 in the Table of Authorities group, then click the **Modify button** on the Table of Authorities tab in the Table of Authorities dialog box
- ☐ In the Style dialog box, enter appropriate information or click the **Modify button** to open the Modify Style dialog box and select options, then click **OK** as needed to close all open dialog boxes

OR
- ☐ To update a Table of Authorities, click the **Update Table of Authorities button** 🔳 in the Table of Authorities group

Shortcut Method
- ☐ To update a Table of Authorities, right-click a section (such as cases, rules, and so on) of the Table of Authorities, then click **Update Field**

MERGE DOCUMENTS AND DATA SOURCES

Create Merged Documents

Ribbon Method
- ☐ Click the **Mailings tab**, click the **Start Mail Merge button** in the Start Mail Merge group, then click **Letters**

☐ Click the **Select Recipients button** in the Start Mail Merge group, click **Type New List** to create a new list, click **Use Existing List** to use a list that was created previously, or click **Select from Outlook Contacts**, then create the list or navigate to the file, select the file, then click **OK**

☐ Position the insertion point where you want to insert a field in the document, then use the buttons in the Write & Insert Fields group to insert an Address Block, a Greeting Line, or select a field from the menu that opens when you click the Insert Merge Field button

☐ Repeat the step in bullet 3 until you have inserted all merge fields in your document

☐ Click the **Preview Results button** in the Preview Results group

☐ Click the **Finish and Merge button** in the Finish group, then click **Edit Individual Documents** to create a merge file that you can edit or click **Print Documents** to send the merged document directly to the printer

Task Pane Method

☐ Click the **Mailings tab**, click the **Start Mail Merge button** in the Start Mail Merge group, then click **Step by Step Mail Merge Wizard**

☐ In the Mail Merge task pane, click the **Letters option button**, then click **Next: Starting Document**

☐ In Step 2 of 6, click the **option button** next to the description of your starting document; if you select Start from a template or Start from an existing document, follow the onscreen directions to navigate to the file you want to use, click it, then click **OK** or **Open**; then click **Next: Select Recipients**

☐ In Step 3 of 6, select the **option button** next to the recipient list you want to use, then follow the onscreen directions to create the list or navigate to and open an existing list, then click **Next: Write your letter**

☐ In Step 4 of 6, write your letter inserting merge fields where appropriate, click **More items** to select individual merge fields to insert, then click **Next: Preview your letters**

☐ In Step 5 of 6, use the **arrow buttons** in the task pane to preview your letters, then click **Next: Complete the merge**

☐ In Step 6 of 6, click **Print** to send the merged document directly to a printer or click **Edit Individual Letters** to merge a new document

Add Name and Address Block

Ribbon Method

☐ Follow the steps in bullets 1–3 of the Create Merged Documents Ribbon Method above

☐ To insert a Name field, position the insertion point where you want, click **Insert Merge Field** in the Write & Insert Fields group, then click **Name**

☐ To insert an Address Block field, position the insertion point where you want the address block to appear, click the **Address Block button** in the Write & Insert Fields group, enter appropriate information in the Insert Address Block dialog box, then click **OK**

Word

MERGE DATA INTO FORM LETTERS

Create or Select Recipients List

Ribbon Method

☐ Follow the steps in bullets 1–2 of the Create Merged Documents Ribbon Method above

Task Pane Method

☐ Follow the steps in bullets 1–4 of the Create Merged Documents Task Pane Method above

Edit Information in Recipients List

Ribbon Method

☐ After a recipient list has been created or selected, click the **Edit Recipient List button** in the Start Mail Merge group
☐ In the Mail Merge Recipients dialog box, enter appropriate changes, then click **OK**

Task Pane Method

☐ Follow the steps in bullets 1–3 of the Create Merged Documents Task Pane Method above
☐ In Step 3 of 6, click **Edit recipient list** to open the Mail Merge Recipients dialog box, enter appropriate changes, then click **OK**

CREATE ENVELOPES AND LABELS

Create a Mail Merge for Envelopes

Ribbon Method

☐ Click the **Start Mail Merge button** in the Start Mail Merge group, then click **Envelopes**
☐ In the Envelope Options dialog box, enter appropriate options, then click **OK**
☐ Follow the steps in bullets 2–6 of the Create Merged Documents Ribbon Method above

Task Pane Method

☐ Click the **Mailings tab**, click the **Start Mail Merge button** in the Start Mail Merge group, then click the **Step by Step Mail Merge Wizard**
☐ In the Mail Merge task pane, click the **Envelopes option button**, then click **Next: Starting Document**
☐ In Step 2 of 6, click the **option button** next to the description of your starting document, click **Envelope options** to open the Envelope Options dialog box, enter appropriate **options**, click **OK**, then click **Next: Select recipients**
☐ Follow the steps in bullets 4–7 of the Create Merged Documents Task Pane Method above

Create a Mail Merge for Labels

Ribbon Method

- ☐ Click the **Start Mail Merge button** in the Start Mail Merge group, then click **Labels**
- ☐ In the Label Options dialog box, enter appropriate options, then click **OK**
- ☐ Follow the steps in bullets 2–6 of the Create Merged Documents Ribbon Method above

Task Pane Method

- ☐ Click the **Mailings tab**, click the **Start Mail Merge button** in the Start Mail Merge group, then click **Step by Step Mail Merge Wizard**
- ☐ In the Mail Merge task pane, click the **Labels option button**, then click **Next: Starting Document**
- ☐ In Step 2 of 6, click the **option button** next to the description of the starting document, click **Label options** to open the Label Options dialog box, enter appropriate options, click **OK**, then click **Next: Select recipients**
- ☐ Follow the steps in bullets 4–7 of the Create Merged Documents Task Pane Method to complete the merge

Create a Single Envelope

Ribbon Method

- ☐ Click the **Mailings tab**, then click the **Envelopes button** in the Create group
- ☐ In the Envelopes and Labels dialog box, click the **Envelopes tab**, type the recipient's address in the Delivery address text box, type the return address in the Return address text box, then click the **Options button**
- ☐ In the Envelope Options dialog box, enter appropriate information, then click **OK** as needed to exit the dialog boxes

Shortcut Method

- ☐ Select the recipient's address in a document, then follow the steps in the Create a Single Envelope Ribbon Method above
  (*Note*: The Recipient address information appears in the Delivery address text box when the Envelopes and Labels dialog box opens)

Create a Single Label

Ribbon Method

- ☐ Click the **Mailings tab**, then click the **Labels button** in the Create group
- ☐ In the Envelopes and Labels dialog box, click the **Labels tab**, type the **address** in the Address text box, then click the **Options button**
- ☐ In the Labels Options dialog box, enter appropriate information, then click **OK** as needed to exit the dialog boxes

Shortcut Method

- ☐ Select the recipient's address in a document, then follow the steps in the Create a Single Label Ribbon Method above
  (*Note*: The Address information appears in the Address text box when the Envelopes and Labels dialog box opens)

WORD OBJECTIVE 5: REVIEWING DOCUMENTS

NAVIGATE DOCUMENTS

Use the Find Command

Ribbon Method
- [ ] Click the **Home tab**, then click the **Find button** in the Editing group
- [ ] In the Find and Replace dialog box, type the text you want to find in the Find what dialog box, then click **Find Next**
- [ ] If prompted to search the document from the beginning, click **OK**
- [ ] Once the term is found, click **Cancel** in the Find and Replace dialog box

Shortcut Method
- [ ] Press **[Ctrl][F]** to open the Find and Replace dialog box, then follow the steps in bullets 2–4 of the Use the Find Command Ribbon Method above

Use the Go To Command

Ribbon Method
- [ ] Click the **Home tab**, click the **Find list arrow** in the Editing group, then click **Go To**
- [ ] On the Go To tab in the Find and Replace dialog box, select the type of item you want to go to, then enter relevant information about that item
- [ ] Click **Go To** or **Next**, then click **Close**

Shortcut Method
- [ ] Press **[Ctrl][G]** to open the Find and Replace dialog box with the Go To tab active, then follow the steps in bullets 2–3 of the Use the Go To Command Ribbon Method above

CHANGE WINDOW VIEWS

Arrange All Windows

Ribbon Method
- [ ] Click the **View tab**, then click the **Arrange All button** in the Window group
- [ ] To view only one document, click the **Maximize button** 🔲 on the title bar of that document

Use Split Screen

Ribbon Method
- [ ] Click the **View tab**, then click the **Split button** in the Window group
- [ ] Drag the horizontal split bar to the location where you want to split the window
- [ ] To adjust the split, drag the horizontal split bar to a new location
- [ ] To remove the split, click the **Remove Split button** in the Window group

Word

Change Zoom Settings

Ribbon Method

☐ Click the **View tab**, then click the **Zoom button** in the Zoom group
☐ In the Zoom dialog box, select appropriate options, then click **OK**

Shortcut Method

☐ Click the **Zoom level button** 100% on the status bar
☐ In the Zoom dialog box, select appropriate options, then click **OK**

COMPARE DOCUMENT VERSIONS

Manage Multiple Documents at the Same Time

Ribbon Method

☐ Click the **View tab**, then click the **Arrange All button** in the Window group

OR

☐ Click the **View tab**, click the **View Side by Side button** in the Window group, then click the **Synchronous Scrolling button** and the **Reset Window Position button**

MERGE DOCUMENT VERSIONS

Merge into a New Document

Ribbon Method

☐ Click the **Review tab**, click the **Compare button** in the Compare group, then click **Combine**
☐ In the Combine documents dialog box, navigate to and select the original document, then navigate to and select the revised document
☐ Click the **New document option button** in the Show changes in section, select other options as appropriate, click **OK**, then click **Yes** if a warning message appears
☐ Click the **Show Source Documents list arrow**, then hide, show the original, show the revised, or show both documents

Merge into an Existing Document

Ribbon Method

☐ Follow the steps in bullets 1–2 of the Merge into a New Document Ribbon Method above
☐ Click the **Original document option button** in the Show changes in section, select other options as appropriate, click **OK**, then click **Yes** if a warning message appears

OR

☐ Click the **Revised document option button** in the Show changes in section, select other options as appropriate, click **OK**, then click **Yes** if a warning message appears

Combine Revisions from Multiple Authors

Ribbon Method

☐ Click the **Review tab**, click the **Compare button** in the Compare group, then click **Combine**
☐ In the Combine documents dialog box, navigate to and select the original document, then navigate to and select the revised document
☐ Select other options as appropriate, click **OK**, then click **Yes** if a warning message appears
☐ Click the **Show Source Documents list arrow**, then hide, show the original, show the revised, or show both documents

DISPLAY MARKUP

Show Tracked Changes and Comments by Reviewer

Ribbon Method

☐ Click the **Review tab**
☐ Click the **Display for Review list arrow** in the Tracking group, then click **Final Showing Markup** to show all tracked changes

OR

☐ Click the **Show Markup list arrow** in the Tracking group, point to **Reviewers**, then **All Reviewers** or select the reviewer(s) you want to view

ENABLE, DISABLE, ACCEPT, AND REJECT TRACKED CHANGES

Turn Track Changes On and Off

Ribbon Method

☐ To turn on the Track Changes feature, click the **Review tab**, then click the **Track Changes button** in the Tracking group
☐ To turn off the Track Changes feature, click the **Review tab**, then click the **Track Changes button** in the Tracking group

Accept and Reject Changes

Ribbon Method

☐ Click the **Review tab**, click the **Next button** in the Changes group, then review the tracked change
☐ Click the **Reject list arrow** in the Changes group, then select the appropriate option

OR

☐ Click the **Accept list arrow** in the Changes group, then select the appropriate option
☐ Click the **Next button** to move to the next tracked change or click the **Previous button** to move to the previous tracked change

CHANGE TRACKING OPTIONS

Change Reviewer Options

Ribbon Method

☐ Click the **Review tab**, click the **Track Changes list arrow** in the Tracking group, then click **Change Tracking Options**
☐ In the Change Tracking Options dialog box, select appropriate color options, then click **OK**

Change Balloon Options

Ribbon Method

☐ Click the **Review tab**, click the **Track Changes list arrow** in the Tracking group, then click **Change Tracking Options**
☐ In the Balloons section in the Change Tracking Options dialog box, select appropriate options, then click **OK**

Change Insertions and Deletions Settings

Ribbon Method

☐ Click the **Review tab**, click the **Track Changes list arrow** in the Tracking group, then click **Change Tracking Options**
☐ In the Markup section in the Change Tracking Options dialog box, click the **Insertions list arrow**, select an appropriate option, then click **OK**
OR
☐ Click the **Deletions list arrow**, select an appropriate option, then click **OK**

Set the Formatting Options

Ribbon Method

☐ Click the **Review tab**, click the **Track Changes list arrow** in the Tracking group, then click **Change Tracking Options**
☐ In the Formatting section in the Change Tracking Options dialog box, click the **Track formatting check box** to select it, click the **Formatting list arrow**, select an appropriate option, then click **OK**

Set the Moves Options

Ribbon Method

☐ Click the **Review tab**, click the **Track Changes list arrow** in the Tracking group, then click **Change Tracking Options**
☐ In the Moves section in the Change Tracking Options dialog box, click the **Track moves check box** to select it, click the **Moved from list arrow**, select an appropriate option, click the **Moved to list arrow**, select an appropriate option, then click **OK**

Word

INSERT, MODIFY, AND DELETE COMMENTS

Insert Comments

Ribbon Method
☐ Select the text you want to comment on, click the **Review tab**, then click the **New Comment button** in the Comments group

Modify Comments

Ribbon Method
☐ Click the **Review tab**, click the **Track Changes list arrow** in the Tracking group, then click **Change Tracking Options**
☐ In the Markup section in the Change Tracking Options dialog box, click the **Comments list arrow**, then select a color

OR

☐ In the Balloons section in the Change Tracking Options dialog box, select appropriate options, then click **OK**

OR

☐ Click in a comment, then make text changes

Delete Comments

Ribbon Method
☐ Click the **Review tab**, click the **Delete list arrow** in the Comments section, then select an appropriate option

WORD OBJECTIVE 6: SHARING AND SECURING CONTENT

SAVE TO APPROPRIATE FORMATS

Select a File Format (.doc, .docx, .xps, .docm, or .dotx) to Save As

Ribbon Method

☐ Click the **Office button** , then click **Save As**
☐ In the Save As dialog box, type an appropriate filename in the File name text box, click the **Save as type list arrow**, select the file format you want to save as, then click **Save**

OR

☐ To save a file as using the .doc format, click the **Office button** , point to **Save As**, then click **Word 97-2003 Document**
☐ In the Save As dialog box, type an appropriate filename in the File name text box, then click **Save**

OR

☐ To save a file using the .docx format, click the **Office button** , point to **Save As**, then click **Word Document**
☐ In the Save As dialog box, type an appropriate filename in the File name text box, then click **Save**

OR

☐ To save a file using the .dotx format, click the **Office button** , point to **Save As**, then click **Word Template**
☐ In the Save As dialog box, type an appropriate filename in the File name text box, then click **Save**

Shortcut Method

☐ To select the Save As file format for a file that has not been saved previously, click the **Save button** on the Quick Access toolbar, then follow the steps in bullet 2 of the Select a File Format (.doc, .docx, .xps, .docm, or .dotx) to Save As Ribbon Method above

OR

☐ To select the Save As file format for a file that has not been saved previously, press **[Ctrl][S]**, then follow the steps in bullet 2 of the Select a File Format (.doc, .docx, .xps, .docm, or .dotx) to Save As Ribbon Method above

Identify Document Features Not Supported by Previous Versions Using the Compatibility Checker

Ribbon Method

☐ Open a Word document, click the **Office button** , point to **Prepare**, then click **Run Compatibility Checker**
☐ Review the information listed in the Microsoft Office Word Compatibility Checker dialog box, then click **OK**

Word

REMOVE INAPPROPRIATE OR PRIVATE INFORMATION USING DOCUMENT INSPECTOR

Delete Hidden Text

Ribbon Method
- [ ] Open a Word document, click the **Office button** , point to **Prepare**, then click **Inspect Document**
- [ ] In the Document Inspector, click the **Hidden Text check box** to select it if necessary, then click **Inspect**
- [ ] In the Document Inspector, click **Remove All** if Hidden Text is found, then click **Reinspect** to inspect the document again or click **Close**

Delete Comments, Revisions, Versions, and Annotations

Ribbon Method
- [ ] Open a Word document, click the **Office button** , point to **Prepare**, then click **Inspect Document**
- [ ] In the Document Inspector, click the **Comments, Revisions, Versions, and Annotations check box** to select it if necessary, then click **Inspect**
- [ ] In the Document Inspector, click **Remove All** if Hidden Text is found, then click **Reinspect** to inspect the document again or click **Close**

Select Inappropriate or Private Information from a List

Ribbon Method
- [ ] Open a Word document, click the **Office button** , point to **Prepare**, then click **Inspect Document**
- [ ] In the Document Inspector, click the **Document Properties and Personal Information check box** to select it if necessary, then click **Inspect**
- [ ] In the Document Inspector, click **Remove All** if Document Properties or Personal Information is found, then click **Reinspect** to inspect the document again or click **Close** to close the Document Inspector

CONTROL DOCUMENT ACCESS

Restrict Permissions to and Password Protect Documents

Ribbon Method
- [ ] Click the **Office button** , click Word Options, select the **Show Developer tab in the Ribbon check box** if necessary, then click **OK**
- [ ] Click the **Developer tab**, be sure the **Design Mode button** in the Controls group is not active, then click **Protect Document** in the Protect group
- [ ] In the Restrict Formatting and Editing task pane, select the appropriate options, then click **Yes, Start Enforcing Protection**

□ Type a password, press **[Tab]**, then type the password again to password protect the document, or click **Cancel** if you do not want to password protect the document

OR

□ Click the **Review tab**, click **Protect Document** in the Protect group,
then follow the steps in bullets 3–4 of the Restrict Permissions to and
Password Protect Documents Ribbon Method above

Mark Documents as Final

Ribbon Method

□ Click the **Office button** 🔘, point to **Prepare**, then click **Mark as Final**

OR

□ Follow the steps in the Restrict Permissions to and Password Protect
Documents Ribbon Method above

□ In the Restrict Formatting and Editing task pane, select the **Allow only
this type of editing in the document check box** in the 2. Editing
restrictions section, then click the list arrow and select **No changes
(Read only)**

Set Passwords

Ribbon Method

□ Follow the steps in bullets 1–4 of the Restrict Permissions to and
Password Protect Documents Ribbon Method above

PROTECT DOCUMENTS

Apply Formatting Restrictions

Ribbon Method

□ Follow the steps in bullets 1–2 of the Restrict Permissions to and
Password Protect Documents Ribbon Method above

□ In the Restrict Formatting and Editing task pane, select the **Limit
formatting to a selection of styles check box** in the
1. Formatting restrictions section, click **Settings**, select the appropriate options in the Formatting Restrictions dialog box, then click **OK**

□ Follow the steps in bullet 4 of the Restrict Permissions to and Password
Protect Documents Ribbon Method above

Apply Editing Restrictions

Ribbon Method

□ Follow the steps in bullets 1–2 of the Restrict Permissions to and
Password Protect Documents Ribbon Method above

□ In the Restrict Formatting and Editing task pane, select the **Allow only
this type of editing in the document check box** in the 2. Editing
restrictions section, click the list arrow to select the type of editing to
allow, then select the users this editing restriction will apply to

□ Follow the steps in bullet 4 of the Restrict Permissions to and Password
Protect Documents Ribbon Method above

ATTACH DIGITAL SIGNATURES

Authenticate Documents Using Digital Signatures

Ribbon Method

- ☐ Open the document, then be sure it is saved in a file format (e.g., .docx) that supports digital signatures
- ☐ Click the **Office button** 🔴, point to **Prepare**, click **Add a Digital Signature**, then click **OK** if a warning message opens
- ☐ In the Sign dialog box, enter appropriate information and review information as needed, then click **Sign**
- ☐ In the Signature Confirmation dialog box, click **OK**

    OR

- ☐ To view a digital signature associated with a document, open the document in Word
- ☐ Click the **Office button** 🔴, point to **Prepare**, then click **View Signatures**

    (*Note*: This option is only available if a document has been digitally signed)
- ☐ In the Signatures task pane, move the pointer over the signature you want to verify, click the list arrow that appears next to the name, then click **Signature Details**
- ☐ In the Signature Details dialog box, review the information, then click **Close**

Insert a Line for a Digital Signature

Ribbon Method

- ☐ Position the insertion point where you want the digital signature line to appear, click the **Insert tab**, click the **Signature Line button** in the Text group, then click **OK** if a warning message appears
- ☐ In the Signature Setup dialog box, fill in the appropriate information, then click **OK**
- ☐ Double-click the **signature box**, read the **message**, then click **OK**
- ☐ Type your name, click **Sign**, then click **OK**

MICROSOFT OFFICE EXCEL 2007
EXAM REFERENCE

Getting Started with Excel 2007

The Excel Microsoft Certified Application Specialist (MCAS) exam assumes a basic level of proficiency in Excel. This section is intended to help you reference these basic skills while you are preparing to take the Excel MCAS exam.

- ☐ Starting and exiting Excel
- ☐ Viewing the Excel window
- ☐ Using the Ribbon
- ☐ Opening, saving, and closing workbooks
- ☐ Navigating in the worksheet window
- ☐ Using views
- ☐ Using keyboard KeyTips
- ☐ Getting Help

START AND EXIT EXCEL

Start Excel

Mouse Method

- ☐ Click the **Start button** 🌀 on the Windows taskbar
- ☐ Point to **All Programs**
- ☐ Click **Microsoft Office**, then click **Microsoft Office Excel 2007**
  OR
- ☐ Double-click the **Microsoft Excel program icon** 🖹 on the desktop

Exit Excel

Ribbon Method

- ☐ Click the **Office button** 🖺, then click **Exit Excel**
  OR
- ☐ Click the **Close button** ✖ on the Excel program window title bar

Shortcut Method

- ☐ Press **[Alt][F4]**

VIEW THE EXCEL WINDOW

Figure EX-1 Excel Window

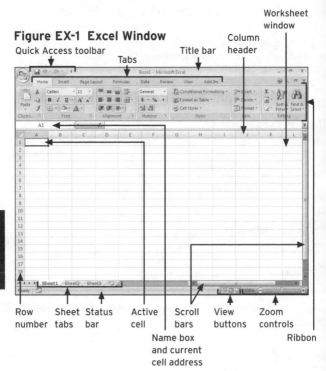

Quick Access toolbar

Tabs

Title bar

Column header

Worksheet window

Row number

Sheet tabs

Status bar

Active cell

Name box and current cell address

Scroll bars

View buttons

Zoom controls

Ribbon

Excel

USE THE RIBBON

Display the Ribbon

Ribbon Method

☐ Double-click any tab

Shortcut Method

☐ Right-click any tab, then click **Minimize the Ribbon** to deselect it

Hide the Ribbon

Ribbon Method

☐ Double-click the active tab

Shortcut Method

□ Right-click any tab, then click **Minimize the Ribbon** to select it

Customize the Quick Access Toolbar

Ribbon Method

□ Right-click any Quick Access toolbar button
□ To remove that button, click **Remove from Quick Access Toolbar**
□ To add or remove a button, click **Customize Quick Access Toolbar**, click a command in the left or right column of the dialog box, then click **Add** or **Remove**

Reposition the Quick Access Toolbar

Ribbon Method

□ Right-click any Quick Access toolbar button
□ Click **Show Quick Access Toolbar Below the Ribbon**

OPEN, SAVE, AND CLOSE WORKBOOKS

Open a New Workbook

Ribbon Method

□ Click the **Office button** 🏐, then click **New**
□ Click **Blank workbook** under Blank and recent, then click **Create**

Shortcut Method

□ Press **[Ctrl][N]**

Open an Existing Workbook

Ribbon Method

□ Click the **Office button** 🏐, then click **Open**
□ In the Open dialog box, navigate to the drive and folder where the file is stored
□ Click the file you want, then click **Open**

Shortcut Method

□ Press **[Ctrl][O]**
□ Follow the steps in bullets 2–3 of the Open an Existing Workbook Ribbon Method above

Use Save As

Ribbon Method

□ Click the **Office button** 🏐, then click **Save As**
□ In the Save As dialog box, navigate to the drive and folder where you want to store the workbook
□ Type an appropriate **file name** in the File name text box, then click **Save**

Shortcut Method

□ Press **[F12]**
□ Follow the steps in bullets 2–3 of the Use Save As Ribbon Method above

Excel

Save an Existing Workbook

Ribbon Method

☐ Click the **Office button** 🔘, then click **Save**

OR

☐ Click the **Save button** 🔲 on the Quick Access toolbar

Shortcut Method

☐ Press **[Ctrl][S]**

Close a Workbook

Ribbon Method

☐ Click the **Office button** 🔘, then click **Close**
☐ If prompted to save the file, click **Yes** or **No** as appropriate

OR

☐ Click the **Close Window button** 🗙 in the document window
☐ If prompted to save the file, click **Yes** or **No** as appropriate

Shortcut Method

☐ Press **[Ctrl][W]** or **[Alt][F4]**
☐ If prompted to save the file, click **Yes** or **No** as appropriate

NAVIGATE IN THE WORKSHEET WINDOW

Ribbon Method

☐ Click the **Home tab**, then click the **Find & Select button** in the Editing group
☐ Click **Go To**
☐ In the Reference text box in the Go To dialog box, type the **address** of the cell you want to go to, then click **OK**

Shortcut Method

☐ Press **[Ctrl][G]**
☐ In the Reference text box in the Go To dialog box, type the **address** of the cell you want to go to, then click **OK**

OR

☐ Use Table EX-1 as a reference to navigate through the worksheet using keyboard shortcuts

Table EX-1 Navigation Keyboard Shortcuts

Keys	Moves the insertion point
[Ctrl][Home]	To the beginning of the worksheet (cell A1)
[Ctrl][End]	To the end of the worksheet area containing data
[Page Up]	One screen up
[Page Down]	One screen down
[Alt][Page Up]	One screen to the left
[Alt][Page Down]	One screen to the right

Mouse Method

To change the view without moving the insertion point, do one of the following:

- [ ] Drag the **scroll box** in a scroll bar to move within the worksheet
- [ ] Click above the scroll box in a scroll bar to jump up a screen
- [ ] Click below the scroll box in a scroll bar to jump down a screen
- [ ] Click the **up scroll arrow** in a scroll bar to move up one row
- [ ] Click the **down scroll arrow** in a scroll bar to move down one row

USE KEYBOARD KEYTIPS

Display KeyTips

- [ ] Press **[Alt]** to display the KeyTips (squares containing numbers or letters) on the active tab on the Ribbon and on the Quick Access toolbar
- [ ] Press the letter or number for a tab to open a tab, then press the letter or number for the specific command on the active tab to perform the command
- [ ] Press additional letters or numbers as needed to complete the command sequence
- [ ] If two letters appear, press each one in order
- [ ] For some commands you have to click an option from a gallery or menu to complete the command sequence
- [ ] The KeyTips turn off automatically at the end of the command sequence

Hide KeyTips

- [ ] Press **[Alt]**

GET HELP

Ribbon Method

☐ Click the **Microsoft Office Excel Help button** 🔘 on the Ribbon
☐ Use Table EX-2 as a reference to select the most appropriate way to
   search for help using the Microsoft Excel Help task pane
   OR
☐ Point to any button on the Ribbon, then read the ScreenTip text
☐ If you see "Press F1 for more help." at the bottom of the ScreenTip,
   continue pointing to the button, then press **[F1]** to see targeted help on
   that button in the Microsoft Excel Help window

Shortcut Method

☐ Press **[F1]**
☐ Use Table EX-2 as a reference to select the most appropriate way to
   search for help using the Microsoft Excel Help window

Table EX-2 Microsoft Help Window Options

Option	To use
Browse Excel Help	Click a **link** representing a topic you want to read about; click **subtopics** that appear until you see help text for the topic
Back button ⬅	Click to return to the previously displayed information
Forward button ➡	Click to go forward in the sequence of previously displayed information
Stop button ✖	Click to stop searching on a topic
Refresh button 🔄	Click to refresh the Help window content
Home button 🏠	Click to return to the Excel Help and How-to window
Print button 🖨	Click to print the current page
Change Font Size button A̋	Click to enlarge or shrink the Help text
Show Table of Contents 📖	Click to show the Table of Contents pane, showing topic links you can click
Keep On Top 📌	Click to keep Help window on top as you work; button becomes the Not On Top button 📌, which you click to let the Help window go behind the current window as you work
Type words to search for box	Type a **word** for which you want Help, then click the **Search button**
Search button list arrow	Click the **list arrow**, then click the area you want Help from, such as Content from Office Online, All Excel, or Excel help

Excel

EXCEL EXAM REFERENCE

Objectives:

1. Creating and manipulating data
2. Formatting data and content
3. Creating and modifying formulas
4. Presenting data visually
5. Collaborating and securing data

EXCEL OBJECTIVE 1: CREATING AND MANIPULATING DATA

INSERT DATA USING AUTOFILL

Fill a Series with or without Formatting

Ribbon Method

☐ Drag to select two or more **cells** in a series you have started and continue dragging to include the range you want to fill, or select one **cell** containing the starting content in an AutoFill series, as described in Table EX-3, and the range you want to fill
☐ Click the **Home tab**, click the **Fill button** 🔽 in the Editing group, then click **Series**
☐ In the Series dialog box, click the **AutoFill option button** in the Type section, then click **OK** to fill in the series with formatting intact

Mouse Method

☐ Select two or more **cells** in a series you have started, or click one **cell** containing the starting content in an AutoFill series, as described in Table EX-3
☐ Point to the cell's **fill handle** until the pointer changes to ➕
☐ Drag the **fill handle** horizontally or vertically to automatically fill in the appropriate values
☐ Click the **AutoFill Options button** 🔳, then click **Fill Series, Fill Formatting Only** or **Fill Without Formatting**

Shortcut Method

☐ Click two or more **cells** in a series you have started, or click one **cell** containing the starting content in an AutoFill series, as described in Table EX-3
☐ Point to the cell's **fill handle** until the pointer changes to ➕
☐ Click and hold the **right mouse button**, then drag in the direction you want to fill
☐ On the shortcut menu, click **Fill Series, Fill Formatting Only**, or **Fill Without Formatting**

Excel

Table EX-3 Built-In AutoFill Series

To fill	Enter and select	Drag to display
Months	January	February, March, April...
Quarters	Q1	Q2, Q3, Q4
Years	2010, 2011	2012, 2013, 2014...
Times	8:00	9:00, 10:00, 11:00...
Text + Numbers	Student 1, Student 2	Student 3, Student 4, Student 5...
Numeric sequence	1, 3	5, 7, 9...

Copy Data Using AutoFill

Ribbon Method
- [ ] Drag to select **data** in one or more adjacent cells, then continue dragging to include the range you want to copy to in the selection
- [ ] Click the **Home tab**, click the **Fill button** 🔽 in the Editing group, then click **Down**, **Right**, **Up**, or **Left**

Mouse Method
- [ ] Drag to select one or more adjacent **cells**
- [ ] Point to the selected range's **fill handle** until the pointer changes to **+**
- [ ] Drag the **fill handle** horizontally or vertically to copy the data to the range you choose

Shortcut Method
- [ ] Click the **cell** whose value or formula you want to copy
- [ ] Press **[Shift][↓]** or **[Shift][→]** as necessary to select the fill range
- [ ] Press **[Ctrl][D]** to fill the range down or **[Ctrl][R]** to fill the range to the right

ENSURE DATA INTEGRITY

Restrict Data Values

Ribbon Method
- [ ] Select the **cell(s)** in which you want to restrict the data entered
- [ ] Click the **Data tab**, then click the **Data Validation button** in the Data Tools group
- [ ] In the Data Validation dialog box, click the **Allow list arrow**, then click a validation option, using Table EX-4 as a guide
- [ ] If desired, click the **Input Message tab** and type a message title and the text you want the user to see when selecting the cell
- [ ] If desired, click the **Error Alert tab** and choose an error alert style, title, and text

Table EX-4 Data Validation Criteria Options

Criteria	Use to	Next action
Any value	Allow user to input any value	Click **OK**
Whole number, Decimal, Date, Time, or Text length	Limit data to a range you specify	Select a Data option, such as "between," enter minimum and maximum values, then click **OK**
List	Limit data to a list of entries you specify	Enter a **list** of allowable entries separated by commas in the Source text box, then click **OK**
Custom	Limit data to a formula you specify	Enter a **formula** in the Formula text box, then click **OK**

Remove Duplicate Rows

Ribbon Method

- ☐ Click inside the table or range from which you want to delete duplicates
- ☐ Click the **Data tab**, then click the **Remove Duplicates button** in the Data Tools group
- ☐ Click **OK** to remove rows that contain duplicate data in all the table or range columns
- ☐ Click **OK** to accept the message

Remove Rows Where Only Some Columns Are Duplicated

Ribbon Method

- ☐ Click inside the table or range from which you want to delete duplicates
- ☐ Click the **Data tab**, then click the **Remove Duplicates button** in the Data Tools group
- ☐ Click **Unselect All**, then click the column(s) in which you want Excel to look for duplicates
- ☐ Click **OK** to remove rows that contain duplicate data in the columns you specified
- ☐ Click **OK**

MODIFY CELL CONTENTS AND FORMATS

Cut and Paste Cell(s)

Ribbon Method

- ☐ Select the **cell(s)** to cut
- ☐ Click the **Home tab**, then click the **Cut button** 🔏 in the Clipboard group
- ☐ Click where you want to paste the cell(s)
- ☐ Click the **Paste button** in the Clipboard group

Excel

Shortcut Method

☐ Select the **cell(s)** to cut
☐ Right-click the **selected cell(s)**, then click **Cut**
☐ Right-click where you want to paste the cell(s), then click **Paste**

OR

☐ Select the **cell(s)** to cut
☐ Press **[Ctrl][X]**
☐ Click where you want to paste the cell(s)
☐ Press **[Ctrl][V]**

Copy and Paste Cell(s)

Ribbon Method

☐ Select the **cell(s)** to copy
☐ Click the **Home tab**, then click the **Copy button** 🔲 in the Clipboard group
☐ Click where you want to paste the cell(s)
☐ Click the **Paste button** in the Clipboard group

Shortcut Method

☐ Select the **cell(s)** to copy
☐ Right-click the **cell(s)**, then click **Copy**
☐ Click where you want to paste the cell(s)
☐ Right-click where you want to paste the cell(s), then click **Paste**

OR

☐ Select the **cell(s)** to copy
☐ Press **[Ctrl][C]**
☐ Click where you want to paste the copied cell(s)
☐ Press **[Ctrl][V]**

Copy Cells without Using the Clipboard

Mouse Method

☐ Select the **cell(s)** to copy
☐ Place the mouse pointer over the edge of the selected range until the pointer becomes ⇱, then press and hold **[Ctrl]**
☐ Drag the selected range to the appropriate location, then release the mouse button and [Ctrl]

Move Cells without Using the Clipboard

Mouse Method

☐ Select the **cell(s)** to move
☐ Place the mouse pointer over any edge of the selected range until the pointer becomes ⇱
☐ Drag the selected range to the appropriate location, then release the mouse button

Use Paste Special to Transpose Data

Ribbon Method

- □ Select the **cell(s)** you want to cut or copy
- □ Click the **Home tab**, then click the **Copy button** 🗐 or the **Cut button** ✂ in the Clipboard group
- □ Click the **cell** where you want to paste the cut or copied cells, click the **Paste button list arrow** in the Clipboard group, then click **Paste Special**
- □ In the Paste Special dialog box, click the **Transpose check box** to select it, then click **OK**

Use Paste Special to Paste Selected Features

Ribbon Method

- □ Select the **cell(s)** from which you want to cut or copy selected features
- □ Click the **Home tab**, then click the **Copy button** 🗐 or the **Cut button** ✂ in the Clipboard group
- □ Click the **cell** where you want to paste the cut or copied cells or features, click the **Paste button list arrow** in the Clipboard group, then click **Paste Special**
- □ In the Paste Special dialog box, click the selected features using Table EX-5 as a guide, then click **OK**

Table EX-5 Selected Paste Special Options

Click	To paste
Formulas option button	Formulas as shown in formula bar
Values option button	Values as shown in cell(s)
Formats option button	Formats only
Validation option button	Validation settings only
All using Source theme option button	Cell contents using theme of source data
All except borders option button	Cell contents and formats except cell borders
Column widths option button	No data or formats, but only column width
Transpose check box	A column of copied data as a row or vice-versa

Excel

CHANGE HOW WORKSHEETS ARE VIEWED

Change Worksheet Views

Refer to Table EX-6 to change worksheet views.

Table EX-6 Worksheet Views

View	What you see	Ribbon method	Status bar method
Normal view	Worksheet without headers, footers, or some graphics; does not show worksheet as it would appear as printed	Click the **View tab**, then click the **Normal button** in the Workbook Views group	Click the **Normal button** on the status bar
Page Layout view	Worksheet with headers, footers, and vertical and horizontal rulers	Click the **View tab**, then click the **Page Layout button** in the Workbook Views group	Click the **Page Layout button** on the status bar
Page Break Preview	Similar to Normal view, except with blue lines indicating page breaks; drag a page break using the resize pointers ↕, ↔, or ↘	Click the **View tab**, then click the **Page Break Preview button** in the Workbook Views group	Click the **Page Break Preview button** on the status bar
Custom views	Saved views	Click the **View tab**, then click the **Custom Views button** in the Workbook Views group	None
Full Screen	Worksheet, title bar, sheet tabs, and scroll bars only	Click the **View tab**, then click the **Full Screen button** in the Workbook Views group	None
Print Preview	Worksheet as it would appear when printed	Click the **Office button**, point to **Print**, then click **Print Preview**	None

Zoom In and Out

Ribbon Method

☐ Click the **View tab**, then click the **Zoom button** in the Zoom group
☐ In the Zoom dialog box, click a **zoom percentage**, then click **OK**
☐ Click the **100% button** in the Zoom group to return the workbook to full size
☐ Click the **Zoom to selection button** in the Zoom group to zoom in on the selected cell(s)

Mouse Method

☐ On the status bar, use the Zoom controls, using Table EX-7 as a reference

Table EX-7 Zoom Options on the Status Bar

To	Do this
Zoom in 10%	Click the ⊕ button once
Zoom out 10%	Click the ⊖ button once
Zoom in or out quickly	Click and hold the ⊕ or ⊖ buttons
Zoom in or out gradually	Drag the Zoom slider ▯ left or right

Hide and Redisplay the Ribbon

Ribbon Method

☐ Double-click the **active tab** to reduce the Ribbon so that only tabs are visible
☐ While the Ribbon is hidden, click **any tab** to display it, then click the worksheet to rehide the tab
☐ To redisplay the Ribbon, double-click **any tab**
  OR
☐ To hide the Ribbon, click the **Customize Quick Access Toolbar button** ▾, then click **Minimize the Ribbon**
☐ Repeat this step to redisplay the Ribbon

Shortcut Method

☐ Right-click any tab, then click **Minimize the Ribbon** to select it (hide the Ribbon) or deselect it (display the Ribbon)
  OR
☐ To hide or redisplay the Ribbon, press **[Ctrl][F1]**

Freeze and Unfreeze Panes, Rows, or Columns

Ribbon Method

☐ Click the **View tab**, then click the **Freeze Panes button** in the Window group
☐ Choose an option, using Table EX-8 as a reference

Excel

Table EX-8 Freeze Panel Options

Click this option	To	To unfreeze
Freeze Panes	Make the rows and columns above and to the left of the selected cell remain visible while the rest of the worksheet scrolls; when panes are frozen, this command becomes Unfreeze Panes	Click the **Freeze Panes button**, then click **Unfreeze Panes**
Freeze Top Row	Make the top row remain visible while cells below it scroll	
Freeze First Column	Make the leftmost column remain visible while cells to its right scroll	

Split a Worksheet into Panes

Ribbon Method

☐ Click the **cell** below and to the right of where you want to split the worksheet
☐ Click the **View tab**, then click the **Split button** in the Window group to split the worksheet horizontally and vertically
☐ To remove the splits, click the **Split button** in the Window group again

Mouse Method

☐ Point to the split box ▯ to the right of the horizontal scroll bar or the split box ▭ above the vertical scroll bar until the pointer becomes ↔ or ↕
☐ Drag left, right, up, or down, releasing the mouse button when the split bar is in the appropriate location
☐ To remove a split, double-click either **split bar**, or double-click the **intersection** of the horizontal and vertical split bars to remove both

Open a New Window Containing the Current Workbook

Ribbon Method

☐ Click the **View tab**, then click the **New Window button** in the Window group

Arrange Workbook Windows

Ribbon Method

☐ With two or more workbooks open, click the **View tab**, then click the **Arrange All button** in the Window group
☐ Using Table EX-9 as a reference, click an **option button** in the Arrange Windows dialog box, then click **OK**

Table EX-9 Arrange Windows Dialog Box Options

Click this option button	To
Tiled	Arrange windows in blocks so all are visible at once
Horizontal	Arrange workbooks horizontally, one above another
Vertical	Arrange workbooks vertically, one next to another
Cascade	Arrange workbooks on top of each other, with title bars visible

MANAGE WORKSHEETS

Move or Copy Worksheets within a Workbook

Ribbon Method

- ☐ Click the **Home tab**, click the **Format button** in the Cells group, then, under Organize Sheets, click **Move or Copy Sheet**
- ☐ In the Move or Copy dialog box, select the **location** to move or copy the worksheet in the Before sheet section
- ☐ Click the **Create a copy check box** to copy the worksheet rather than move it if desired
- ☐ Click **OK**

Shortcut Method

- ☐ Right-click the **sheet tab** of the worksheet to move or copy, then click **Move or Copy** on the shortcut menu
- ☐ Follow the steps in bullets 2–4 of the Move or Copy Worksheets within a Workbook Ribbon Method above

   OR

- ☐ Position the pointer over the **sheet tab** to be moved or copied
- ☐ Use ⬚ to drag the tab to the appropriate location in the workbook, then release the mouse button
- ☐ Press **[Ctrl]** and use ⬚ to drag a worksheet copy to the desired location

Move or Copy Worksheets to Another Workbook

Ribbon Method

- ☐ Open the source and destination workbooks
- ☐ In the source workbook, click the **sheet tab** of the sheet you want to move
- ☐ Click the **Home tab**, click the **Format button** in the Cells group, then, under Organize Sheets, click **Move or Copy Sheet**
- ☐ In the Move or Copy dialog box, click the **To book list arrow**, then click the destination workbook name
- ☐ Click the **Create a copy check box** to copy the worksheet rather than move it if desired
- ☐ Click **OK**

Excel

Mouse Method

☐ Open the source and destination workbooks
☐ Click the **View tab**, click the **Arrange All button** in the Window group, click the **Tiled option button**, then click **OK**
☐ Drag to move (or press **[Ctrl]** while dragging to copy) the source worksheet to the destination workbook window

Assign a New Name to a Worksheet

Mouse Method

☐ Double-click a **sheet tab**
☐ Type a new worksheet **name**, then press **[Enter]**

Shortcut Method

☐ Right-click a **sheet tab**, then click **Rename**
☐ Type a new worksheet **name**, then press **[Enter]**

Hide a Worksheet

Shortcut Method

☐ Right-click any **worksheet tab**
☐ Click **Hide**

Redisplay a Hidden Worksheet

Shortcut Method

☐ Right-click any **sheet tab**
☐ Click **Unhide**
☐ In the Unhide dialog box, click the **sheet** you want to unhide, then click **OK**

Insert a New Worksheet into a Workbook

Ribbon Method

☐ Click the **Home tab**, click the **Insert list arrow** in the Cells group, then click **Insert Sheet**

Shortcut Method

☐ Right-click the **sheet tab** to the right of where you want the new one to appear
☐ Click **Insert** on the shortcut menu
☐ In the Insert dialog box, click the **Worksheet icon** on the General tab if necessary, then click **OK**

Delete a Worksheet from a Workbook

Ribbon Method

☐ Click the **Home tab**, click the **Delete list arrow** in the Cells group, then click **Delete Sheet**

Shortcut Method

☐ Right-click the **sheet tab** to delete, then click **Delete** on the shortcut menu
☐ Click **Delete** in the message box if necessary

EXCEL OBJECTIVE 2: FORMATTING DATA AND CONTENT

FORMAT WORKSHEETS

Use a Workbook Theme

Ribbon Method

- ☐ Click the **Page Layout tab**, then click the **Themes button** in the Themes group
- ☐ Click a **theme** to apply it to the workbook, using Table EX-10 as a reference

Table EX-10 Theme Selection Options

Click this option	To
A theme in the Custom group	Apply a theme you previously customized or that you downloaded from the Microsoft Office Web site
A theme in the Built-In group	Apply a predefined theme
More Themes on Microsoft Office Online	Download a theme from the Microsoft Office Web site and place it in the Custom category
Browse for Themes	Browse for a theme or themed document in another location

Customize and Save a Workbook Theme

Ribbon Method

- ☐ Click the **Page Layout tab**, then click the **Theme Colors button**, **Theme Fonts button**, or **Theme Effects button** in the Themes group
- ☐ Select or create new theme colors, fonts, or effects to be applied to the current workbook
- ☐ Click the **Themes button** in the Themes group, then click **Save Current Theme**
- ☐ In the Save Current Theme dialog box, type a **name** for the customized theme in the File name text box, then click **Save** to place the new theme in the Custom section of the Theme gallery

Create New Theme Colors

Ribbon Method

- ☐ Click the **Page Layout tab**, click the **Themes button**, then click a **theme**
- ☐ Click the **Theme Color button** in the Themes group, then click **Create New Theme Colors**

Excel

☐ In the Create New Theme Colors dialog box, click the **button arrow** for a theme color to change, click a new **color**, then adjust other theme colors as desired

☐ Type a **custom theme color name** in the Name text box, then click **Save** to save the custom color set in the Custom section of the Theme Colors menu

Create New Theme Fonts

Ribbon Method

☐ Click the **Page Layout tab**, click the **Themes button**, then click a **theme**

☐ Click the **Theme Fonts button** in the Themes group, then click **Create New Theme Fonts**

☐ In the Create New Theme Fonts dialog box, select new Heading and/or Body fonts

☐ Type a **custom font theme name** in the Name text box, then click **Save** to save the custom theme set in the Custom section of the Theme Fonts menu

Delete a Custom Theme, Color Set, or Font Set

☐ Click the **Page Layout tab**

☐ Click the **Themes button**, **Theme Colors button**, or **Theme Fonts button** in the Themes group

☐ Right-click the **theme**, **theme color set**, or **theme font set** to delete, click **Delete**, then click **Yes**

Display and Hide Gridlines

Ribbon Method

☐ Click the **Page Layout tab**

☐ Click the **View check box** in the Gridlines section of the Sheet Options group to select it or deselect it

OR

☐ Click the **View tab**

☐ Click the **Gridlines check box** in the Show/Hide group to select it or deselect it

Display and Hide Column and Row Headings

Ribbon Method

☐ Click the **Page Layout tab**

☐ Click the **View check box** in the Headings section of the Sheet Options group to select it or deselect it

OR

☐ Click the **View tab**

☐ Click the **Headings check box** in the Show/Hide group to select it or deselect it

Change Sheet Tab Color

Shortcut Method

□ Right-click the **sheet tab** to change
□ Point to **Tab Color**, then click a **theme color** or a **standard color**, or click **More Colors** to select a color from the Colors dialog box

Format Worksheet Backgrounds

Ribbon Method

□ Click the **Page Layout tab**, then click the **Background button** in the Page Setup group
□ In the Sheet Background dialog box, browse to a picture if necessary, then double-click the **picture** to create a sheet background that appears on the screen, but does not print

Create a Sheet Watermark

Ribbon Method

□ Click the **Insert tab**, then click the **Header & Footer button** in the Text group
□ Click in the **left**, **center**, or **right** header section, then click the **Picture button** in the Header & Footer Elements group
□ Browse to a picture if necessary, then double-click the **picture** to add a picture that does not appear on the screen, but that does appear in Print Preview and when the worksheet is printed

---

INSERT AND MODIFY ROWS AND COLUMNS

Insert Cells

Ribbon Method

□ Click where you want to insert cells
□ Click the **Home tab**, click the **Insert list arrow** in the Cells group, then click **Insert Cells**
□ In the Insert dialog box, select the appropriate option button, then click **OK**

Shortcut Method

□ Right-click where you want to insert cells
□ Click **Insert** on the shortcut menu
□ In the Insert dialog box, select the appropriate option button, then click **OK**

Delete Cells

Ribbon Method

□ Select the **cell(s)** you want to delete
□ Click the **Home tab**, click the **Delete list arrow** in the Cells group, then click **Delete Cells**
□ In the Delete dialog box, select the appropriate option button, then click **OK**

Shortcut Method

- [ ] Select the **cell(s)** you want to delete, then right-click the selected cell(s)
- [ ] Click **Delete** on the shortcut menu
- [ ] In the Delete dialog box, select the appropriate option button, then click **OK**

Insert One Row or Column

Ribbon Method

- [ ] Select the **column** (or a **cell** in the column) to the right of where you want the new column to appear, or select the **row** (or a **cell** in the row) below where you want the new row to appear
- [ ] Click the **Home tab**, then click the **Insert list arrow** in the Cells group
- [ ] Click **Insert Sheet Rows**

Shortcut Method

- [ ] Select the **column** (or a **cell** in the column) to the right of where you want the new column to appear, or select the **row** (or a **cell** in the row) below where you want the new row to appear
- [ ] Right-click, then click **Insert** on the shortcut menu
- [ ] In the Insert dialog box, select the **Entire row option button** or the **Entire column option button**, then click **OK**

  OR

- [ ] Select the **column** (or a **cell** in the column) to the right of where you want the new column to appear, or select the **row** (or a **cell** in the row) below where you want the new row to appear
- [ ] Press **[Ctrl][Shift][+]**
- [ ] In the Insert dialog box, select the **Entire row option button** or the **Entire column option button**, then click **OK**

Insert Multiple Columns or Rows at Once

Ribbon Method

- [ ] Select two or more **rows** or **columns** to the right of or below where you want the new ones to appear
- [ ] Click the **Home tab**, click the **Insert list arrow** in the Cells group, then click **Insert Sheet Rows** or **Insert Sheet Columns** to insert the same number of rows or columns as you selected

Shortcut Method

- [ ] Select two or more **rows** or **columns** to the right of or below where you want the new ones to appear
- [ ] Right-click the **selected area**, then click **Insert**

  OR

- [ ] Select two or more **rows** or **columns** to the right of where you want the new ones to appear
- [ ] Press **[Ctrl][Shift][+]**

Excel

Apply Formats to Entire Rows and Columns

Ribbon Method

☐ Select an entire **row** or **column**, or select two or more **rows** or **columns**
☐ Click the **Home tab**, then click the appropriate formatting commands in the Font, Alignment, Number, and Styles groups

Shortcut Method

☐ Select an entire **row** or **column**, or select two or more **rows** or **columns**
☐ Right-click the **selected row(s) or column(s)**, then click **Format Cells**
☐ In the Format Cells dialog box, select options to apply number, alignment, font, border, or fill formats to the selected row(s) or column(s)

OR

☐ Select an entire **row** or **column**, or select two or more **rows** or **columns**
☐ Right-click the **selected row(s) or column(s)**
☐ Click a formatting command on the Mini toolbar

Hide Rows and Columns

Ribbon Method

☐ Click a **cell** in the row or column to hide, select a **range** of cells spanning the rows or columns to hide, select an entire **row** or **column**, or select two or more **rows** or **columns**
☐ Click the **Home tab**, then click the **Format button** in the Cells group
☐ Point to **Hide & Unhide**, then click **Hide Rows** or **Hide Columns**

Redisplay Hidden Rows and Columns

Ribbon Method

☐ Drag to select two **cells**, one on either side of the hidden row(s) or column(s)
☐ Click the **Home tab**, then click the **Format button** in the Cells group
☐ Point to **Hide & Unhide**, then click **Unhide Rows** or **Unhide Columns**

Changing Row Height

Ribbon Method

☐ Click a **row heading** to select the row to change or click any **cell** in a row to change
☐ Click the **Home tab**, click the **Format button** in the Cells group, then click **Row Height**
☐ In the Row Height dialog box, type the **height** you want, then click **OK**

Mouse Method

☐ Position the mouse pointer over the bottom edge of a **row heading**, until the pointer changes to ✛
☐ Drag ✛ downward to increase the row height to the desired size, or drag upward to decrease the row height

Excel

AutoFit Row Height

- [ ] Position the mouse pointer over the bottom edge of a **row heading**, until the pointer changes to ✛
- [ ] Double-click to automatically adjust the row height to fit the size of the row contents

Change Column Width

Ribbon Method

- [ ] Click a **column heading** to select the column or click any **cell** in the column to change
- [ ] Click the **Home tab**, click the **Format button** in the Cells group, then click **Column Width**
- [ ] In the Column Width dialog box, type the **width** you want, then click **OK**

Mouse Method

- [ ] Move the mouse pointer over the right edge of a column heading until the pointer changes to ✛
- [ ] Drag the column heading divider to the right to increase the column width or to the left to decrease the column width

AutoFit Column Width

- [ ] Move the mouse pointer over the divider on the right edge of a column heading until the pointer changes to ✛
- [ ] Double-click to automatically adjust the column width to fit the size of the column contents

FORMAT CELLS AND CELL CONTENT

Use Number Formats

Ribbon Method

- [ ] Select the **cell(s)** to format
- [ ] Click the **Home tab**, then click a button in the Number group, using Table EX-11 as a guide

Table EX-11 Number Format Options on the Home Tab

Click this option	To apply	Example
$	Accounting Number Format	$ 10,000.00
%	Percent Style	Displays .06 as 6%
,	Comma Style	10,000.00
.00→.0	One additional decimal place	Changes 5.0 to 5.00
.00→.0	One less decimal place	Changes 5.0 to 5
Number Format list arrow	General, Number, Currency, Accounting, Short & Long Date, Time, Percentage, Fraction, and Scientific Formats	Various; see also Table EX-12

OR

☐ Click the **Home tab**, then click the **Launcher** 🖻 in the Number group
☐ In the Format Cells dialog box, click a **category** and select options on the Number tab using Table EX-12 as a guide

Table EX-12 Number Tab Categories in the Format Cells Dialog Box

Category	To Apply
General	No number format
Number	General number format with or without decimal places or comma separators
Currency	General number format with currency symbols ($, €, etc.)
Accounting	Currency format but aligns currency symbols and decimal points
Date	Various month, day, and year formats
Time	Various hour, minute, and date formats
Percentage	Number multiplied by 100 and displayed with %
Fraction	Fractions in various formats (halves, quarters, etc.)
Scientific	Scientific format such as displaying 5500 as 5.50E+03
Text	Numbers treated as text, exactly as entered
Special	Zip code, phone number, or social security number formats
Custom	Special number, date, and time formats that user customizes

Create Custom Cell Formats

Ribbon Method

☐ Click the **cell(s)** to format
☐ Click the **Home tab**, then click the **Launcher** 🖻 in the Number group
☐ On the Number tab, click the **Custom category**
☐ Click a **format** that is close to the format you want to create
☐ In the Type text box, edit the format as necessary, using Table EX-13 as a reference for some symbols

Excel

Table EX-13 Symbols to Use in Custom Formats

Use this symbol	To represent	How it appears in worksheet
mm	Month displayed as a 2-digit number	01
mmmm	Displays full month name	January
dd	Day of the month as a 2-digit number	01
0	Digit that shows # of decimal places	0.000 format would display .732

Apply Cell Quick Styles

Ribbon Method

☐ Click the **cell(s)** to format
☐ Click the **Cell Styles button** in the Styles group, then click a **style** in one of the groups

Create and Apply a Custom Style

Ribbon Method

☐ Click the **cell(s)** to format
☐ Click the **Home tab**, click the **Cell Styles button** in the Styles group, then click **New Cell Style**
☐ Type a **name** in the Style name text box, then click **Format**
☐ Choose settings on the tabs of the Format Cells dialog box, then click **OK**
☐ Click any check box to not include that parameter, then click **OK**
☐ Click the **Cell Styles button** in the Styles group, then click the **custom style** in the Custom group

Format Cells and Cell Text

Ribbon Method

☐ Select the **cell(s)** to format
☐ Click the **Home tab**, then use the buttons in the Font and Alignment groups to apply the appropriate formats using Table EX-14 as a reference

Shortcut Method

☐ Select the **cell(s)** to format
☐ Right-click the **selected range**, then use the buttons on the Mini toolbar to apply the appropriate formats using Table EX-14 as a reference

Table EX-14 Applying Cell Formats Using the Home Tab or Mini Toolbar

Button	Formatting	Effect
Font list arrow	Font	Changes font style
Font Size list arrow	Font Size	Changes font size
B	Bold	Bold
I	Italic	*Italic*
U	Underline	<u>Underline</u>
≡	Align Left	Aligns to left cell edge
≡	Center	Aligns between left and right cell edges
≡	Align Right	Aligns to right cell edge
⊞	Merge and Center	Merges selected cells and centers text in merged cell
$ ▾	Accounting Number Format	$1234.56
%	Percent Style	123456%
,	Comma Style	1,234.56
.00→.0	Increase Decimal	1234.560
.00←.0	Decrease Decimal	1234.6
手	Decrease Indent	Decreases indentation from left cell edge
手	Increase Indent	Indents from left cell edge
⊞	Borders	Adds borders to edge(s) of selected cell(s)
◇	Fill Color	Fills cell(s) with color
A	Font Color	Changes font color

Excel

Convert Text into Columns

Ribbon Method

☐ Select the **cells** containing the text to convert
☐ Click the **Data tab**, then click the **Text to Columns button** in the Data Tools group
☐ In screen 1 of the Convert Text to Columns Wizard, select the **Delimited option button** or **Fixed width option button**, then click **Next**
☐ In screen 2 of the wizard, select the **delimiter** or create, delete, and move **break lines** to set field widths, then click **Next**
☐ In screen 3 of the wizard, set the **data format** for each column, then click **Finish**

Split and Merge Cells

Ribbon Method

- ☐ Select the **cells** to merge or the **merged cell** to be split
- ☐ Click the **Home tab**, then click the **Merge and Center list arrow** in the Alignment group
- ☐ Click an option, using Table EX-15 as a reference

Table EX-15 Merge Options

Option	Action
Merge & Center	Merges selected cells and centers content in the newly merged call
Merge Across	Merges cells in a range horizontally only
Merge Cells	Merges content across selected cell range
Unmerge Cells	Removes merge and restores column or row structure

Format Cell Borders and Fill Colors

Ribbon Method

- ☐ Select the **cell(s)** to format
- ☐ Click the **Home tab**, click the **Borders list arrow** 🔲 ▾ in the Font group, then click the appropriate border option
- ☐ Click the **Home tab**, click the **Fill Color list arrow** 🎨 ▾ in the Font group, then click the appropriate color

OR

- ☐ Select the **cell(s)** to format
- ☐ Click the **Home tab**, then click the **Launcher** ⬛ in the Font group
- ☐ In the Format Cells dialog box, click the **Border tab** or the **Fill tab**
- ☐ Make the appropriate selections, then click **OK**

Shortcut Method

- ☐ Select the **cell(s)** to format
- ☐ Press **[Ctrl][1]**
- ☐ Follow the steps in bullets 3–4 of the second Format Cell Borders and Fill Colors Ribbon Method above

OR

- ☐ Right-click the **cell(s)** to format
- ☐ On the Mini toolbar, click the **Borders list arrow** 🔲 ▾ in the Font group, then click the appropriate border option
- ☐ On the Mini toolbar, click the **Fill Color list arrow** 🎨 ▾ in the Font group, then click the appropriate color

Insert Hyperlinks

Ribbon Method

- ☐ Select the appropriate **cell**, **range**, **chart**, or **graphic**
- ☐ Click the **Insert tab**, then click the **Hyperlink button** in the Links group

Excel

□ In the Insert Hyperlink dialog box, specify the appropriate options using Table EX-16 as a reference, then click **OK**

Shortcut Method

□ Select the appropriate **cell**, **range**, **chart**, or **graphic**
□ Press **[Ctrl][K]**
□ In the Insert Hyperlink dialog box, specify the appropriate options using Table EX-16 as a reference, then click **OK**

Table EX-16 Inserting Hyperlinks Using the Insert Hyperlink Dialog Box

To link to	Instructions
Another place in the document	Click **Place in This Document**, select a **location** in the Or select a place in this document list, then click **OK**
Another document	Click **Existing File or Web Page**, navigate to the appropriate drive and folder, click the **file name** in the list, then click **OK**
A new document	Click **Create New Document**, name the document and verify the drive and folder, choose to edit it now or later, then click **OK**
A Web page	(*Note*: Make sure you are connected to the Internet) Click **Existing File or Web Page**, click the **Address text box**, type the URL, then click **OK**
An e-mail address	Click **E-mail Address**, type the **address** and any other text to display, then click **OK**

Edit Hyperlinks

Shortcut Method

□ Right-click the **hyperlink**, then click **Edit Hyperlink** on the shortcut menu
□ In the Edit Hyperlink dialog box, make modifications, then click **OK**

Remove Hyperlinks

Shortcut Method

□ Right-click the **hyperlink**, then click **Remove Hyperlink** on the shortcut menu

FORMAT DATA AS A TABLE

Create a Table

Ribbon Method

□ Click inside (or drag to select) the range of cells you want to change to a table
□ Click the **Insert tab**, then click the **Table button** in the Tables group
□ In the Create Table dialog box, verify that the range is correct and that the My table has headers check box is checked if appropriate, then click **OK**

Excel

Shortcut Method

- ☐ Click inside (or drag to select) the range of cells you want to change to a table
- ☐ Press **[Ctrl][T]**
- ☐ In the Create Table dialog box, verify that the range is correct and that the My table has headers check box is checked if appropriate, then click **OK**

Apply and Change Table Quick Styles

Ribbon Method

- ☐ Click inside the table
- ☐ Click the **Table Tools Design tab**, then click the **More button** ▼ in the Table Styles group
- ☐ Click a **table style** in the Light, Medium, or Dark section of the gallery
- ☐ To change styles, click ▼ again and click another **style**

Hide and Display Table Header Rows

Ribbon Method

- ☐ Click inside the table, observing that the header row appears in all tables by default
- ☐ Click the **Table Tools Design tab**, then click the **Header Row check box** in the Table Style Options group to remove the check mark and hide the header row
- ☐ Click the **Header Row check box** again to select it and redisplay the header row

Add and Remove Banded Table Rows

Ribbon Method

- ☐ Click inside the table, then, if the table does not have a style applied, apply a **table style** that features banded rows
- ☐ Click the **Table Tools Design tab**, then click the **Banded Rows check box** in the Table Style Options group to remove the check mark and remove banded rows from the table
- ☐ Click the **Banded Rows check box** again to add banded rows back to the table

Add and Remove Banded Table Columns

Ribbon Method

- ☐ Click inside the table, then, if the table does not have a style applied, apply a **table style** that features banded rows
- ☐ Click the **Table Tools Design tab**, then click the **Banded Columns check box** in the Table Style Options group to select it and add banded columns to the table
- ☐ Click the **Banded Columns check box** again to remove the check mark and remove banded columns from the table

Switch from Banded Table Rows to Banded Table Columns

Ribbon Method

☐ Click inside a table that has banded rows
☐ Click the **Table Tools Design tab**, then click the **Banded Rows check box** in the Table Style Options group to deselect it
☐ Click the **Banded Columns check box** in the Table Style Options group to select it

Modify a Table Range

Ribbon Method

☐ Click inside the table, then click the **Table Tools Design tab**
☐ Click the **Resize Table button** in the Properties group
☐ With the Resize Table dialog box open, drag across a new range on the worksheet, then click **OK** (*Note*: The headers for the resized table must be in the same row as the headers in the original table, and the resized table must overlap the original table)

Shortcut Method

☐ Point to the lower-right corner of a table, until the pointer becomes ↘
☐ Drag up, down, left, or right until the table encompasses the desired cell range, then release the mouse button

OR

☐ Click in the row immediately below or the column immediately to the right of a table
☐ Enter **data**, then press **[Enter]**

Emphasize the First and Last Table Columns

Ribbon Method

☐ Click inside the table
☐ Click the **Table Tools Design tab**, then click the **First Column check box** in the Table Style Options group to select it and add formatting to the first table column
☐ Click the **Last Column check box** in the Table Style Options group to select it and add formatting to the last table column
☐ To remove formatting from the first or last column, click the **First Column check box** or the **Last Column check box** to deselect it

Add a Table Total Row

Ribbon Method

☐ Click inside the table
☐ Click the **Table Tools Design tab**, then click the **Total Row check box** in the Table Style Options group to select it

Shortcut Method

☐ Click inside the table
☐ Press **[Ctrl][Shift][T]**

Excel

OR
☐ Right-click the **table**, point to **Table**, then click **Totals Row**

Change a Table Summary Function

Mouse Method
☐ Click a **cell** in the totals row of a table
☐ Click the cell's **list arrow**
☐ Click another summary function

Shortcut Method
☐ Click a **cell** in the totals row of a table
☐ Press **[Alt][↓]**
☐ Use the keyboard arrow keys to select the summary function you want, then press **[Enter]**

Insert Table Rows and Columns

Ribbon Method
☐ Select the **table row(s)** (or select a **cell** in the table row) above which you want to insert a row, or select a **table column** (or a **cell** in the table column) to the right of which you want to insert a column
☐ Click the **Home tab**, then click the **Insert list arrow** in the Cells group
☐ Click **Insert Table Rows Above** or **Insert Table Columns to the Left**
☐ If the table row you selected was the last row in the table, you also see an **Insert Table Row Below** command; if you selected the rightmost table column, you see an **Insert Table Column to the Right** command

Shortcut Method
☐ Right click a **cell** in the table row above which you want to insert a row or to the right of which you want to insert a column
☐ Point to **Insert** on the shortcut menu, then click **Table Rows Above** or **Table Columns to the Left**
☐ If the table row you selected was the last row in the table, you also see an **Insert Table Row Below** command; if you selected the rightmost table column, you see an **Insert Table Column to the Right** command

Delete Table Rows and Columns

Ribbon Method
☐ Select the **table row(s)** (or select a **cell** in the table row) you want to delete, or select the **table column(s)** (or click a **cell** in the table column) you want to delete
☐ Click the **Home tab**, then click the **Delete list arrow** in the Cells group
☐ Click **Delete Table Rows** or **Delete Table Columns**

Shortcut Method
☐ Right-click a **cell** in the table row or column you want to delete
☐ Point to **Delete** on the shortcut menu, then click **Table Rows** or **Table Columns**

EXCEL OBJECTIVE 3: CREATING AND MODIFYING FORMULAS

REFERENCE DATA IN FORMULAS

Note: Use Figure EX-2 as a reference for using relative and absolute references in formulas.

Use Relative References

Shortcut Method

☐ Click the appropriate **cell**, then click the **formula bar** and type **=**, or type **=** directly in the cell

☐ To insert a cell reference in the formula, type the **cell address** you want to reference in the formula bar or in the cell that contains the formula, or click the **cell** you want to reference

☐ Complete the formula using appropriate operators, values, and additional cell references, then click the **Enter button** ✅ on the formula bar

Use Absolute References in Formulas

Shortcut Method

☐ Click a **cell** where you want to enter a formula, then enter the **formula** in the formula bar or type the **formula** directly in the cell

☐ In the formula bar, select the **cell reference** that you want to make an absolute reference

☐ Press **[F4]**, then verify that the cell reference now reads **A1** (where A1 is the cell address)

☐ Press **[Enter]** or **[Tab]**

Use Mixed References in Formulas

Shortcut Method

☐ Click a **cell** where you want to enter a formula, then enter the **formula** in the formula bar or type the **formula** directly in the cell

☐ In the formula bar, select the **cell reference** that you want to make into a mixed reference

☐ Press **[F4]** until the cell reference reads **A$1** or **$A1** (where A1 is the cell address)

☐ Press **[Enter]** or **[Tab]**

Excel

Figure EX-2 Relative and Absolute References

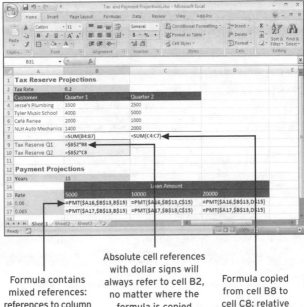

Formula contains mixed references: references to column A and rows 13 and 15 are absolute; reference to row 16 and second reference to column B are relative

Absolute cell references with dollar signs will always refer to cell B2, no matter where the formula is copied

Formula copied from cell B8 to cell C8; relative cell reference has changed to reflect column C

Excel

Troubleshoot Formulas by Tracing Precedents

Ribbon Method

☐ Click a **cell** that contains a formula
☐ Click the **Formulas tab**, then click the **Trace Precedents button** in the Formula Auditing group
☐ Double-click one of the **blue arrows** to navigate between the cell containing the formula and the precedent cells

Troubleshoot Formulas by Tracing Dependents

Ribbon Method

☐ Click a **cell** that is referenced in a formula
☐ Click the **Formulas tab**, then click the **Trace Dependents button** in the Formula Auditing group
☐ Double-click the **blue arrow** to navigate between the cells

Troubleshoot Formulas by Tracing Locate and Resolve Errors

Ribbon Method

☐ Click the **cell** that shows an error, using Table EX-17 as a reference
☐ Click the **Formulas tab**, click the **Error Checking list arrow** in the Formula Auditing group, then click **Trace Error**
☐ Use the formula bar to correct the formula

Table EX-17 Common Cell Errors

Error	Means
#DIV/0!	Value is divided by zero
#NAME?	Excel does not recognize text
#N/A	Value is not available for the formula
#NULL!	When a formula specifies an intersection of two areas that do not intersect
#NUM!	Invalid formula number(s)
#REF!	Invalid cell reference
#VALUE!	Operand or argument is incorrect

Excel

Remove All Tracer Arrows

Ribbon Method

☐ Click the **Formulas tab**, then click the **Remove Arrows button**

Troubleshoot Formulas Using Error Checking

Ribbon Method

☐ Click the **Formulas tab**, then click the **Error Checking button** in the Formula Auditing group
☐ In the Error Checking dialog box, click the appropriate button, using Table EX-18 as a reference, fix or view the error as prompted, then click **OK**
☐ Click the **Next** and **Previous buttons** to navigate through the errors

Table EX-18 Error Checking Dialog Box Options

Button	Action
Help on this error	Opens the Microsoft Excel Help Window and displays an article about this type of function or formula
Show Calculation Steps	Opens the Evaluate Formula dialog box
Ignore Error	Move to the next error without modifying the current error
Edit in Formula Bar	Activates the cell containing the error in the formula bar

Troubleshoot Formulas by Evaluating Formulas

Ribbon Method

☐ Click the **cell** that contains the formula
☐ Click the **Formulas tab**, then click **Evaluate Formula** in the Formula Auditing group
☐ In the Evaluate Formula dialog box, click the appropriate button, using Table EX-19 as a reference

Table EX-19 Evaluate Formula Dialog Box Options

Button	Action
Evaluate	Shows the result of the underlined value; click repeatedly to display additional levels of the formula
Step In	View the formula that supports the highlighted argument; available when there is a formula within the formula you are evaluating
Step Out	Display the previous cell and formula; available after you have clicked Step In

Troubleshoot Formulas by Using Cell Watch

Ribbon Method

- ☐ Select the **cells** to watch
- ☐ Click the **Formulas tab**, then click the **Watch Window button** in the Formula Auditing group
- ☐ Click **Add Watch** in the Watch Window, select the **cells** you want to watch, then click **Add**

Use References to Data in Other Worksheets in a Formula

- ☐ If necessary, open the **workbook** containing the data you want to reference
- ☐ In the current workbook, click the **cell** that will contain the formula, then type **=**
- ☐ Click the **workbook** (if necessary) and **worksheet** containing the value you want to include, then click the **cell** containing the value
- ☐ Type another **operand** (such as + or –) to continue the formula in the current workbook, then select other **cells** as necessary
- ☐ Press **[Enter]**

Create Summary Formulas Using 3-D References to the Same Cell

Mouse Method

- ☐ Create a summary worksheet with the same structure as the sheets with the supporting data
- ☐ Click the **cell** that will contain the summary formula, then type **=**
- ☐ Type the **function**, such as SUM, followed by **(**
- ☐ If you are referencing sheets in another workbook, click that workbook's button on the taskbar
- ☐ Click the **sheet tab** of the first supporting sheet, press and hold **[Shift]**, click the **sheet tab** for the last supporting sheet, then release **[Shift]**
- ☐ Click the **cell** containing the value you want to summarize, then type **)**
- ☐ Press **[Enter]**

Create Summary Formulas Using 3-D References to Different Cells

Mouse Method

- ☐ Create a summary worksheet with the same structure as the sheets with the supporting data
- ☐ Click the **cell** that will contain the summary formula, then type **=**
- ☐ Type the **function**, such as SUM, followed by **(**
- ☐ If you are referencing sheets in another workbook, click that workbook's button on the taskbar
- ☐ Click the **sheet tab** of the first supporting sheet, click the **cell** containing the value to summarize, then type **,**
- ☐ Click the **sheet tab** and **cell** for any other supporting sheet values
- ☐ Type **)**
- ☐ Press **[Enter]**

Excel

Name One or More Cell Ranges

Ribbon Method

- [ ] Select a **range**
- [ ] Click the **Formulas tab**, then click the **Define Name button** in the Defined Names group
- [ ] In the New Name dialog box, type the **range name** in the Name text box, then click **OK**

  OR

- [ ] Click the **Formulas tab**, then click the **Name Manager button** in the Defined Names group
- [ ] Click **New**
- [ ] In the New Name dialog box, type the **range name** in the Name text box, then click **OK**

Shortcut Method

- [ ] Select the **range** you want to name
- [ ] Click the **Name box** to the far left of the formula bar, type the **range name** using numbers and letters and without using spaces, then press **[Enter]**

  OR

- [ ] Click the **Formulas tab**, then press **[Ctrl][F3]**
- [ ] Press **[Alt][N]**
- [ ] In the New Name dialog box, type the **range name** in the Name text box, then press **[Enter]**

  OR

- [ ] Click a **cell** containing the name you want to use as a range name
- [ ] Right-click the **cell**, then click **Name a Range** in the shortcut menu
- [ ] Change the range name or range as necessary, then click **OK**

Use Labels to Create Range Names

Ribbon Method

- [ ] Select the **range**, including any row or column labels
- [ ] Click the **Formulas tab**, then click the **Create from Selection button** in the Defined Names group
- [ ] In the Create Names from Selection dialog box, click the appropriate **check box** to use as the range name, then click **OK**

Shortcut Method

- [ ] Select the **range**, including any row or column labels
- [ ] Click the **Formulas tab**, then press **[Ctrl][Shift][F3]**
- [ ] In the Create Names from Selection dialog box, click the appropriate **check box** to use as the range name, then click **OK**

Add a Column to a Named Range

Ribbon Method

- [ ] Click the **Formulas tab**, then click the **Name Manager button** in the Defined Names group

□ In the Name Manager dialog box, click the **name** of the range to which you want to add a column, then click **Edit**
□ Edit the cell range in the Refers to text box
□ Click **OK**

Shortcut Method

□ Click the **Formulas tab**, then press **[Ctrl][F3]**
□ Follow the steps in bullets 2–4 of the Add a Column to a Named Range Ribbon Method above

Delete a Named Range

Ribbon Method

□ Click the **Formulas tab**, then click the **Name Manager button** in the Defined Names group
□ Click the **name** of the range you want to delete
□ Click **Delete**, click **OK**, then click **Close**

Shortcut Method

□ Click the **Formulas tab**, then press **[Ctrl][F3]**
□ Follow the steps in bullets 2–3 of the Delete a Named Range Ribbon Method above

Insert a Named Range in a Formula

Ribbon Method

□ Click in the **cell** where the formula will appear
□ Begin typing the formula, then when you need to insert the range name, click the **Formulas tab**
□ Click the **Use in Formula button** in the Defined Names group, then click the **range name** in the drop-down menu
□ Complete the formula as appropriate

OR

□ Click in the **cell** where the formula will appear
□ Begin typing the formula, then when you need to insert the range name, click the **Formulas tab**
□ Click the **Use in Formula button** in the Defined Names group, click **Paste Names**, then in the Paste Name dialog box, double-click the **range name**
□ Complete the formula as appropriate

Shortcut Method

□ Click the **cell** where the formula will appear
□ As you type the formula in the cell, type the first letter of the range name, and use **[↓]** to select the range name that appears in the drop-down menu
□ Press **[Tab]**, then type the rest of the formula and press **[Enter]**

Summarize Data Using Range Names

Ribbon Method

□ Create a **range name** for one group of related data, such as JanuarySales

Excel

- [ ] Create a **range name** for another group of related data, such as FebruarySales
- [ ] Create any additional **range names** for related data
- [ ] Click a **blank cell**, then create a **formula** that adds the sums of each range, using the Use in Formula button to insert range names, such as =SUM(rangename1)+SUM(rangename2)+SUM(rangename3)

SUMMARIZE DATA USING A FORMULA

Create a Formula

Mouse Method

- [ ] Click the **cell** where you want the formula result to appear
- [ ] Type =
- [ ] Click the **cell** containing the first value you want to include
- [ ] Type an **operand** such as +, −, * (for multiplication), or / (for division)
- [ ] Click the **cell** containing the second value you want to include
- [ ] Enter operands and other cells as necessary
- [ ] Press **[Enter]**

Keyboard Method

- [ ] Click the **cell** where you want the formula result to appear
- [ ] Type =
- [ ] Type the **cell address** or use the keyboard arrow keys to navigate to the cell containing the first value you want to include
- [ ] Type an **operand** such as +, −, * (for multiplication), or / (for division)
- [ ] Type the **cell address** or use the keyboard arrow keys to navigate to the cell containing the second value you want to include
- [ ] Press **[Enter]**

Create a Formula Using a Function

Ribbon Method

- [ ] Click the **cell** where you want the formula result to appear
- [ ] Click the **Formulas tab**, then click the **Insert Function button** in the Function Library group
- [ ] In the Insert Function dialog box, select the appropriate function using Table EX-20 as a reference, then click **OK**
- [ ] In the Function Argument dialog box, specify the appropriate settings or the appropriate cells if necessary, then click **OK**
  OR
- [ ] Click the **Formulas tab**, click the appropriate **Function Category button** in the Function Library group, then click the function name in the drop-down menu, using Table EX-20 as a reference
- [ ] In the Function Argument dialog box, specify the appropriate settings or the appropriate cells if necessary, then click **OK**

Shortcut Method

- [ ] Click the appropriate **cell**
- [ ] Click the **Insert Function button** f_x on the formula bar

☐ Follow the steps in bullets 3–4 of the first Create a Formula Using a Function Ribbon Method above

OR

☐ Type **=**, start to type a function name, then observe the function drop-down menu
☐ Press **[↓]** until the desired function name is highlighted, then press **[Tab]**
☐ Type or drag to enter the argument cell or range, then press **[Enter]**

Table EX-20 Examples of Commonly Used Excel Functions

Function	Example	Results
SUM	=SUM(A4:C4)	The total of the values in cells A4, B4, and C4
MIN	=MIN(B10,B13,B15)	The lowest value in the cells B10, B13, and B15
MAX	=MAX(C14,C18:C20)	The highest value in the cells C14, C18, C19, and C20
COUNT	=COUNT(A4:C4)	The number of cells in a range that contain numbers
COUNTA	=COUNTA(A4:C4)	The number of cells in a range that are not empty
DATE	=DATE(A2,A3,A4)	The date as a sequential serial number (as in 2008, 4, 2), where cells A2, A3, and A4 have the year (2008), month (4), and day (2), respectively
NOW	=NOW()	The current date and time
PMT	=PMT(rate,nper,pv,fv,type)	Payment for a loan where **rate** is the interest rate, **Nper** is the number of payments, **Pv** is the principal on the loan, **Fv** is the cash balance after the last payment (if omitted, is assumed to be zero), **Type** is the number 0 (zero) or 1 and indicates when payments are due
AVERAGE	=AVERAGE(D2:D10)	The average of the values for the cell range D2 through D10

Excel

SUMMARIZE DATA USING SUBTOTALS

Create a List

Keyboard Method

☐ Type related **data** in rows and columns, with column headers describing each column if desired
☐ Type additional rows and columns as necessary, being sure that there are no empty rows or columns

Filter a List

Ribbon Method

- ☐ Click inside the list range
- ☐ Click the **Data tab**, then click the **Filter button** in the Sort & Filter group
- ☐ Click the **list arrow** at the top of the column on which you want to filter
- ☐ Click **(Select All)** to remove all check marks
- ☐ Click the **check boxes** for the items you want to display
- ☐ Click **OK**

Shortcut Method

- ☐ Click inside the list range, then press **[Ctrl][Shift][L]**
- ☐ Follow the steps in bullets 3–6 of in the Filter a List Ribbon Method above

  OR

- ☐ Right-click in a cell that contains the value, color, font color, or icon on which you want to filter
- ☐ Point to **Filter**, then click **Filter by Selected Cell's Value** (or **Color, Font Color**, or **Icon**)

Remove a Filter

Ribbon Method

- ☐ Click in the filtered list range
- ☐ Click the **Data tab**, then click the **Filter button** in the Sort & Filter group to deselect the button and remove the filter arrows

Sort a List

Ribbon Method

- ☐ Click inside the list range
- ☐ Click the **Data tab**, then click the **Sort button** in the Sort & Filter group
- ☐ In the Sort dialog box, click the **Sort by list arrow**, then click the **column** on which to sort
- ☐ Select appropriate values in the Sort On and Order lists, then click **OK**
- ☐ To sort within the groupings you created, click **Add Level**, then select another column on which to sort and specify Sort On and Order values
- ☐ Continue adding levels as necessary, then click **OK**

Shortcut Method

- ☐ Right-click a **cell value** on which you want to sort
- ☐ Point to **Sort**, then click the appropriate option

Subtotal a List

Ribbon Method

- ☐ Click in the list range, then sort the list on the column where you want to group the data (See "Sort a List" above)
- ☐ Filter the list if necessary (See "Filter a List" above)
- ☐ Click the **Subtotal button** in the Outline group on the Data tab
- ☐ In the Subtotal dialog box, click the **At each change in list arrow**, then select the field on which you sorted
- ☐ Click the **Use function list arrow**, then click the function to use to summarize the data, using Table EX-21 as a reference
- ☐ In the Add subtotal to box, click the **check boxes** of the fields you want to subtotal, then click **OK**

Table EX-21 Functions Available for Subtotaled Lists

Function	Finds for each sorted group
SUM	Total of the items
COUNT	Number of instances
AVERAGE	Average of the values
MAX	The highest value
MIN	The lowest value

Remove Subtotals

Ribbon Method

- ☐ Click in the list range containing subtotals
- ☐ Click the **Data tab**, then click the **Subtotal button** in the Outline group
- ☐ In the Subtotal dialog box, click **Remove All**

CONDITIONALLY SUMMARIZE DATA USING A FORMULA

Summarize Data That Meets Certain Conditions

Ribbon Method

- ☐ Verify that your worksheet has a range to search and numerical values to summarize
- ☐ Click in the cell that will contain the conditional formula result
- ☐ Type **=**, then type a conditional function, using Table EX-22 as a reference

Table EX-22 Functions to Summarize Data Based on Conditions

Conditional function and arguments	Example	Tells Excel to
SUMIF(range, criteria, sum_range)	=SUMIF(A1:A50,H2, D1:D50)	Look in the range A1:A50, if the value specified in cell H2 is found, then sum the values of those items that are in the range D1:D50
SUMIFS(sum_range, criteria_range1, criteria1, criteria_range2, criteria2...)	=SUMIFS(D1:D50, E1:E5,">2",E1:E5,"<5")	Add the amounts from the range D1:D50, for instances where the amounts in E1:E5 are between 2 and 5
COUNTIF(range, criteria)	=COUNTIF(A1:A4,A4)	Count the number of cells in the range A1:A4 that contain the value in cell A4
COUNTIFS(range1, criteria1, range2, criteria 2...)	=COUNTIFS(A1:A4, "=Wiley")	Count the number of cells in the range A1:A4 that contain "Wiley"
AVERAGEIF(range, criteria)	=AVERAGEIF(A1: A4,<10)	Average the values in the range A1:A4 that are less than 10
AVERAGEIFS(average_ range, criteria_range1, criteria1,criteria_range2, criteria2...)	=AVERAGEIFS(A1:A4, A1:A4,">10",A1: A4,"<20")	Average the values in A1:A4 if the values are between 10 and 20

LOOK UP DATA USING A FORMULA

Use VLOOKUP or HLOOKUP to Find Values in a List

Ribbon Method

- ☐ Click the **cell** where the formula will appear
- ☐ Click the **Formulas tab**, then click the **Insert Function button** in the Function Library group
- ☐ In the Insert Function dialog box, click the **Or select a category list arrow**, then click **All**
- ☐ Double-click **VLOOKUP** or **HLOOKUP** from the Select a function list box
- ☐ In the Function Arguments dialog box, select the appropriate options using Table EX-23 as a reference, then click **OK**

OR

☐ Click the **cell** where the formula is to appear

☐ Click the **Insert Function button** f_x on the formula bar

☐ Follow the steps in bullets 3–5 of the Use VLOOKUP or HLOOKUP to Find Values in a List Ribbon Method above

Table EX-23   VLOOKUP and HLOOKUP Function Arguments

Argument	Definition
Lookup_value	The value in the first column or row of the array; can be a value, a reference, or a text string
Table_array	The table of information in which data is looked up; use a reference to a range or range name; there are sorting requirements depending on the range_lookup value
Col_index_num (VLOOKUP) OR Row_index_num (HLOOKUP)	The column or row number in table_array from which the matching value must be returned
Range_lookup (optional)	A logical value that specifies whether you want VLOOKUP to find an exact match or an approximate match; if range_lookup is TRUE, or if there is no value in the formula, the match is approximate; if FALSE is entered as the range_lookup, the match returned will be exact, or there will be an error if there is no exact value

Excel

USE CONDITIONAL LOGIC IN A FORMULA

Create Formulas Using Conditional Functions

Ribbon Method

☐ Click the **cell** where you want the formula result to appear

☐ Click the **Formulas tab**, then click the **Insert Function button** in the Function Library group (or click the **Insert Function button** f_x on the formula bar)

☐ In the Insert Function dialog box, select the appropriate function using Table EX-24 as a reference, then click **OK**

☐ In the Function Arguments dialog box, specify the appropriate settings or the appropriate cells if necessary, then click **OK**

OR

☐ Click the **Formulas tab**, click the **Logical button** in the Function Library group, then click the function name in the drop-down menu, using Table EX-24 as a reference

☐ In the Function Arguments dialog box, specify the appropriate settings or the appropriate cells if necessary, then click **OK**

Table EX-24 Functions for Conditional Logic

Function	Example	Results
IF	=IF(logical_test,value_if_true, value_if_false)	Performs the logical test, then returns (displays) a value if it is true or false, such as whether a budget is within limits
AND	=AND(A1>10,B1>25)	Checks two or more conditions; if all are true, then returns TRUE; if one of the conditions is not true, then returns FALSE
OR	=OR(A1>10,B1>25)	Checks two or more conditions; if any are true, then returns TRUE; if all of the conditions are not true, then returns FALSE
NOT	=NOT(A1=25)	Checks the condition; and reverses the TRUE result and reports FALSE
IFERROR	=IFERROR(Formula, "ERRORMESSAGE")	Checks a formula for correctness; if it would result in an Excel error message (such as #DIV/0!), it displays your ERRORMESSAGE text instead of the Excel error

FORMAT OR MODIFY TEXT USING FORMULAS

Change Text Formats Using Text Functions

Ribbon Method

- ☐ Click the **cell** where you want the formula result to appear
- ☐ Click the **Formulas tab**, click the **Text button** in the Function Library group, then click a text function, using Table EX-25 as a reference
- ☐ In the Function Arguments dialog box, click the **cell** containing the text to convert, if necessary type old and new text, using Table EX-25 as a reference, then click **OK**

Shortcut Method

- ☐ Click the **cell** where you want the formula result to appear
- ☐ Click the **Insert Function button** 𝑓ₓ on the formula bar
- ☐ In the Insert Function dialog box, click the **Or select a category list arrow**
- ☐ Click **All**, then double-click the **function name** in the Select a function list, using Table EX-25 as a reference
- ☐ In the Function Arguments dialog box, click the **cell** containing the text to convert, if necessary type old and new text, using Table EX-25 as a reference, then click **OK**

  OR

- ☐ Click the **cell** where you want the formula result to appear
- ☐ Type **=**

□ Begin typing the appropriate text function, using Table EX-25 as a
reference
□ When the desired text function is selected, press **[Tab]**
□ Click the **cell** containing the text to convert, then press **[Enter]**

Table EX-25 Text Functions

Function example	Converts this in cell A1	To this
PROPER(A1)	roberto gonzales	Roberto Gonzales
UPPER(A1)	roberto gonzales	ROBERTO GONZALES
LOWER(A1)	ROBERTO GONZALES	roberto gonzales
SUBSTITUTE(A1, "Roberto","Pedro")	Roberto	Pedro

Convert Text into Columns

Ribbon Method

□ Select the **cell** or **range** containing the text to convert to columns
□ Click the **Data tab**, then click the **Text to Columns button** in the
Data Tools group
□ In screen 1 of the Convert Text to Columns Wizard, select the **Delimited
option button** or **Fixed width option button**, then click **Next**
□ In screen 2 of the wizard, select the **delimiter** or create, delete, and
move **break lines** to set field widths, then click **Next**
□ In screen 3 of the wizard, set the **data format** for each column, then
click **Finish**

Combine Columnar Text into One Column

Ribbon Method

□ Click the **cell** where you want the formula result to appear
□ Click the **Formulas tab**, click the **Text button** in the Function Library
group, then click **CONCATENATE**
□ In the Function Arguments dialog box, click the **cell** containing the
first text string to combine, press **[Tab]**, click the **cell** containing the
second text string, then click **OK**

Shortcut Method

□ Click the **cell** where you want the formula result to appear
□ Click the **Insert Function button** *fx* on the formula bar
□ In the Insert Function dialog box, click the **Or select a category
list arrow**
□ Click **All**, then double-click **CONCATENATE** in the Select a
function list
□ In the Function Arguments dialog box, click the **cell** containing the
first text string to combine, press **[Tab]**, click the **cell** containing the
second text string, then click **OK**

Excel

OR

☐ Click the **cell** where you want the formula result to appear
☐ Type **=**
☐ Type **CONCATENATE(**
☐ Click the **cell** containing the first text string to combine, type **,** (comma), click the **cell** containing the second text string, type **)**, then press **[Enter]**

DISPLAY AND PRINT FORMULAS

Display and Hide Formulas

Ribbon Method

☐ Click the **Formulas tab**, then click the **Show Formulas button** in the Formula Auditing group to display formulas
☐ Click the **Show Formulas button** again to hide the formulas

Shortcut Method

☐ Press **[Ctrl][`]** to display formulas or to hide them if they are displayed

Print Formulas

☐ Display formulas as described in the previous section
☐ Click the **Office button** 🪟, point to **Print**, click **Print Preview**, adjust the Page Setup if necessary, then click the **Print button** in the Print group

EXCEL OBJECTIVE 4: PRESENTING DATA VISUALLY

CREATE AND FORMAT CHARTS

Create a Chart

Ribbon Method

☐ Select the **data range** you want to use to create a chart
☐ Click the **Insert tab**, click a **chart type button** in the Charts group, using Table EX-26 as a guide, then click a **chart subtype** from the drop-down menu

Table EX-26 Common Chart Types

Chart type	Looks like	Could be used to
Column	Column	Show relative amounts for one or multiple values at different points in time (displays vertically)
Line	Line	Show growth trends over time
Pie	Pie	Show proportions or percentages of parts to a whole
Bar	Bar	Show relative amounts for one or multiple values at different points in time (displays horizontally)
Area	Area	Show differences between several sets of data over time
Scatter	Scatter	Show values that are not in categories and where each data point is a distinct measurement

Create a Chart Using Selected Data

Ribbon Method

☐ Drag to select a **column** or **row** containing value data, such as cells A1:A4 in Table EX-27
☐ Press and hold **[Ctrl]**, then drag to select the corresponding **row** or **column** of numeric data you want to chart, such as cells C1:C4 in Table EX-27
☐ Click the **Insert tab**, then click a **chart type button** in the Charts group, using Table EX-26 as a guide, then click a **chart subtype** from the drop-down menu

Create a Chart Showing a Trend Over Time

Ribbon Method

- □ Select a **range** containing categories and data over a time period (such as cells A1:D4 in Table EX-27)
- □ Click the **Insert tab**, then click the **Line button** in the Charts group
- □ Click a **2-D** or **3-D line chart type**

Chart Two Sets of Data

- □ Select a **range** containing categories and two data series (such as cells A1:C4 in Table EX-27)
- □ Click the **Insert tab**, then click the **Column button** in the Charts group
- □ Click a **column chart type**

Table EX-27 Data for Charts

	A	B	C	D
1	Month	Chicago	San Francisco	Brisbane
2	January	10,000	9,000	8000
3	February	5,000	7,000	6,000
4	March	15,000	4000	4,000

Use Quick Layouts to Format Charts

Ribbon Method

- □ With a chart selected, click the **Chart Tools Design tab**, then click the **More button** in the Chart Layouts group
- □ Click a **chart layout** in the gallery

Use Quick Styles to Format Charts

Ribbon Method

- □ With a chart selected, click the **Chart Tools Design tab**, then click the **More button** in the Chart Styles group
- □ Click a **chart style** in the gallery

MODIFY CHARTS

Insert or Delete a Chart Axis Title

Ribbon Method

- □ With the chart selected, click the **Chart Tools Layout tab**
- □ Click the **Axis Titles button** in the Labels group
- □ To add a horizontal axis title, point to **Primary Horizontal Axis Title** click **Title Below Axis**, type the axis title **text**, then press **[Enter]**
- □ To add a vertical axis title, point to **Primary Vertical Axis Title**, then click the appropriate selection to create a **Rotated**, **Vertical**, or **Horizontal Title**

☐ To delete an axis title, click the **Axis Titles button** in the Labels group, point to **Primary Horizontal Axis Title** or **Primary Vertical Axis Title** and then click **None**, or select the **axis title** on the chart and then press **[Delete]**

Insert or Delete a Chart Title

Ribbon Method

☐ With the chart selected, click the **Chart Tools Layout tab**
☐ Click the **Chart Title button** in the Labels group, then click **Centered Overlay Title** or **Above Chart**
☐ Type the chart title **text**, then press **[Enter]**
☐ To delete a chart title, click the **Chart Title button** in the Labels group and then click **None**, or click the chart title on the chart and then press **[Delete]**

Insert or Delete a Chart Legend

Ribbon Method

☐ With the chart selected, click the **Chart Tools Layout tab**
☐ Click the **Legend button** in the Labels group, then click an appropriate legend placement option
☐ To delete a legend, click the **Legend button** in the Labels group and then click **None**, or click the **chart legend** and then press **[Delete]**

Insert Percentages on a Pie Chart

Ribbon Method

☐ With the pie chart selected, click the **Chart Tools Layout tab**
☐ Click the **Data Labels button** in the Labels group, then click **More Data Label Options**
☐ In the Label Options section of the Format Data Labels dialog box, click the **Percentage check box** to select it, then deselect any other check boxes under Label Contains
☐ Click **Close**

Move a Chart on a Worksheet

Mouse Method

☐ Point to the edge of a chart until the pointer becomes ⁺⅍, then drag the chart to another location

Move a Chart to a Newly Created Sheet

Ribbon Method

☐ Click a **chart** on a worksheet, then click the **Chart Tools Design tab**
☐ Click the **Move Chart button** in the Location group
☐ In the Move Chart dialog box, click the **New Sheet option button**, type a **sheet name** in the New sheet text box, then click **OK**

Excel

Shortcut Method

☐ Right-click a **chart edge**, then click **Move Chart**
☐ In the Move Chart dialog box, click the **New Sheet option button**, type a **sheet name** in the New sheet text box, then click **OK**

Move a Chart to an Existing Worksheet

Ribbon Method

☐ Click a **chart** on a worksheet, then click the **Chart Tools Design tab**
☐ Click the **Move Chart button** in the Location group
☐ In the Move Chart dialog box, click the **Object in option button**, click the **Object in list arrow**, click a **sheet name**, then click **OK**

Resize Charts

Ribbon Method

☐ Click a **chart**, then click the **Chart Tools Format tab**
☐ Click the **Shape Height text box**, type a new vertical dimension, then press **[Enter]**
☐ Click the **Shape Width text box**, type a new horizontal dimension, then press **[Enter]**

OR

☐ Click a **chart**, then click the **Chart Tools Format tab**
☐ Click the **Launcher** 🔲 in the Size group
☐ On the Size tab in the Size and Properties dialog box, adjust the **Height** and **Width values** under Size and Rotate

Shortcut Method

☐ Click the **chart**, then position the pointer over a corner, side, top, or bottom sizing handle
☐ Drag the **sizing handle** to resize the chart

Resize Charts Proportionally

Ribbon Method

☐ Click a **chart**, then click the **Chart Tools Format tab**
☐ Click the **Launcher** 🔲 in the Size group
☐ On the Size tab in the Size and Properties dialog box, click the **Lock aspect ratio check box** to select it
☐ Adjust the **Height** and **Width percentages** under Scale, then click **Close**

Mouse Method

☐ Click a **chart**, then position the pointer over a corner, side, top, or bottom sizing handle
☐ Press and hold **[Shift]**, then drag to resize the chart

Change Chart Types

Ribbon Method

☐ Click a **chart**, click the **Chart Tools Design tab**, then click the **Change Chart Type button** in the Type group

☐ In the Change Chart Type dialog box, click a **chart type** on the left, click a **chart subtype** in the center pane, then click **OK**

Shortcut Method

☐ Right-click a **chart** (not a series on the chart), then click **Change Chart Type**

☐ In the Change Chart Type dialog box, click a **chart type** on the left, click a **chart subtype** in the center pane, then click **OK**

APPLY CONDITIONAL FORMATTING

Create a Conditional Formatting Rule

Ribbon Method

☐ Select a **data range**

☐ Click the **Conditional Formatting button** in the Styles group on the Home tab, then click **New Rule**

☐ In the New Formatting Rule dialog box, click a **rule type** in the Select a Rule Type section

☐ In the Edit the Rule Description section, specify the values that you want formatted

☐ Click the **Format button** in the Edit the Rule Description section, then specify a format in the Format Cells dialog box

☐ Click **OK**, then click **OK**

Edit a Conditional Formatting Rule

Ribbon Method

☐ Click any worksheet **cell**

☐ Click the **Conditional Formatting button** in the Styles group on the Home tab, then click **Manage Rules**

☐ In the Conditional Formatting Rules Manager dialog box, click the **Show formatting rules for list arrow**, then click **This Worksheet**

☐ In the Conditional Formatting Rules Manager dialog box, click a **rule**, click **Edit Rule**, then edit the rule type and description

☐ Click **OK**, then click **OK**

Delete a Conditional Formatting Rule

Ribbon Method

☐ Click any worksheet **cell**

☐ Click the **Conditional Formatting button** in the Styles group on the Home tab, point to **Clear Rules**, then click **Clear Rules from Selected Cells** or **Clear Rules from Entire Sheet**

OR

☐ Click any worksheet **cell**

☐ Click the **Conditional Formatting button** in the Styles group on the Home tab, then click **Manage Rules**

☐ In the Conditional Formatting Rules Manager dialog box, click the **Show formatting rules for list arrow**, then click **This Worksheet**

☐ Click the rule to delete, click **Delete Rule** or press **[Delete]**, then click **OK**

Excel

Create and Apply Multiple Conditional Formatting Rules

Ribbon Method

- ☐ Select a **data range**
- ☐ Click the **Conditional Formatting button** in the Styles group on the Home tab, then click **Manage Rules**
- ☐ In the Conditional Formatting Rules Manager dialog box, click the **Show formatting rules for list arrow**, then click **Current Selection** if necessary
- ☐ Click **New Rule**, create a rule for the selected cells in the New Formatting Rule dialog box, then click **OK**
- ☐ Click **New Rule**, create another rule for the selected cells, then click **OK**
- ☐ In the Conditional Formatting Rules Manager dialog box, use the **Move Up button** 🔼 and **Move Down button** 🔽 as necessary to put the rules in order of precedence (rules higher on the list have precedence over lower rules; if rules conflict, the rule higher on the list takes precedence)
- ☐ Click **OK**

Apply Conditional Formatting to Data

Ribbon Method

- ☐ Select a **cell range** to format conditionally
- ☐ Click the **Conditional Formatting button** in the Styles group on the Home tab
- ☐ Point to a conditional formatting category, then click a category option, using Table EX-28 as a reference

Table EX-28 Conditional Formatting Options

Formatting category	Options	Available formatting
Highlight Cells Rules	Greater Than, Less Than, Between, Equal To, Text that Contains, A Date Occurring, Duplicate Values	Colored text and fills, or custom formats
Top/Bottom Rules	Top 10 Items, Top 10%, Bottom 10 Items, Bottom 10%, Above Average, Below Average	Colored text and fills, or custom formats
Data Bars	6 built-in types	Existing colors or click More Rules to create custom formats
Color Scales	8 built-in types	Existing scales or click More Rules to create custom formats
Icon Sets	17 built-in icon styles	Click More Rules to modify rules for icon display

INSERT AND MODIFY ILLUSTRATIONS

Embed Pictures from Files

Ribbon Method

☐ Click the **Insert tab**, then click the **Picture button** in the Illustrations group
☐ In the Insert Picture dialog box, navigate to the location of the picture you want to insert
☐ Click the **picture**, then click **Insert**

Link to Pictures from Files

Ribbon Method

☐ Click the **Insert tab**, then click the **Picture button** in the Illustrations group
☐ In the Insert Picture dialog box, navigate to the location of the picture you want to insert
☐ Click the **picture**, click the **Insert list arrow**, then click **Link to File**

Resize a Picture

Ribbon Method

☐ Select a **picture**, then on the **Picture Tools Format tab**, click the **Shape Height** or **Shape Width text box** in the Size group
☐ Type a new **height** or **width**, then press **[Enter]**
   OR
☐ Click a **picture**, then on the **Chart Tools Format tab**, click the **Launcher** 🔲 in the Size group
☐ On the Size tab in the Size and Properties dialog box, under Size and Rotate, adjust the **Height** and **Width**, or specify a **percentage** under Scale

Mouse Method

☐ Click a **picture**, then position the pointer over a corner sizing handle
☐ Drag the **sizing handle** to resize the chart

Format a Picture

Ribbon Method

☐ Click a **picture**, click the **Picture Tools Format tab**, then, using Table EX-29 as a reference, click an option and adjust its settings

Excel

Table EX-29 Picture Formatting Options

Format tab group	Options
Adjust	Brightness, Contrast, Recolor, Compress Pictures, Change Picture, Reset Picture
Picture Styles	28 predesigned picture formats; Picture Shape, Picture Border, Picture Effects
Arrange	Bring to Front, Send to Back, Selection Pane, Align, Group, Rotate
Size	Crop, Shape Height, Shape Width

Add SmartArt Graphics

Ribbon Method
☐ Click the **Insert tab**, then click the **SmartArt button** in the Illustrations group
☐ In the Choose a SmartArt Graphic dialog box, click a **category** on the left, using Table EX-30 as a reference
☐ Click a **SmartArt style** in the center, then click **OK**
☐ Click shapes and add text as necessary

Table EX-30 SmartArt Categories

SmartArt Category	Use to illustrate
List	Related data in hierarchical, sequential or nonsequential groups
Process	Data in a progression, sequence, timeline, flow, process, or other directional relationship
Cycle	Data that flow in a circular sequence, form dependent or sequential ideas, or that together form a whole
Hierarchy	Data that is related in horizontal or vertical hierarchical form
Relationship	Data in interrelated, opposing, or concurring relationships
Matrix	Part of a whole along two axes
Pyramid	Data in proportional, interconnected, or hierarchical relationships

Apply SmartArt Quick Styles

Ribbon Method
☐ Click a **SmartArt object**, then click the **SmartArt Tools Design Tab**
☐ Click the **SmartArt Styles More button** 🔽, then click a **style**
☐ Click the **Change Colors button**, then click a **new color scheme** if desired

Excel

Apply SmartArt Effects

Ribbon Method

☐ Click a **SmartArt object**, then click the **SmartArt Tools Format Tab**
☐ Click the **Shape Effects button** in the Shape Styles group, point to an **effect category**, then click an **effect**

Add SmartArt Shapes

Ribbon Method

☐ Click a **SmartArt object**, then click the **SmartArt Tools Design Tab**
☐ Click the **Add Shape button** in the Create Graphic group, or click the **Add Shape button arrow**, then click **Add Shape After** or **Add Shape Before**

OUTLINE DATA

Group Data

Ribbon Method

☐ Select a **data range** that you want to group
☐ On the Data tab, click the **Group button** in the Outline group
☐ In the Group dialog box, select whether you want to group rows or columns, then click **OK**
☐ Use the **[+]** and **[-]** symbols to expand and collapse individual groups in the outline

Outline Totaled Data

Ribbon Method

☐ Verify that the data contains data structured with detail data and summary data, such as totals calculated using a formula
☐ Click inside the data range
☐ Click the **Data tab**, click the **Group list arrow** in the Outline group, then click **AutoOutline**
☐ Use the outline symbols **[1]**, **[2]**, and **[3]** to collapse and display detail in the outlined list
☐ Use the **[+]** and **[-]** symbols to expand and collapse individual groups in the outline

Sort, Subtotal, and Outline Grouped Data

Ribbon Method

☐ Verify that the data has column headers, that the same type of information is in every column, that the data contains groups according to which data can be combined, and that there are no blank cells in the data range
☐ Click inside the data range, click the **Data tab**, then click the **Sort button** in the Sort & Filter group
☐ In the Sort dialog box, specify the **column** on which to sort, specify a **sort order**, then click **OK**
☐ Click the **Subtotal button** in the Outline group

☐ In the Subtotal dialog box, click the **At each change in list arrow**,
then select the **column** you want to group by
☐ Verify that the Use function text box contains "Sum"
☐ In the Add subtotal to list, click the **check box** for the column that you
want to subtotal, then click **OK**
☐ Use the outline symbols **[1]**, **[2]**, and **[3]** to collapse and display detail
in the outlined list
☐ Use the **[+]** and **[-]** symbols to expand and collapse individual groups
in the outline

Ungroup Data

Ribbon Method

☐ Select the **grouped data range**
☐ Click the **Data tab**, then click the **Ungroup button** in the Outline group
☐ In the Ungroup dialog box, click the **Rows** or **Columns option
button**, then click **OK**

Clear an Outline

Ribbon Method

☐ Select the **outlined data range**
☐ Click the **Ungroup list arrow** in the Outline group, then click **Clear
Outline**

Remove Subtotals

Ribbon Method

☐ Click in the data range
☐ Click the **Subtotal button** in the Outline group
☐ In the Subtotal dialog box, click **Remove All**

SORT AND FILTER DATA

Sort Data Using a Single Criterion

Ribbon Method

☐ Select the **column** on which you wish to sort
☐ Click the **Data tab**, then click the **Sort A to Z** ⬛ or **Sort Z to A
button** ⬛ in the Sort & Filter group

Shortcut Method

☐ Verify that the data has column headers, that the same type of information is in every column, and that there are no blank cells in the
data range
☐ Right-click the **column** on which you wish to sort
☐ Point to **Sort**, then click **Sort A to Z** or **Sort Z to A** if the data contains text values, or click **Sort Smallest to Largest** or **Sort Largest
to Smallest** if the data contains numeric values

Sort Data Using Multiple Criteria

Ribbon Method

☐ Click in the data range, then click the **Sort button** in the Sort & Filter group
☐ In the Sort dialog box, click the **Sort by list arrow**, then click a field name on which to sort
☐ Click the **Order list arrow**, then select **A to Z** or **Z to A**
☐ Click **Add Level**, then follow the steps in bullets 2–3 of this section to select another field
☐ Repeat if necessary, then click **OK**

Shortcut Method

☐ Right-click the **column** on which you wish to sort
☐ Point to **Sort**, then click **Custom Sort**
☐ Follow the steps in bullets 2-5 of the Sort Data Using Multiple Criteria Ribbon Method above

Sort Data Using Cell Formatting

Ribbon Method

☐ Select the **data range**, click the **Data tab**, then click the **Sort button** in the Sort & Filter group
☐ In the Sort dialog box, click the **Sort by list arrow**, then select a **column name** on which to sort
☐ Click the **Sort on list arrow**, then click **Cell Color**, **Font Color**, or **Cell Icon**
☐ Click the **Order list arrow**, then select an option
☐ To add a second sort level, click **Add Level**, then repeat the steps in bullets 2–4 of this section to select another field
☐ Repeat if necessary, then click **OK**

Shortcut Method

☐ Right-click the **column** on which you wish to sort
☐ Point to **Sort**, then click **Custom Sort**
☐ Follow the steps steps in bullets 2–6 of the Sort Data Using Cell Formatting Ribbon Method above

AutoFilter Cell Values

☐ To filter a table, go to the next bullet; to filter a cell range, select the **range**, click the **Home tab**, click the **Sort & Filter button** in the Editing group, then click **Filter**
☐ Click a **column heading list arrow**, click the **(Select All) check box** to deselect it, click to select the **check box(es)** for the value(s) in the list you want to display, then click **OK**

AutoFilter Text Data Using Criteria

☐ To filter a table, go to the next bullet; to filter a cell range, select the **range**, click the **Home tab**, click the **Sort & Filter button** in the Editing group, then click **Filter**
☐ Click a **column heading list arrow**, point to **Text Filters**, then click a criterion, such as **Equals** or **Begins With**

Excel

☐ In the Custom AutoFilter dialog box, click in the upper text box, then type a **letter** or **word** representing the text you want to display, or click the **list arrow** and select a **value**

☐ To use more than one criterion, click the **And** or **Or option button**, then enter another criterion in the lower text box

☐ Click **OK**

AutoFilter Numeric Data Using Criteria

☐ To filter a table, go to the next bullet; to filter a cell range, select the **range**, click the **Home tab**, click the **Sort & Filter button** in the Editing group, then click **Filter**

☐ Click a **column heading list arrow**, point to **Number Filters**, then click a criterion, such as **Equals** or **Greater Than**

☐ In the Custom AutoFilter dialog box, click in the upper text box, then type a **number** representing the values you want to display, or click the **list arrow** and select a **value**

☐ To use more than one criterion, click the **And** or **Or option button**, then enter another criterion in the lower text box

☐ Click **OK**

AutoFilter Data Using Cell Formatting

☐ To filter a table, go to the next bullet; to filter a cell range, select the **range**, click the **Home tab**, click the **Sort & Filter button** in the Editing group, then click **Filter**

☐ Click a **column heading list arrow** of a column that has color applied to its values or cell backgrounds

☐ Point to **Filter by Color**, then click the color of the data you want to display

Excel

EXCEL OBJECTIVE 5: COLLABORATING AND SECURING DATA

MANAGE CHANGES TO WORKBOOKS

Track Workbook Changes

Ribbon Method

☐ Click the **Review tab**, click the **Track Changes button** in the Changes group, then click **Highlight Changes**
☐ In the Highlight Changes dialog box, click to select the **Track changes while editing check box**
☐ Make sure the **Highlight changes on screen check box** is selected, then click **OK**
☐ In the message box, click **OK**

Insert or Modify Tracked Changes

Ribbon Method

☐ Turn on change tracking, as described in the Track Workbook Changes section above
☐ Click any **cell** and type revised data, then press **[Enter]**

Accept and Reject Changes

Ribbon Method

☐ Click the **Review tab**, click the **Track Changes button** in the Changes group, then click **Accept or Reject Changes**
☐ If you get a message box to save the workbook, click **OK**
☐ In the Select Changes to Accept or Reject dialog box, in the When list box, make sure **Not yet reviewed** is selected, then click **OK**
☐ In the Accept or Reject Changes dialog box, click the appropriate options until all changes have been reviewed

Review Changes

Ribbon Method

☐ Click the **Review tab**, click the **Track Changes button** in the Changes group, then click **Highlight Changes**
☐ In the Highlight Changes dialog box, make sure the **Track changes while editing check box** is selected
☐ Make sure the **Highlight changes on screen check box** is selected, then click **OK**
☐ Position the insertion point over a cell with a colored triangle in the corner, then read the screen tip to review the change

Insert Cell Comments

Ribbon Method

☐ Select the **cell** to which you want to attach a comment

Excel

□ Click the **Review tab**, then click the **New Comment button** in the Comments group
□ Type the appropriate **text** in the comment box
□ Click outside the comment box

Shortcut Method

□ Right-click the **cell** to which you want to attach a comment
□ Click **Insert Comment** on the shortcut menu
□ Follow the steps in bullets 3–4 of the Insert Cell Comments Ribbon Method above

Edit Cell Comments

Ribbon Method

□ Click a **cell** marked with a comment (a red triangle in the upper-right corner of the cell)
□ Click the **Review tab**, then click the **Edit Comment button** in the Comments group
□ Modify the comment
□ Click outside the comment box

Shortcut Method

□ Right-click a **cell** marked with a comment (a red triangle in the upper-right corner of the cell), then click **Edit Comment** on the shortcut menu
□ Follow the steps in bullets 3–4 of the Edit Cell Comments Ribbon Method above

Display a Single Comment

Ribbon Method

□ Click the **Review tab**, then click a **cell** marked with a comment (a red triangle in the upper-right corner of the cell)
□ Click the **Show/Hide Comment button** in the Comments group; the comment remains displayed when you click other cells

Shortcut Method

□ Point to a **cell** containing the comment, then read the comment that appears

OR

□ Right-click a **cell** marked with a comment (a red triangle in the upper-right corner of the cell), then click **Show/Hide Comments** on the shortcut menu

Display All Workbook Comments

Ribbon Method

□ Click a **cell** marked with a comment (a red triangle in the upper-right corner of the cell)
□ Click the **Review tab**, then click the **Show All Comments button** in the Comments group; the comments remain displayed when you click other cells

Hide Cell Comments

Ribbon Method

☐ If all workbook comments are displayed, click the **Review tab**, then click the **Show All Comments button** in the Comments group to hide all comments

☐ If all workbook comments are displayed, click the **cell** whose comment you want to hide, click the **Review tab**, then click the **Show/Hide Comment button** in the Comments group to hide only one comment and leave the other comments displayed

Shortcut Method

☐ If all workbook comments are displayed, right-click the **cell** whose comment you want to hide, then click **Hide Comment** on the shortcut menu to hide only one comment and leave the other comments displayed

Delete Cell Comments

Ribbon Method

☐ Click the **cell** marked with a comment (a red triangle in the upper-right corner of the cell)

☐ Click the **Review tab**, then click the **Delete Comment button** in the Comments group

Shortcut Method

☐ Right-click the **cell** marked with a comment (a red triangle in the upper-right corner of the cell), then click **Delete Comment** on the shortcut menu

---

PROTECT AND SHARE WORKBOOKS

Unprotect Worksheet Cells in a Protected Worksheet

Ribbon Method

☐ Select the **range** you want to be editable by others in the protected worksheet

☐ Click the **Home tab**, then click the **Format button** in the Cells group

☐ Click **Lock cell** to deselect it

☐ Click the **Review tab**, then click the **Protect Sheet button** in the Changes group

☐ In the Protect Sheet dialog box, click to select the **Protect worksheet and contents of locked cells check box** if necessary, then type a **password** in the Password to unprotect sheet text box

☐ Click **OK**

☐ In the Confirm Password dialog box, retype the **password**, then click **OK**

Protect Worksheets

Ribbon Method

☐ Click the **Review tab**, then click the **Protect Sheet button** in the Changes group

□ In the Protect Sheet dialog box, click to select the **Protect worksheet and contents of locked cells check box** if necessary, then type a **password** in the Password to unprotect sheet text box
□ Click **OK**
□ In the Confirm Password dialog box, retype the **password**, then click **OK**

OR

□ Click the **Home tab**, click the **Format button** in the Cells group, then click **Protect Sheet**
□ Follow the steps in bullets 2–4 of the Protect Worksheets Ribbon Method above

Shortcut Method

□ Right-click a **sheet tab**, then click **Protect Sheet** on the shortcut menu
□ Follow the steps in bullets 2–4 of the first Protect Worksheets Ribbon Method above

Protect Workbooks and Workbook Elements

Ribbon Method

□ Click the **Review tab**, then click the **Protect Workbook button** in the Changes group
□ In the Protect Structure and Windows dialog box, select the appropriate **check boxes**
□ If desired, click the **Password text box**, type a **password**, then click **OK**
□ If desired, type the **password** to confirm it, then click **OK**

Create a Shared Workbook

Ribbon Method

□ Click the **Review tab**, then click the **Share Workbook button** in the Changes group
□ On the Editing tab in the Share Workbook dialog box, click the **Allow changes by more than one user at the same time check box** if necessary, then click **OK**
□ Click **OK** if prompted to save the file

Modify a Shared Workbook

Ribbon Method

□ Open the **workbook** from its network location
□ Click the **Office button** , then click **Excel Options**
□ Click **Popular**, if necessary, under **Personalize your copy of Office**, click in the **User Name** box, then type the user name that you want to use to identify your work in the shared workbook, and then click **OK**
□ Enter and edit data on the worksheets as usual
□ Make the modifications to the workbook, then save the workbook
□ If prompted, resolve any conflicts in the Resolve Conflicts dialog box

Remove Workbook Sharing

Ribbon Method

□ Open a **shared workbook**, click the **Review tab**, then click the **Share Workbook button** in the Changes group

□ Click to deselect the **Allow changes by more than one user at the same time check box**, then click OK
□ Click **Yes** to confirm the action

PREPARE WORKBOOKS FOR DISTRIBUTION

Remove Private Information from Workbooks Using the Document Inspector

Ribbon Method

□ Determine if your open document will be shared with others via e-mail, an intranet or server, or the Internet; if so, proceed with the next step
□ Save the document, click the **Office button** , point to **Prepare**, then click **Inspect Document**
□ In the Document Inspector dialog box, make sure the **check boxes** are selected for the features for which you want to check
□ Click **Inspect**
□ In the list of inspection results, look for items flagged by a red exclamation point
□ Click **Remove All** next to each item type you want to remove
□ Click **Close**

Restrict Workbook Permissions

□ Save the workbook you want to restrict
□ Click the **Office button** , point to **Prepare**, point to **Restrict Permission**, and then click **Do Not Distribute**
□ Select the **Restrict permission to this document check box**, assign the access levels that you want for each user, using Table EX-31 as a reference, then click **OK**

Table EX-31 Workbook Permission Levels

Level	Meaning
Read	Users can read the workbook but not edit, print, or copy it
Change	Users can read, edit, and save changes to the document, but cannot print it
Full Control	Users can perform all functions that the author can, including setting expiration dates, preventing printing, or giving permission to other users, until the document expires

Add Workbook Properties

Ribbon Method

□ Click the **Office button** , point to **Prepare**, then click **Properties**
□ In the Document Properties pane, click and type in any **text box** to add an author name, title, document subject, keywords, category, status, or comments

Excel

☐ To add more properties, click the **Document Properties list arrow**, then click **Advanced Properties**
☐ In the workbook's Properties dialog box, click a tab and type additional property information, then click **OK**

Insert a Digital Signature

Ribbon Method

☐ Click the **Office button** 📄, point to **Prepare**, then click **Add a Digital Signature**
☐ In the Sign dialog box, if desired type a purpose for signing the document in the **Purpose for signing this document text box**
☐ Click **Sign**

Mark a Workbook as Final

Ribbon Method

☐ Click the **Office button** 📄, point to **Prepare**, then click **Mark as Final**
☐ In the dialog box, click **OK**
☐ If you see a dialog box explaining the Mark as Final status, click **OK**
☐ Check the status bar for the Marked as Final icon 🖉

SAVE WORKBOOKS

Use the Compatibility Checker

Ribbon Method

☐ Click the **Office button** 📄, point to **Prepare**, then click **Run Compatibility Checker**
☐ In the Compatibility Checker dialog box, click one of the **options** listed in Table EX-32
☐ Click **Help** next to any item to learn more about what will be lost if you save the document in an earlier workbook format
☐ To have Excel check compatibility each time the document is saved, click to select the **Check compatibility when saving this workbook check box**
☐ Click **OK**

Table EX-32 Compatibility Dialog Box Options

Option	To do this
Find	Highlight the object in the workbook
Help	Open a Help window showing detail on that item
Check compatibility when saving this workbook	Have Excel advise on compatibility each time you save
Copy to New Sheet	Copy the compatibility information to a new worksheet titled Compatibility Report

Save a Workbook in Excel 97-2003 Format

Ribbon Method

☐ Open the **workbook** you want to save, click the **Office button** 🔘, point to **Save As**, then click **Excel 97-2003 Workbook**

☐ Enter a **file location** and **file name**, then verify that the Save as type is **Excel 97-2003 Workbook (*.xls)**

☐ Click **Save**

Save a Workbook in Other Formats

Ribbon Method

☐ Open the **workbook** you want to save to another format, click the **Office button** 🔘, then click **Save As**

☐ Enter a **file location** and **file name**, then click the **Save as type list arrow**

☐ Choose a **format**, using Table EX-33 as a reference, then click **Save**

Table EX-33 Document Type Options in Save As dialog box

Option	To save a workbook...
Excel Macro-Enabled Workbook (*.xlsm)	With macros that you can enable for use
Excel template (*.xltx)	As a template that you can use to create duplicate workbooks with the same design and content
PDF (*.pdf)	In the Portable Document Format that can be easily opened by people with Adobe Acrobat Reader on their computer
Single File Web Page (*.mht, *.mhtml)	As a page that you can place on the World Wide Web, with the page and all supporting files and graphics in one file
Web Page (*.htm, *.html)	As a page that you can place on the World Wide Web, with the page in one .htm file and all supporting files and graphics in a separate folder
Text (Tab delimited) (*.txt)	As a file that can be opened in most word processors and spreadsheets, and that has tabs in place of column breaks
XML Data (*.xml)	In XML format, which allows it to be used by others to extract only the information they need

Excel

Save a Workbook in PDF Format

☐ Verify that your machine has the Publish as PDF or XPS add-in for the Microsoft Office 2007 system

☐ Click the **Office button** 🔘, point to **Save As**, then click **PDF or XPS**

☐ If you want to open the file immediately after saving it, select the **Open file after publishing** check box; (this check box is available only if you have a PDF reader installed on your computer)

☐ Next to **Optimize for**, select **Standard (publishing online and printing)** or **Minimum size (publishing online)**
☐ Click **Options**, select publishing options, then click **OK**
☐ Click **Publish**

SET PRINT OPTIONS FOR PRINTING DATA, WORKSHEETS AND WORKBOOKS

Set a Print Area

Ribbon Method

☐ Select the **worksheet area** you want to print
☐ Click the **Page Layout tab**, then click the **Print Area button** in the Page Setup group
☐ Click **Set Print Area** to print only that worksheet area

Insert a Page Break

Ribbon Method

☐ Click the **cell** below and to the right of the location where you want to insert a page break
☐ Click the **Page Layout tab**, click the **Breaks button** in the Page Setup group, then click **Insert Page Break**

Move a Page Break

Ribbon Method

☐ Click the **View tab** and click the **Page Break Preview button** in the Workbook Views group, or click the **Page Break Preview button** 🔲 on the status bar
☐ If you see a dialog box saying Welcome to Page Break Preview, click **OK**
☐ Drag the **blue dotted line** representing a page break to a new location
☐ Click the **Normal button** in the Workbook Views group on the View tab or click the **Normal button** 🔲 on the status bar

Set Workbook Margins

Ribbon Method

☐ Click the **Page Layout tab**, then click the **Margins button** in the Page Setup group
☐ Click **Custom Margins**
☐ In the Margins tab of the Page Setup dialog box, enter **values** for the Top, Left, Right, and Bottom margins, then click **OK**

Add Worksheet Headers and Footers

Ribbon Method

☐ Click the **Insert tab**, then click the **Header & Footer button** in the Text group
☐ Click in the left, center, or right **header section** and type **text**, or click one of the **buttons** in the Header & Footer Elements group

☐ Click an **option** in the Options group if desired
☐ Click the **Go to Footer button** in the Navigation group
☐ Click a footer **section** and type **text**, or click one of the **buttons** in the Header & Footer Elements group
☐ Click the **Normal View button** in the status bar

Modify Worksheet Headers and Footers

Ribbon Method

☐ Click the **View tab**, then click the **Page Layout button** in the Workbook Views group
☐ Click any **header section** and modify the information
☐ Scroll to the footer, click any **section**, then modify the information
☐ Click the **Normal button** 🔲 in the status bar

Change Worksheet Orientation

Ribbon Method

☐ Click the **Page Layout tab**, then click the **Orientation button** in the Page Setup group
☐ Click **Portrait** (to make the worksheet taller than it is wide) or **Landscape** (to make the worksheet wider than it is tall)

Scale a Worksheet to Fit One Printed Page

Ribbon Method

☐ Click the **Page Layout tab**
☐ Click the **Width list arrow** in the Scale to Fit group, then click **1 page**
☐ Click the **Height list arrow** in the Scale to Fit group, then click **1 page**
OR
☐ Click the **Page Layout tab**, then click the **Size button** in the Page Setup group
☐ Click **More Paper Sizes**
☐ On the Page tab in the Page Setup dialog box, under Scaling, click **Fit to** and enter **1** in the pages(s) wide and tall text boxes
☐ Click **OK**

MICROSOFT OFFICE ACCESS 2007
EXAM REFERENCE

Getting Started with Access 2007

The Access Microsoft Certified Application Specialist (MCAS) exam assumes a basic level of proficiency in Access. This section is intended to help you reference these basic skills while you are preparing to take the Access MCAS exam.

- ☐ Starting and exiting Access
- ☐ Viewing the Getting Started with Microsoft Office Access window
- ☐ Opening a database
- ☐ Viewing the database window
- ☐ Using the Navigation Pane
- ☐ Using the Ribbon
- ☐ Saving and closing objects and databases
- ☐ Using keyboard KeyTips
- ☐ Getting Help

START AND EXIT ACCESS

Start Access

Shortcut Method

- ☐ Click the **Start button** 😊 on the Windows taskbar
- ☐ Point to **All Programs**
- ☐ Click **Microsoft Office**, then click **Microsoft Office Access 2007**
  OR
- ☐ Double-click the **Microsoft Office Access program icon** 📄 on the desktop

Exit Access

Ribbon Method

- ☐ Click the **Office button** 🔘, then click **Exit Access**

Shortcut Method

- ☐ Click the **Close button** ☒ on the Access program window title bar

VIEW THE GETTING STARTED WITH MICROSOFT OFFICE ACCESS WINDOW

Figure AC-1 Getting Started with Microsoft Office Access Window

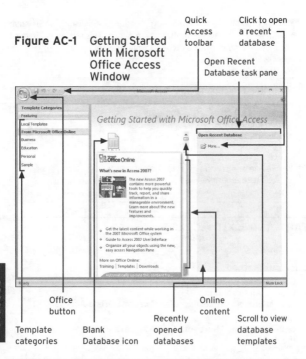

OPEN A DATABASE

Open an Existing Database

Ribbon Method

□ Click the **Office button** , then click **Open**
□ In the Open dialog box, navigate to the appropriate drive and folder
□ Click the file you want, then click **Open**

OR

□ Click the **Office button** , then click the file you want in the Recent Documents list

Shortcut Method

- ☐ Click the **More link** in the Open Recent Database task pane
- ☐ In the Open dialog box, navigate to the appropriate drive and folder
- ☐ Click the file you want, then click **Open**

  OR

- ☐ Click a recently opened database in the Open Recent Database task pane

VIEW THE DATABASE WINDOW

Figure AC-2 Access Database Window

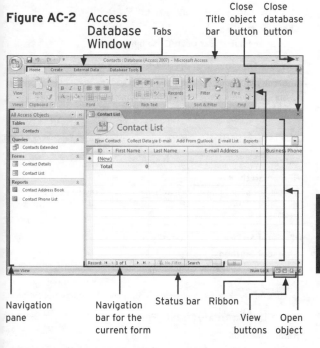

USE THE NAVIGATION PANE

Open an Object

Shortcut Method

- ☐ Double-click the object in the Navigation Pane

  OR

- ☐ Right-click the object in the Navigation Pane, then click **Open**

Open an Object in Design View or Layout View

Ribbon Method

☐ Double-click the object in the Navigation Pane

☐ Click the **View button arrow** in the Views group on the Home tab, then click **Design View** or **Layout View**, as appropriate

Shortcut Method

☐ Right-click the object in the Navigation Pane, then click **Design View** or **Layout View**

Open and Close the Navigation Pane

Shortcut Method

☐ Click the **Shutter Bar Open/Close button** ⨠

Change the View of Objects in the Navigation Pane

Shortcut Method

☐ Click the **Navigation Pane arrow button** ▾, click a **Navigate To Category option**, then click a **Filter By Group option**

USE THE RIBBON

Change Tabs

Ribbon Method

☐ Click the name of a tab, such as Home, Create, External Data, or Database Tools, or the name of a contextual tab, such as Table Tools Datasheet

Open and Close the Ribbon

Shortcut Method

☐ Right-click a blank area of the Ribbon, then click **Minimize the Ribbon**

OR

☐ Click the Quick Access toolbar arrow, then click **Minimize the Ribbon**

Open a Dialog Box or Task Pane

Ribbon Method

☐ Click the **launcher icon** ▣ in a group on a tab, such as the Clipboard group on the Home tab

SAVE AND CLOSE OBJECTS AND DATABASES

Save an Object

Ribbon Method
□ With the object open in the database window, click the **Office button** 🏛, then click **Save**

Shortcut Method
□ Click the **Save button** 🖫 on the Quick Access toolbar

Save an Object with a Different Name

Ribbon Method
□ Click the **Office button** 🏛, point to **Save As**, then click **Save Object As**
□ In the Save As dialog box, enter a name for the object, then click **Save**

Save a Database

Ribbon Method
□ Click the **Office button** 🏛, then click **Save**

Note: Access automatically saves changes you make to database settings, so you rarely need to save a database; however, you should save changes to a database object before you close it.

Save a Database with a Different Name, Location, or Format

Ribbon Method
□ Click the **Office button** 🏛, point to **Save As**, then click a database format
□ In the Save As dialog box, enter a database name, navigate to the appropriate drive and folder, if necessary, then click **Save**

Close an Object

Shortcut Method
□ Click the **Close object button** ⊠
    OR
□ Click the **Close Window button** ⊠ if the window is maximized; otherwise, click the **Close button** ⊠ on the object's title bar

Close a Database

Ribbon Method
□ Save and close all database objects
□ Click the **Office button** 🏛, then click **Close Database**
    OR
□ Click the **Close button** ⊠ on the object's title bar

Access

USE KEYBOARD KEYTIPS

Display KeyTips

Shortcut Method

- □ Press **[Alt]** to display the KeyTips for each command on the active tab of the Ribbon and on the Quick Access toolbar
- □ Press the letter or number for the specific command for the active tab on the Ribbon
- □ Press additional letters or numbers as needed to complete the command sequence
- □ If two letters appear, press each one in order; for some commands you will find that you have to click an option from a gallery or menu to complete the command sequence
- □ The KeyTips turn off automatically at the end of the command sequence

Hide KeyTips

Shortcut Method

- □ Press **[Alt]** to hide the KeyTips for each Ribbon command

GET HELP

Ribbon Method

- □ Click the **Microsoft Office Access Help button** 🔘
- □ Use Table AC-1 as a reference to select the most appropriate way to get help using the Access Help window

Shortcut Method

- □ Press **[F1]**
- □ Use Table AC-1 as a reference to select the most appropriate way to get help using the Access Help window

Table AC-1 Access Help Window Options

Option	To use
Type words to search for	Type one or more keywords, click the Search button arrow, click the Help source you want to search, click Search, then click a topic in the search results
Browse Access Help	Click a topic category, then click a topic
Table of Contents	Click the Show Table of Contents button 🔘 on the Help window toolbar, click a topic category in the Table of Contents pane, then click a topic

ACCESS EXAM REFERENCE

Objectives:

1. Structuring a database
2. Creating and formatting database elements
3. Entering and modifying data
4. Creating and modifying queries
5. Presenting and sharing data
6. Managing and maintaining databases

ACCESS OBJECTIVE 1: STRUCTURING A DATABASE

DEFINE DATA NEEDS AND TYPES

Identify Fields

Planning

- ☐ Determine fields for the data—each single characteristic of a person, place, object, event, or idea that you want to store
- ☐ Make sure each field contains the smallest useful part of the data you want to store
- ☐ Decide which fields belong together in a table—a collection of fields that describe a person, place, object, event, or idea
- ☐ Data that is updated often or the result of a calculation, such as sales tax, should not be stored in fields, but calculated in queries

Define Data Types

Planning

- ☐ Identify the data type of the values the fields will contain
- ☐ Identify multivalued fields, which let you store more than one value in a field
- ☐ Use Table AC-2 as a reference to select data types

Access

Table AC-2 Data Types

Data type	Description
Text	Text, combinations of text and numbers, or formatted numbers such as phone numbers
Memo	Text longer than 255 characters
Number	Numeric information to be used in calculations
Date/Time	Dates and times
Currency	Monetary values
AutoNumber	Integers assigned by Access to sequentially order each record added to a table
Yes/No	Only two values (Yes/No, On/Off, True/False) can be chosen for this type of field
OLE Object	Files created in other programs (OLE stands for Object Linking and Embedding)
Attachment	Files of any supported type, including .jpg, .docx, and .xlsx
Hyperlink	Web and e-mail addresses

Identify Tables

Planning

- □ Design each table to contain fields that describe only one subject
- □ Organize the fields as columns in the table and provide a unique field name for each column
- □ Recognize that each row in the table is a record, and each record should be unique
- □ Normalize the design of each table by arranging data into rows and columns, removing redundant data and storing it in a separate related table, then removing calculated fields
- □ Determine a primary key for each table
- □ Include a common field in related tables
- □ Identify external sources of the data you need, such as worksheets or other databases

DEFINE AND PRINT TABLE RELATIONSHIPS

Create a One-to-Many Relationship Between Tables

Ribbon Method

- □ Open a database that contains two tables for which you want to establish a one-to-many relationship
- □ Click the **Database Tools tab**, then click the **Relationships button** in the Show/Hide group
- □ If necessary, click the **Show Table button** in the Relationships group on the Relationship Tools Design tab

☐ In the Show Table dialog box, double-click the object(s) you want to relate, then click **Close**

☐ To create a one-to-many relationship, drag the "one" field (usually the primary key) from its field list to the "many" field (usually the foreign key) in another field list

☐ In the Edit Relationships dialog box, click **Create**

☐ Close and save the Relationships window

Shortcut Method

☐ In a database that contains two tables for which you want to establish a one-to-many relationship, open one of the tables in Design View

☐ If necessary, click the **Restore Window button** 🗗 to resize the table window so it is not maximized

☐ Right-click the **title bar** of the table window, then click **Relationships**

☐ Follow the steps in bullets 3–7 of the Create a One-to-Many Relationship Between Tables Ribbon Method above

Create a One-to-One Relationship Between Tables

Ribbon Method

☐ Open a database that contains two tables for which you want to establish a one-to-one relationship

☐ Click the **Database Tools tab**, then click the **Relationships button** in the Show/Hide group

☐ If necessary, click the **Show Table button** in the Relationships group on the Relationship Tools Design tab

☐ In the Show Table dialog box, double-click the object(s) you want to relate, then click **Close**

☐ To create a one-to-one relationship, drag the "one" field (usually the primary key) from its field list to the "one" field (usually the primary key) in another field list

☐ In the Edit Relationships dialog box, click **Create**

☐ Close and save the Relationships window

Shortcut Method

☐ In a database that contains two tables for which you want to establish a one-to-many relationship, open one of the tables in Design View

☐ If necessary, click the **Restore Window button** 🗗 to resize the table window so it is not maximized

☐ Right-click the **title bar** of the table window, then click **Relationships**

☐ Follow the steps in bullets 3–7 of the Create a One-to-One Relationship Between Tables Ribbon Method above

Access

Modify Relationships

Ribbon Method

- ☐ Click the **Database Tools tab**, then click the **Relationships button** in the Show/Hide group
- ☐ In the Relationships window, click the **join line** for the relationship you want to modify, then click the **Edit Relationships button** in the Tools group on the Relationship Tools Design tab

  OR

- ☐ Double-click the **join line** for the relationship you want to modify
- ☐ In the Edit Relationships dialog box, make the appropriate modifications, then click **OK**

Shortcut Method

- ☐ Open a related table in Design View, restore its window, if necessary, right-click the **title bar**, then click **Relationships**
- ☐ Follow the steps in bullets 2–3 of the Modify Relationships Ribbon Method above

Enforce Referential Integrity

Ribbon Method

- ☐ Click the **Database Tools tab**, then click the **Relationships button** in the Show/Hide group
- ☐ In the Relationships window, click the **join line** for the relationship you want to modify, then click the **Edit Relationships button** in the Tools group on the Relationship Tools Design tab

  OR

- ☐ Double-click the **join line** for the relationship you want to modify
- ☐ In the Edit Relationships dialog box, click the **Enforce Referential Integrity check box** to select it, then click **OK**

Shortcut Method

- ☐ Open a related table in Design View, restore its window, if necessary, right-click the **title bar**, then click **Relationships**
- ☐ Follow the steps in bullets 2–3 of the Enforce Referential Integrity Ribbon Method above

Set Cascade Update and Delete Options

Ribbon Method

- ☐ Click the **Database Tools tab**, then click the **Relationships button** in the Show/Hide group
- ☐ In the Relationships window, click the **join line** for the relationship you want to modify, then click the **Edit Relationships button** in the Tools group on the Relationship Tools Design tab

  OR

- ☐ Double-click the **join line** for the relationship you want to modify
- ☐ In the Edit Relationships dialog box, click the **Enforce Referential Integrity check box** to select it, if necessary

Access

☐ Click the **Cascade Update Related Fields check box** to select it

☐ Click the **Cascade Delete Related Records check box** to select it

☐ Click **OK**

Shortcut Method

☐ Open a related table in Design View, restore its window, if necessary, right-click the **title bar**, then click **Relationships**

☐ Follow the steps in bullets 2–6 of the Set Cascade Update and Delete Options Ribbon Method above

Change the Join Type

Ribbon Method

☐ Click the **Database Tools tab**, then click the **Relationships button** in the Show/Hide group

☐ In the Relationships window, click the **join line** for the relationship you want to modify, then click the **Edit Relationships button** in the Tools group on the Relationship Tools Design tab

OR

☐ Double-click the **join line** for the relationship you want to modify

☐ In the Edit Relationships dialog box, click **Join Type**

☐ In the Join Properties dialog box, click the **1**, **2**, or **3 option buttons**, then click **OK**

Shortcut Method

☐ Open a related table in Design View, restore its window, if necessary, right-click the title bar, then click **Relationships**

☐ Follow the steps in bullets 2–5 of the Change the Join Type Ribbon Method above

Print Relationships

Ribbon Method

☐ Click the **Database Tools tab**, then click the **Relationships button** in the Show/Hide group

☐ In the Relationships window, click the **Relationship Report button** in the Tools group on the Relationship Tools Design tab

☐ Click the **Print button** in the Print group on the Print Preview tab

ADD, SET, CHANGE, OR REMOVE PRIMARY KEYS

Set the Primary Key for a Table

Ribbon Method

☐ Open a table in Design View

☐ Click the field you want to set as the primary key

☐ Click the **Primary Key button** in the Tools group on the Table Tools Design tab

Shortcut Method

☐ Open a table in Design View

☐ Right-click the field you want to set as the primary key, then click **Primary Key**

Note: When you create a table in Datasheet View, Access automatically creates a primary key for you and assigns it the AutoNumber data type.

Modify the Primary Key for a Table

Ribbon Method

☐ Open a table in Design View

☐ Click the current primary key field

☐ Click the **Primary Key button** in the Tools group on the Table Tools Design tab to remove the primary key from this field

☐ Click the field you want to change to the primary key field

☐ Click the **Primary Key button** in the Tools group on the Table Tools Design tab

Shortcut Method

☐ Open a table in Design View

☐ Right-click the current primary key field, then click **Primary Key** to remove the primary key from this field

☐ Right-click the field you want to set as the primary key, then click **Primary Key**

Note: Before you can remove or modify a primary key field, you need to delete any relationships in which it participates. See the Define and Print Table Relationships section for instructions.

Setting and Changing a Multifield Primary Key

Ribbon Method

☐ Open a table in Design View

☐ Hold down **[Ctrl]** and click the **row selector** for each field you want to include in the primary key

☐ Click the **Primary Key button** in the Tools group on the Table Tools Design tab to set the selected fields as the primary key

☐ To change one of the primary key fields, click an appropriate field, then click the **Primary Key button** in the Tools group on the Table Tools Design tab

Shortcut Method

☐ Open a table in Design View

☐ Hold down **[Ctrl]**, then click the **row selector** for each field you want to include in the primary key

☐ Right-click a selected field, then click **Primary Key**

☐ To change one of the primary key fields, right-click an appropriate primary key field, then click **Primary Key**

SPLIT DATABASES

Ribbon Method

☐ Click the **Database Tools tab**, then click the **Access Database button** in the Move Data group

☐ Follow the instructions in the Database Splitter Wizard dialog boxes, then click **Finish**

ACCESS OBJECTIVE 2: CREATING AND FORMATTING DATABASE ELEMENTS

CREATE DATABASES

Create a Database Using a Template

Shortcut Method

☐ Open the Getting Started with Microsoft Office Access page (start Access or, if you have a database open, close the database)

☐ Click the template you want to use

☐ Change the database name in the File Name text box, if necessary, then specify where you want to save the database

☐ Click **Create** if you selected a local template; click **Download** if you selected an online template

Create a Blank Database

Ribbon Method

☐ Click the **Office button** 🏛, then click **New**

☐ Follow the steps in bullets 2–3 of the Create a Blank Database Shortcut Method above

Shortcut Method

☐ Open the Getting Started with Microsoft Office Access page (Start Access or, if you have a database open, close the database)

☐ In the New Blank Database section, click **Blank Database**

☐ In the Blank Database pane, click the **Browse button** 📂 to navigate to the appropriate drive and folder, type the filename in the File Name text box, then click **Create**

OR

☐ Press **[Ctrl][N]**

☐ Follow the steps in bullets 2–3 of the Create a Blank Database Shortcut Method above

CREATE TABLES

Create Tables in Design View

Ribbon Method

☐ Click the **Create tab**, then click the **Table Design button** in the Tables group

☐ For each field you want in the table, type the field name in the Field Name column, then press **[Enter]**

☐ To specify the type of data for a field, click the **Data Type list arrow**, then click the appropriate data type for the field, using Table AC-2 as a reference

☐ To set properties for data that is entered in a field, click the appropriate property text box in the Field Properties pane, then specify and modify the property for that field using Table AC-3 as a reference

☐ Click the field you want to define as the primary key, then click the **Primary Key button** in the Tools group on the Table Tools Design tab

Table AC-3 Selected Field Properties

Field property	Can be used to	Used for data type(s)
Field Size	Set the maximum size for data stored in a field set	Text, Number, and AutoNumber
Format	Customize the way numbers, dates, times, and text are displayed and printed, or use special symbols to create custom formats, such as to display information in all uppercase	Text, Memo, Date/Time, AutoNumber, Yes/No, Hyperlink, and Number
Decimal Places	Specify the number of decimal places that are displayed, but not how many decimal places are stored	Number and Currency
New Values	Specify whether an AutoNumber field is incremented or assigned a random value	AutoNumber
Input Mask	Make data entry easier and to control the values users can enter in a text box control, such as (___) ___-____ for a phone number	Text and Date
Caption	Provide helpful information to the user through captions on objects in various views	All fields
Default Value	Specify a value that is entered in a field automatically when a new record is added; (for example, in an Addresses table you can set the default value for the State field to Massachusetts); when a new record is added to the table, you can either accept this value or enter a new state	All fields except AutoNumber or OLE object
Validation Rule	Specify requirements for data entered into a record, field, or control	All fields except AutoNumber or OLE object

(continued)

Access

Table AC-3 Selected Field Properties (continued)

Field property	Can be used to	Used for data type(s)
Validation Text	Specify a message to be displayed when the user enters data that violates the Validation Rule property	All fields where a Validation Rule is specified
Required	Specify whether a value is required in a field	All fields except AutoNumber
Allow Zero Length	Allow users to enter a zero-length string ("")	Text and Memo
Indexed	Set a single-field index that will speed up queries on the indexed fields, as well as sorting and grouping operations	Text, Number, Date/Time, Currency, AutoNumber, Yes/No, Hyperlink, and Memo
Smart Tags	Specify that certain data be marked as a Smart Tag	Text, Currency, Number, Date/Time, AutoNumber, and Hyperlink

Create a Table Based on Another Table

Ribbon Method

- ☐ Click a table in the Navigation Pane, then click the **Copy button** 🔳 in the Clipboard group on the Home tab
- ☐ Click the **Paste button** in the Clipboard group on the Home tab
- ☐ In the Paste Table As dialog box, click the **Structure Only option button**
- ☐ Enter a name for the table in the Table Name text box, then click **OK**

Shortcut Method

- ☐ Right-click a table in the Navigation Pane, then click **Copy**
- ☐ Right-click a blank area of the Navigation Pane, then click **Paste**
- ☐ Follow the steps in bullets 3–4 of the Create a Table Based on Another Table Ribbon Method above

Create a Table Based on a Table Template

Ribbon Method

- ☐ Click the **Create tab**, click the **Table Templates button arrow** in the Tables group, then click a template

MODIFY TABLES

Change Table Properties

Ribbon Method

- ☐ In the Navigation Pane, double-click the table whose properties you want to modify

☐ Click the **View button arrow** in the Views group on the Home tab, then click **Design View**

☐ In Design View, use the Field Properties pane to change the table properties, click the **Save button** 🖫 on the Quick Access toolbar, then close the table

Shortcut Method

☐ In the Navigation Pane, right-click the table whose properties you want to modify, then click **Design View**

☐ In Design View, use the Field Properties pane to change the table properties, click the **Save button** 🖫 on the Quick Access toolbar, then close the table

Use the Table Analyzer

Ribbon Method

☐ In the Navigation Pane, click the table you want to analyze

☐ Click the **Database Tools tab**, then click the **Analyze Table button** in the Analyze group

☐ Follow the instructions in the Table Analyzer Wizard dialog boxes, then click **Finish**

Rename a Table

Shortcut Method

☐ In the Navigation Pane, right-click the table you want to rename, then click **Rename**

☐ Type a name for the table and press **[Enter]**

Delete a Table

Ribbon Method

☐ In the Navigation Pane, click the table you want to delete

☐ Click the **Delete button** in the Records group on the Home tab

☐ Click **Yes** to confirm the deletion

Shortcut Method

☐ In the Navigation Pane, right-click the table you want to delete, then click **Delete**

☐ Click **Yes** to confirm the deletion

Add a Total Row to a Table

Ribbon Method

☐ Open a table in Datasheet View

☐ Click the **Totals button** in the Records group on the Home tab

☐ In the Total row, click the field for which you want to display a total, click the list arrow, then click a calculation, such as **Sum** or **Count**

CREATE FIELDS AND MODIFY FIELD PROPERTIES

Create Fields in Datasheet View

Ribbon Method

☐ Open a table in Datasheet View, double-click the Add New Field column heading, then enter the name of the field

☐ Click a row in the new column, if necessary

☐ Click the **Table Tools Datasheet tab**, click the **Data Type list arrow** in the Data Type & Formatting group, then select a data type (see Table AC-2)

☐ Select other settings as necessary in the Data Type & Formatting group on the Table Tools Datasheet tab

Create Fields in Design View

Ribbon Method

☐ Open a table in Design View, then enter a field name in a blank row of the Field Name column

☐ Click in the Data Type column, click the **Data Type list arrow**, then select a data type (see Table AC-2)

☐ Click the **Save button** 🔲 on the Quick Access toolbar

Select an Input Mask for a Field

Shortcut Method

☐ Open a table in Design View

☐ Click a field with a Currency, Date/Time, Number, or Text data type

☐ Click the **Input Mask property text box** in the Field Properties pane

☐ Click the **Build button** 🔳, click **Yes** if prompted to save the table, follow the instructions in the Input Mask Wizard dialog boxes, then click **Finish**

OR

☐ Modify the Input Mask as appropriate using Table AC-4 as a reference

Table AC-4 Parts of the Input Mask Entry

Part	Description	Options	Example	Sample entry
First	Controls display of data and data type that can be entered	9: an optional number 0: a required number ?: an optional letter L: a required letter \: the next character will display as entered	Telephone Number \(999\)\-000\-0000;1;*	(978)-555-7000 OR ( ) 555-7000
Second	Establishes whether all displayed characters (such as slashes in the Date field) are stored in the field, or just the part you type	0: stores all characters 1: stores only typed characters	Zip Code 00000\-9999;0;	56178- OR 56178-7157
Third	Establishes the placeholder characters that will display to represent characters that will be typed in a field	* (asterisk) _ (underscore) # (pound sign)	Social Security Number 000\-00\-0000;0;#	Before typing, appears as: ###-##-#### After typing, appears as: 444-33-1111

Set the Field Size of a Text or Number Field

Shortcut Method

- ☐ Open a table in Design View
- ☐ Click a field with a Number or Text data type
- ☐ Click the **Field Size text box** in the Field Properties pane
- ☐ For a Text field, type the maximum number of characters to allow in the field (up to 255); for a Number field, click the **list arrow**, then click a field size

Allow Zero-Length Entries in a Field

Shortcut Method

- ☐ Open a table in Design View
- ☐ Click a field with a Hyperlink, Memo, or Text data type
- ☐ Click the **Allow Zero Length text box** in the Field Properties pane, click the **list arrow**, then click **Yes**

Access

Set Memo Fields to Append Only

Shortcut Method
- Open a table in Design View
- Click a field with a Memo data type
- Click the **Append Only text box** in the Field Properties pane, click the **list arrow**, then click **Yes**

Apply a Data Validation Rule to a Field

Ribbon Method
- Open a table in Design View
- Click a field (except for those with an AutoNumber, OLE Object, or Attachment data type, or a Number field set to ReplicationID)
- Click the **Validation Rule text box** in the Field Properties pane, then click the **Builder button** in the Tools group on the Table Tools Design tab, use the Expression Builder dialog box to create a validation expression, then click **OK**

Shortcut Method
- Open a table in Design View
- Click a field (except for those with an AutoNumber, OLE Object, or Attachment data type, or a Number field set to ReplicationID)
- Click the **Validation Rule text box** in the Field Properties pane, then enter a validation rule

  OR

- Click the **Validation Rule text box** in the Field Properties pane, click the **Build button** [...], use the Expression Builder dialog box to create a validation expression, then click **OK**

Assign a Caption to a Field

Shortcut Method
- Open a table in Design View
- Click a field
- Click the **Caption text box** in the Field Properties pane, then type the caption

Create a Multivalued Field

Ribbon Method
- Open a table in Datasheet View
- Click the **Table Tools Datasheet tab**
- Click the **Lookup Column button** in the Fields & Columns group
- Follow the instructions in the Lookup Wizard dialog boxes; in the last dialog box, click the **Allow Multiple Values check box**
- Click **Finish**

Shortcut Method

- □ Open a table in Design View
- □ Enter a field name in a blank row of the Field Name column, click in the Data Type column, click the **Data Type list arrow**, then click **Lookup Wizard**
- □ Follow the instructions in the Lookup Wizard dialog boxes; in the last dialog box, click the **Allow Multiple Values check box**
- □ Click **Finish**

Change a Multivalued Field

Shortcut Method

- □ Open a table in Design View
- □ Click the multivalued field
- □ Click the **Lookup tab** in the Field Properties pane
- □ Change the properties, pressing **[F1]** for Help as necessary

Create an Attachment Field

Ribbon Method

- □ Open a table in Datasheet View
- □ Click the **Table Tools Datasheet tab**
- □ In the Data Type & Formatting group, click the **Data Type list arrow**, then click **Attachment**

Shortcut Method

- □ Open a table in Design View
- □ Enter a field name in a blank row of the Field Name column, click in the Data Type column, click the **Data Type list arrow**, then click **Attachment**

Modify an Attachment Field

Ribbon Method

- □ Open a table in Datasheet View
- □ Click the **Table Tools Datasheet tab**
- □ Click the Attachment field, then click the **Is Required check box** in the Data Type & Formatting group, which is the only change you can make to an Attachment field in Datasheet View

Shortcut Method

- □ Open a table in Design View
- □ Click the **Attachment field**
- □ In the Field Properties pane, change the Caption or the Required property, which are the only properties you can change for an Attachment field in Design View

Access

CREATE FORMS

Create a Form in Design View

Ribbon Method

- ☐ Click the **Create tab**, then click the **Form Design button** in the Forms group
- ☐ On the Form Design Tools Design tab, click the **Property Sheet button** in the Tools group, if necessary, to open the Property Sheet
- ☐ In the Property Sheet, click the **Selection type list arrow**, if necessary, then click **Form**
- ☐ Click the **Data tab**
- ☐ To base the form on an existing database object, click the **Record Source list arrow**, then click the object's name

  OR
- ☐ To base the form on a new query, click the **Build button** [...] in the Record Source property, create the query, then save and close the query
- ☐ On the Form Design Tools Design tab, click the **Add Existing Fields button** in the Tools group to open the Field List
- ☐ Drag one or more fields from the Field List to the appropriate location on the form
- ☐ Click the **Save button** 🔲 on the Quick Access toolbar, type an appropriate name for the form in the Save As dialog box, then click **OK**

Create a Datasheet Form

Ribbon Method

- ☐ In the Navigation Pane, click an object on which you want to base a datasheet form
- ☐ Click the **Create tab**, click the **More Forms button** in the Forms group, then click **Datasheet**
- ☐ Click the **Save button** 🔲 on the Quick Access toolbar, type an appropriate name for the form in the Save As dialog box, then click **OK**

Create a Multiple Item Form

Ribbon Method

- ☐ In the Navigation Pane, click an object on which you want to base a multiple item form
- ☐ Click the **Create tab**, then click the **Multiple Items button** in the Forms group
- ☐ Click the **Save button** 🔲 on the Quick Access toolbar, type an appropriate name for the form in the Save As dialog box, then click **OK**

Create a Split Form

Ribbon Method

- ☐ In the Navigation Pane, click an object on which you want to base a split form

- □ Click the **Create tab**, then click the **Split Form button** in the Forms group
- □ Click the **Save button** 🖫 on the Quick Access toolbar, type an appropriate name for the form in the Save As dialog box, then click **OK**

Create a Form Containing a Subform

Ribbon Method

- □ Click the **Create tab**, click the **More Forms button** in the Forms group, then click **Form Wizard**
- □ Follow the instructions in the Form Wizard dialog boxes, making sure to create a form based on two or more tables or on a multitable query, then click **Finish**

Shortcut Method

- □ In Design View, open the form you want to use as the main form
- □ Drag a form from the Navigation Pane to the main form to create a subform

Create a PivotTable Form

Ribbon Method

- □ In the Navigation Pane, click an object on which you want to base a PivotTable form
- □ Click the **Create tab**, click the **More Forms button** in the Forms group, then click **PivotTable**
- □ Drag fields to the Filter, Column, Row, and Totals or Details areas in the PivotTable
- □ Click the **Save button** 🖫 on the Quick Access toolbar, type an appropriate name for the form in the Save As dialog box, then click **OK**

Create a Form in Layout View

Ribbon Method

- □ In the Navigation Pane, click an object on which you want to create a form
- □ Click the **Create tab**, then click the **Blank Form button** in the Forms group
- □ If necessary, click the **Add Existing Fields button** in the Controls group on the Form Layout Tools Format tab to open the Field List
- □ If necessary, click **Show all tables** in the **Field List**
- □ Expand the list of tables and fields as necessary to display the fields you want to add to the form
- □ Drag one or more fields from the Field List to the appropriate location on the form
- □ Click the **Save button** 🖫 on the Quick Access toolbar, type an appropriate name for the form in the Save As dialog box, then click **OK**

Create a Simple Form Using the Form Tool

Ribbon Method
- ☐ In the Navigation Pane, click an object on which you want to base a simple form
- ☐ Click the **Create tab**, then click the **Form button** in the Forms group
- ☐ Click the **Save button** 🖫 on the Quick Access toolbar, type an appropriate name for the form in the Save As dialog box, then click **OK**

CREATE REPORTS

Create a Simple Report Using the Report Tool

Ribbon Method
- ☐ In the Navigation Pane, click an object on which you want to base a simple report
- ☐ Click the **Create tab**, then click the **Report button** in the Reports group
- ☐ Click the **Save button** 🖫 on the Quick Access toolbar, type an appropriate name for the report in the Save As dialog box, then click **OK**

Create a Report Using the Report Wizard

Ribbon Method
- ☐ Click the **Create tab**, then click the **Report Wizard button** in the Reports group
- ☐ Follow the instructions in the Report Wizard dialog boxes, specifying the fields, grouping levels, sort order, layout, style, and title to create the report, then click **Finish**

Create a Report in Design View

Ribbon Method
- ☐ Click the **Create tab**, then click the **Report Design button** in the Reports group
- ☐ On the Report Design Tools Design tab, click the **Property Sheet button** in the Tools group, if necessary, to open the Property Sheet
- ☐ In the Property Sheet, click the **Selection type list arrow**, if necessary, then click **Report**
- ☐ Click the **Data tab**
- ☐ To base the report on an existing database object, click the **Record Source list arrow**, then click the object's name

  OR
- ☐ To base the report on a new query, click the **Build button** 🔲 in the Record Source property, create the query, then save and close the query
- ☐ On the Report Design Tools Design tab, click the **Add Existing Fields button** in the Tools group to open the Field List

☐ Drag one or more fields from the Field List to the appropriate location on the report, using Table AC-5 as a reference

☐ Click the **Save button** 🖫 on the Quick Access toolbar, type an appropriate name for the report in the Save As dialog box, then click **OK**

Table AC-5 Report Sections

Section	Information that can appear here	Location in printed report
Report Header	Report title, company graphics, graphic line to separate the title	Only on the first page of the report at the top of the page
Page Header	Page numbers, author information, a date field	On the top of every page; on the first page, it appears below the report header
Group Header	Text boxes for the grouped records	Before each record group
Detail	Text boxes for the fields in the table or query that the report is based on	For each record
Group Footer	Any calculations for a group of records	After each group of records
Page Footer	Page numbers, author information, a date field	On the bottom of each page
Report Footer	Summary information or calculations for all of the records and groups in the report	Only on the last page of the report, at the bottom of the page

Include a Group Header on a Report

Ribbon Method

☐ Open a report in Layout View or Design View

☐ On the Format tab, click the **Group & Sort button** in the Grouping & Totals group, if necessary, to open the Group, Sort, and Total pane

☐ In the Group, Sort, and Total pane, click **Add a group**

☐ Click the field you want to use as the group header

Shortcut Method

☐ Open a report in Layout View

☐ Right-click the field on which you want to group the records, then click **Group on** *field,* where *field* is the field name

Add an Aggregate Calculation to a Report

Ribbon Method

☐ Open a report in Design View

☐ On the Report Design Tools Design tab, click the **Text Box button** 🔳 in the Controls group

☐ To calculate a total or average for a group of records, click in the Group Header or Group Footer section to insert the text box

OR

☐ To calculate a grand total or average for all records in the report, click in the Report Header or Report Footer section to insert the text box

☐ Click the text box, then type an expression that uses an aggregate function, such as =Sum([Price])

Shortcut Method

☐ Open a report in Layout View

☐ Right-click a field for which you want to display a calculation, then click an aggregate function, such as **Sum** or **Count**

Format a Report for Printing

Ribbon Method

☐ Open a report in Print Preview

☐ To set the page orientation, click the **Portrait button** or the **Landscape button** in the Page Layout group on the Print Preview tab

☐ To change the margins, click the **Margins button arrow** in the Page Layout group on the Print Preview tab, then click a margin setting

☐ To specify the page orientation, margins, and other print settings, click the **Page Setup button** in the Page Layout group on the Print Preview tab, select settings in the Page Setup dialog box, then click **OK**

OR

☐ Open a report in Layout View or Design View

☐ Click the **Report Layout Tools Page Setup tab** or the **Report Design Tools Page Setup tab**

☐ To set the page orientation, click the **Portrait button** or the **Landscape button** in the Page Layout group

☐ To change the margins, click the **Margins button arrow** in the Page Layout group, then click a margin setting

☐ To specify the page orientation, margins, and other print settings, click the **Page Setup button** in the Page Layout group, select settings in the Page Setup dialog box, then click **OK**

Create Mailing Labels

Ribbon Method

☐ In the Navigation Pane, click an object on which you want to base mailing labels

☐ Click the **Create tab**, then click the **Labels button** in the Reports group

☐ Follow the instructions in the Label Wizard dialog boxes, selecting a label type, specifying text font and color, arranging fields for the labels, choosing a sort field, and providing a name to create the mailing label report, then click **Finish**

MODIFY THE DESIGN OF REPORTS AND FORMS

Add Controls to a Report or Form

Ribbon Method

- ☐ Open a report or form in Design View
- ☐ Click a button in the Controls group on the Form Design Tools tab or the Report Design Tools tab, then click where you want to place the control

Add Fields to a Report or Form as Controls

Ribbon Method

- ☐ Open a report or form in Layout View or Design View
- ☐ In Layout View, click the **Add Existing Fields button** in the Controls group on the Report Layout Tools tab or the Form Layout Tools tab to open the Field List, if necessary

  OR

- ☐ In Design View, click the **Add Existing Fields button** in the Tools group on the Report Design Tools tab or the Form Design Tools tab to open the Field List, if necessary
- ☐ Drag a field from the Field List to the report or form

Bind a Control to a Field in a Report or Form

Shortcut Method

- ☐ Open a report or form in Layout View or Design View
- ☐ Right-click the control you want to bind to a field, then click **Properties**
- ☐ In the Property Sheet, click the **Data tab**, if necessary
- ☐ Click the **Control Source list arrow**, then click a field included in the record source for the report or form

  OR

- ☐ Click the **Build button** 🔲 in the Control Source text box, then use the Expression Builder dialog box to select a field store in a different object in the database

Set the Tab Order on a Form

Ribbon Method

- ☐ Open a form in Layout View, click the **Form Layout Tools Arrange tab**, then click the **Tab Order button** in the Control Layout group

  OR

- ☐ Open a form in Design View, click the **Form Design Tools Arrange tab**, then click the **Tab Order button** in the Control Layout group
- ☐ In the Tab Order dialog box, click the **form section** you want to change, click a **field selector button** (drag to select more than one), then drag the fields to a new location
- ☐ To create a left-to-right and top-to-bottom tab order, click **Auto Order**
- ☐ Click **OK**

Shortcut Method

☐ Open a form in Design View, right-click a blank area in the form, then click **Tab Order**

☐ Follow the steps in bullets 3–5 of the Set the Tab Order on a Form Ribbon Method above

Change the Appearance of Controls

Ribbon Method

☐ Open a report or form in Layout View or Design View

☐ To change the font or foreground color of a control, click the control, click the **Font Color button arrow** in the Font group on the Home tab, then click a color

☐ To change the background or fill color of a control, click the control, click the **Fill/Back Color button arrow** in the Font group on the Home tab, then click a color

☐ To change the format of the control contents in Layout View only, click the control, click the **Format list arrow** in the Formatting group on the Report Layout Tools Format tab, then click a format, such as Currency or Standard

☐ Use Table AC-6 as a reference to modify the control appropriately

Shortcut Method

☐ Open a report or form in Design View

☐ To change the font or foreground color of a control, right-click the control, point to **Font/Fore Color**, then click a color

☐ To change the background or fill color of a control, right-click the control, point to **Fill/Back Color**, then click a color

Table AC-6 Common Formatting Buttons for Forms and Reports

Button	Name	Used to
Calibri (Body)	Font list box	Change the font
11 ▾	Font Size list box	Change font size
B	Bold	Apply bold formatting
I	Italic	Apply italic formatting
U	Underline	Apply underline formatting
◇	Fill/Back Color	Change background color
A	Font/Fore Color	Change font color
◢	Line Color	Change border color
≡ ▾	Line Thickness	Change border widths
▦ ▾	Line Type	Change line style
▭	Special Effect	Apply shadowed, etched, and other special effects

Access

Change the Arrangement of Controls

Ribbon Method

- ☐ Open a report or form in Layout View or Design View
- ☐ Click the **Arrange tab**
- ☐ To align controls, select two or more controls, then click the appropriate button in the Control Alignment group
- ☐ To group controls in a control layout, select two or more controls, then click the **Tabular button** or the **Stacked button** in the Control Layout group
- ☐ To remove one or more controls from a group, select the controls in the control layout, then click the **Remove button** in the Control Layout group
- ☐ To anchor controls on a form only, group them in a control layout, click the **Anchoring button arrow** in the Size group, then click an option in the Anchoring gallery

Shortcut Method

- ☐ Open a report or form in Layout View or Design View
- ☐ To align controls in Design View only, select two or more controls, right-click a selected control, point to **Align**, then click the appropriate alignment
- ☐ To group controls in a control layout, select two or more controls, right-click a selected control, point to **Layout**, then click **Tabular** or **Stacked**
- ☐ To remove one or more controls from a group, select the controls in the control layout, right-click a selected control, point to **Layout**, then click **Remove**
- ☐ To anchor controls on a form only, group them in a control layout, right-click the group, point to **Anchoring**, then click an anchoring option

Use Conditional Formatting

Ribbon Method

- ☐ Open a report or form in Layout View or Design View
- ☐ Click a control, then click the **Conditional button** in the Font group on the Home tab or on the Design tab
- ☐ In the Conditional Formatting dialog box, set the format of the field if no conditions are met, if necessary
- ☐ Click the **Condition 1 list arrow**, then click **Field Value Is**, **Expression Is**, or **Field Has Focus**, if necessary
- ☐ Specify the rest of the condition
- ☐ Set the format of the field if the condition is met
- ☐ Click **Add** to add other conditions and formats
- ☐ Click **OK**

Shortcut Method

☐ Open a report or form in Design View

☐ Right-click a control, then click **Conditional Formatting**

☐ Follow the steps in bullets 4–8 of the Use Conditional Formatting Ribbon Method above

Use AutoFormats

Ribbon Method

☐ Open a report or form in Layout View, click the **More button** in the AutoFormat group on the Form Layout Format tab or the Report Layout Format tab, then click an option in the AutoFormat gallery

OR

☐ Open a report or form in Design View, click the **Arrange tab**, click the **AutoFormat button arrow** in the AutoFormat group, then click an option in the AutoFormat gallery

ACCESS OBJECTIVE 3: ENTERING AND MODIFYING DATA

ENTER, EDIT, AND DELETE RECORDS

Enter Records in Datasheet View or Form View

Shortcut Method

- ☐ Open the table in Datasheet View or Form View
- ☐ Click in the first blank field in the table or form

  OR

- ☐ Click the **New (blank) record button** 📭 on the navigation bar
- ☐ Type the data for the first field, then press **[Tab]** to go to the next field in the record

Delete Records in Datasheet View or Form View

Ribbon Method

- ☐ Open the table in Datasheet View or Form View
- ☐ Click to the left of the record you want to delete
- ☐ Click the **Delete button** in the Records group on the Home tab
- ☐ Click **Yes** in the dialog box to confirm the deletion

Shortcut Method

- ☐ Open the table in Datasheet View or Form View
- ☐ Right-click to the left of the record you want to delete, then click **Delete Record**
- ☐ Click **Yes** in the dialog box to confirm the deletion

Edit Records in Datasheet View or Form View

Shortcut Method

- ☐ Open the table in Datasheet View or Form View, then use Table AC-7 as a reference to edit the records

Access

Table AC-7 Editing Records in Form View or Datasheet View

Action	Keyboard	Button
Deletes one character to the left of the insertion point	[Backspace]	
Deletes one character to the right of the insertion point	[Delete]	
Toggles between Edit and Navigation mode	[F2]	
Reverses the change to the current field	[Esc]	Undo button 🔄 on the Quick Access toolbar
Undoes all changes to the current record	[Esc][Esc]	
Starts the Spell Check feature	[F7]	Spelling button on the Home tab
Inserts the value from the same field in the previous record into the current field	[Ctrl][']	
Inserts the current date in a date field	[Ctrl][;]	

NAVIGATE AMONG RECORDS

Shortcut Method

☐ Open the table in Datasheet View or Form View, then use Table AC-8 as a reference to navigate among the records

Table AC-8 Navigation Buttons on the Record Navigation Bar

Button	Name
⏮	First Record button
◀	Previous Record button
▶	Next Record button
⏭	Last Record button

Shortcut Method

☐ Open the table in Datasheet or Form View, then use Table AC-9 as a reference to navigate among the records (*Note*: In Form View, you need to press [F2] so that you are in Edit mode before using these methods)

Table AC-9 Common Keyboard Navigation Techniques

Keyboard key or key combination	Moves to the following location
[↑]	Same field in the previous record (Datasheet View)
[↓]	Same field in the next record (Datasheet View)
[→], [Enter], or [Tab]	Next field in same record
[←] or [Shift][Tab]	Previous field in same record
[↑] or [Shift][Tab]	Previous field (Form View)
[↓] or [Tab]	Next field (Form View)
[Ctrl][Home]	First field of the first record
[Home]	First field of the current record
[Ctrl][End]	Last field of the last record
[End]	Last field of the current record
[Page Down] or [Page Up]	Down or up one screen at a time

FIND AND REPLACE DATA

Find Data

Ribbon Method

- □ Open a table in Datasheet View or a form in Form View
- □ Click the **Find button** in the Find group on the Home tab
- □ In the Find and Replace dialog box, enter the value you want to find in the Find What text box
- □ To search using wildcards, enter the value using * (asterisk) to stand for any number of characters and ? (question mark) to stand for a single character
- □ To specify additional criteria, click the **Look In list arrow**, then select a field name; click the **Match list arrow**, then select which part of the field you want to search; click the **Search list arrow**, then select the direction you want to search
- □ Click **Find Next**

Shortcut Method

- □ Open a table in Datasheet View or a form in Form View
- □ Press **[Ctrl][F]**
- □ Follow the steps in bullets 3–6 of the Find Data Ribbon Method above

Replace Data

Ribbon Method

- □ Open a table in Datasheet View or a form in Form View
- □ Click the **Replace button** in the Find group on the Home tab

Access

- [ ] In the Find and Replace dialog box, enter the value you want to find in the Find What text box
- [ ] Click in the Replace With text box, then enter the value you want to use as a replacement
- [ ] To specify additional criteria, click the **Look In list arrow**, then select a field name; click the **Match list arrow**, then select which part of the field you want to search; click the **Search list arrow**, then select the direction you want to search
- [ ] Click **Find Next**, then click **Replace** or click **Replace All**

Shortcut Method
- [ ] Open a table in Datasheet View or a form in Form View
- [ ] Press **[Ctrl][H]**
- [ ] Follow the steps in bullets 3–6 of the Replace Data Ribbon Method above

ATTACH DOCUMENTS TO AND DETACH FROM RECORDS

Attach Files to Records

Shortcut Method
- [ ] Open a table containing an attachment field in Datasheet View
- [ ] Double-click the **attachment field** in a datasheet or click the **attachment field** in a form
- [ ] In the Attachments dialog box, click **Add**
- [ ] In the Choose Files dialog box, navigate to the drive and folder containing the file(s) you want to attach to the record, select one or more files, then click **Open**
- [ ] In the Attachments dialog box, click **OK** to attach the file(s) to the record

Detach Files from Records

Shortcut Method
- [ ] Open a table containing an attachment field in Datasheet View
- [ ] Double-click the **attachment field** in a datasheet or click the **attachment field** in a form
- [ ] In the Attachments dialog box, click the file you want to delete, then click **Remove**
- [ ] Click **OK**

Export Files Attached to Records

Shortcut Method
- [ ] Open a table or form containing an attachment field in Datasheet View or Form View

☐ Double-click the **attachment field** in a datasheet or click the **attachment field** in a form, then click the **attachment icon** 📎

☐ In the Attachments dialog box, click the file you want to export, then click **Save As**

☐ In the Save Attachment dialog box, navigate to where you want to save the file, then click **Save**

☐ Click **OK**

Navigate Multiple Attachments

Shortcut Method

☐ Open a form containing two or more attachment fields in Form View

☐ Click the **attachment field**, then click the **Previous button** 📎 or the **Next button** 📎 on the Attachments toolbar

IMPORT DATA

Import Data from an Excel Workbook

Ribbon Method

☐ Click the **External Data tab**, then click the **Excel button** in the Import group

☐ In the Get External Data - Excel Spreadsheet dialog box, click **Browse** to navigate to the appropriate drive and folder, click the file you want to import, then click **Open**

☐ If you want to import the data as a new table in the database, click the **Import the source data into a new table in the current database option button**

☐ If you want to add the records to an existing table in the database, click the **Append a copy of the records to the table option button**, click the **list arrow**, then select a table

☐ Click **OK**

☐ Follow the instructions in the Import Spreadsheet Wizard dialog boxes, then click **Finish**

☐ Click **Close**

Import Data from a CSV Text File

Ribbon Method

☐ Click the **External Data tab**, then click the **Text File button** in the Import group

☐ In the Get External Data - Text File dialog box, click **Browse** to navigate to the appropriate drive and folder, click the file you want to import, then click **Open**

☐ If you want to import the data as a new table in the database, click the **Import the source data into a new table in the current database option button**

□ If you want to add the records to an existing table in the database, click the **Append a copy of the records to the table option button**, then click the **list arrow**, and select a table

□ Click **OK**

□ Follow the instructions in the Import Text File Wizard dialog boxes, then click **Finish**

□ Click **Close**

Link to an Excel Workbook

Ribbon Method

□ Click the **External Data tab**, then click the **Excel button** in the Import group

□ In the Get External Data - Excel Spreadsheet dialog box, click **Browse** to navigate to the appropriate drive and folder, click the file you want to import, then click **Open**

□ Click the **Link to the data source by creating a linked table option button**

□ Click **OK**

□ Follow the instructions in the Import Text File Wizard dialog boxes, then click **Finish**

□ Click **Close**

Save Import Steps

Ribbon Method

□ Follow the steps in bullets 1–5 of the Import Data from an Excel Workbook or Import Data from a CSV Text File Ribbon Methods above

□ Click the **Save import steps check box**

□ In the Save As text box, enter a name for the import, then click **Save Import**

Run a Saved Import

Ribbon Method

□ Click the **External Data tab**, then click the **Saved Imports button** in the Import group

□ In the Manage Data Tasks dialog box, click the **Saved Imports tab**, if necessary, click the import you want to run, then click **Run**

ACCESS OBJECTIVE 4: CREATING AND MODIFYING QUERIES

CREATE QUERIES

Create Queries Using Design View

Ribbon Method

- ☐ Click the **Create tab**, then click the **Query Design button** in the Other group
- ☐ In the Show Table dialog box, double-click each object you want to query, then click **Close**
- ☐ Move the fields into the query design grid by dragging the fields from the field list to the appropriate column in the query design grid

  OR

- ☐ To add all fields from a table to a query, double-click the title bar of the field list, then drag the selected fields to the query design grid
- ☐ To specify a sort order for a field, click the **Sort cell list arrow**, then click the sort order
- ☐ Click the **Run button** in the Results group on the Query Tools Design tab
- ☐ Click the **Save button** 🔲 on the Quick Access toolbar, type an appropriate name for the query in the Save As dialog box, then click **OK**

Create Queries Using the Query Wizard

Ribbon Method

- ☐ Click the **Create tab**, then click the **Query Wizard button** in the Other group
- ☐ In the New Query dialog box, click the query wizard option you want, using Table AC-10 as a reference, then click **OK**
- ☐ Navigate through the Query Wizard, making changes or accepting the defaults as appropriate to create the query, then click **Finish**

Note: When two related tables have fields with the same name, use the field from the "one" (or parent) table in the query.

Table AC-10 New Query Dialog Box Options

Option	Description
Simple Query Wizard	Wizard that helps you create a query by choosing fields
Crosstab Query Wizard	Wizard that helps you create a crosstab query in a format similar to a spreadsheet
Find Duplicates Query Wizard	Wizard that helps you create a query to locate records that contain duplicate values in a table or query
Find Unmatched Query Wizard	Wizard that helps you create a query to find records in a table that have no related records in another specified table

Create a Make Table Query

Ribbon Method

☐ Follow the steps in the Create Queries Using Design View or Create Queries Using the Query Wizard Ribbon Methods above to create a query

☐ Switch to Design View, if necessary

☐ To preview the new table before you create it, click the **View button arrow** in the Results group on the Query Tools Design tab, then click **Datasheet View**

☐ Return to Design View, make any necessary changes, then click the **Make Table button** in the Query Type group on the Query Tools Design tab

☐ In the Make Table dialog box, enter or select the name of the table you want to make

☐ To create the table in the current database, click the **Current Database option button**; to create a table in a different database, click the **Another Database option button**, then type the path of the database where you want to make the new table or click Browse to locate the database

☐ Click the **Run button** in the Results group on the Query Tools Design tab

☐ Click **Yes**

Create an Append Query

Ribbon Method

☐ Follow the steps in the Create Queries Using Design View or Create Queries Using the Query Wizard Ribbon Methods above to create a query

☐ Switch to Design View, if necessary

☐ To preview the records before you append them, click the **View button arrow** in the Results group on the Query Tools Design tab, then click **Datasheet View**

☐ Return to Design View, make any necessary changes, then click the **Append button** in the Query Type group on the Query Tools Design tab

☐ In the Append dialog box, enter or select the name of the table to which you want to append records

☐ To add records to the table in the current database, click the **Current Database option button**; to add records to a table in a different database, click the **Another Database option button**, then type the path of the database where you want to append records or click Browse to locate the database

☐ Click the **Run button** in the Results group on the Query Tools Design tab

☐ Click **Yes**

Create an Update Query

Ribbon Method

☐ Follow the steps in the Create Queries Using Design View or Create Queries Using the Query Wizard Ribbon Methods above to create a query

☐ In Design View, specify the conditions for updating records

☐ To preview the updates before you apply them, click the **View button arrow** in the Results group on the Query Tools Design tab, then click **Datasheet View**

☐ Return to Design View, make any necessary changes, then click the **Update button** in the Query Type group on the Query Tools Design tab

☐ Enter the updated values for the fields you need to update in the Update To text boxes

☐ Click the **Run button** in the Results group on the Query Tools Design tab

☐ Click **Yes**

Create a Delete Query

Ribbon Method

☐ Follow the steps in the Create Queries Using Design View or Create Queries Using the Query Wizard Ribbon Methods above to create a query

☐ In Design View, specify the conditions for deleting records

☐ To preview the records you will delete, click the **View button arrow** in the Results group on the Query Tools Design tab, then click **Datasheet View**

☐ Return to Design View, make any necessary changes, then click the **Delete button** in the Query Type group on the Query Tools Design tab

☐ Click the **Run button** in the Results group on the Query Tools Design tab

☐ Click **Yes**

Create a Crosstab Query

Ribbon Method

☐ Click the **Create tab**, then click the **Query Wizard button** in the Other group

☐ In the New Query dialog box, click **Crosstab Query Wizard**, then click **OK**

☐ Follow the instructions in the Crosstab Query Wizard dialog boxes above, then click **Finish**

Create a Subquery

Ribbon Method

☐ Click the **Create tab**, then click the **Query Design button** in the Other group

☐ In the Show Table dialog box, click the **Queries tab**

☐ Double-click the query you want to use as the subquery, then click **Close**

☐ Select the fields and specify criteria as necessary for the query

☐ Click the **Run button** in the Results group on the Query Tools Design tab

Save a Filter as a Query

Ribbon Method

□ Open the object you want to filter
□ On the Home tab, click the **Advanced button arrow** in the Sort & Filter group, then click **Advanced Filter/Sort**
□ In the query design grid, select fields and specify criteria as necessary for the filter
□ On the Home tab, click the **Advanced button arrow** in the Sort & Filter group, then click **Save As Query**
□ In the Save As Query dialog box, enter a name for the query, then click **OK**

MODIFY QUERIES

Add a Table to a Query

Ribbon Method

□ Open a query in Design View
□ Click the **Show Table button** in the Query Setup group on the Query Tools Design tab
□ In the Show Table dialog box, double-click the table you want to add to the query
□ To add a second copy of a table, double-click the table name in the Show Table dialog box
□ Click **Close**

Shortcut Method

□ Open a query in Design View
□ Right-click a blank area of the query window, then click **Show Table**
□ In the Show Table dialog box, double-click the table you want to add to the query
□ To add a second copy of a table, double-click the table name in the Show Table dialog box
□ Click **Close**

Remove a Table from a Query

Shortcut Method

□ Open a query in Design View
□ Right-click the title bar of the field list for the table you want to remove, then click **Remove Table**

Set Conditions for a Query

Shortcut Method

□ Open a query in Design View
□ Enter criteria in the Criteria and/or rows of the query design grid, using Table AC-11 as a guide

Table AC-11 Query Condition Operators

Condition name	Operator
Exact match	=
Range of values	<, >, <=, >=, <>, Between...And
List of values	In ( )
Pattern match	Like (can include wildcards)
Logical	And, Or, Not

Create a Parameter Query

Shortcut Method

☐ Open a query in Design View

☐ In the Criteria text box for a field, enter a prompt between brackets; the prompt appears in a message box when you run the query

Change a Query's Join Type

Shortcut Method

☐ Open a query in Design View

☐ Right-click the **join line** between two tables, then click **Join Properties**

☐ In the Join Properties dialog box, make sure the **1 option button** is selected for an inner join

☐ To create an outer left join, click the **2 option button**

☐ To create an outer right join, click the **3 option button**

☐ Click **OK**

Add Calculated Fields to a Query

Ribbon Method

☐ Open a query in Design View

☐ Click the first blank field in the query design grid, type the heading for the calculated field, then type **:** (colon)

☐ Click the **Builder button** in the Query Setup group on the Query Tools Design tab

☐ In the Expression Builder dialog box, use the expression elements and common operators to build the expression, then click **OK**, or type the exact expression

☐ In the expression, use arithmetic operators (+, -, /, *), comparison operators (=, <, >, <=, >=, < >), and logical operators (And, Or, Not, Like) as necessary to create the calculation

Shortcut Method

☐ Open a query in Design View

☐ Click the first blank field in the query design grid, type the heading for the calculated field, then type **:** (colon)

☐ Enter an expression, enclosing field names in brackets

Access

OR

☐ Right-click the field, click **Zoom**, type the expression, enclosing field names in brackets, then click **OK**

OR

☐ Right-click the first blank field in the query design grid, click **Build**, use the Expression Builder dialog box to create an expression, then click **OK**

☐ In the expression, use arithmetic operators (+, -, /, *), comparison operators (=, <, >, <=, >=, < >), and logical operators (And, Or, Not, Like) as necessary to create the calculation

Use an Alias in a Query

Ribbon Method

☐ Open a query in Design View

☐ Click the **Show Table button** in the Query Setup group on the Query Tools Design tab, double-click the table in the Show Table dialog box for which you want to add a second copy, then click **Close**

☐ Click the second copy of the field list, then click the **Property Sheet button** in the Show/Hide group on the Query Tools Design tab

☐ In the Alias text box, enter a new name for the table

Shortcut Method

☐ Open a query in Design View

☐ Right-click a blank area of the query window, click **Show Table**, double-click the table in the Show Table dialog box for which you want to add a second copy, then click **Close**

☐ Right-click the second copy of the field list, then click **Properties**

☐ In the Alias text box, enter a new name for the table

Use Aggregate Functions in Queries

Ribbon Method

☐ Open the query in Design View

☐ Click the **Totals button** in the Show/Hide group on the Query Tools Design tab

☐ Click **Group By** in the Total row for the field, click the **Group By list arrow**, then click the appropriate aggregate function, using Table AC-12 as a reference

Shortcut Method

☐ Open the query in Design View

☐ Right-click a field in the query design grid, then click **Totals**

☐ Click **Group By** in the Total row for the field, click the **Group By list arrow**, then click the appropriate aggregate function, using Table AC-12 as a reference

Access

Table AC-12   Aggregate Functions

Function	Used to calculate the	Used for field types
Sum	Total value	Number, Date/Time, Currency, and AutoNumber
Avg	Average value	Number, Date/Time, Currency, and AutoNumber
Min	Lowest value in a field	Text, Number, Date/Time, Currency, and AutoNumber
Max	Highest value in a field	Text, Number, Date/Time, Currency, and AutoNumber
Count	Number of values in a field (not counting null values)	Text, Memo, Number, Date/Time, Currency, AutoNumber, Yes/No, and OLE Object
StDev	Standard deviation of values	Number, Date/Time, Currency, and AutoNumber
Var	Variance of values	Number, Date/Time, Currency, and AutoNumber

ACCESS OBJECTIVE 5: PRESENTING AND SHARING DATA

SORT DATA

Sort Data in a Table or Query Datasheet

Ribbon Method

☐ Open the table or query in Datasheet View

☐ Click any value in the field you want to sort

☐ In the Sort & Filter group on the Home tab, click the **Ascending button** 🔼 or the **Descending button** 🔽

☐ To remove the sort, click the **Clear All Sorts button** 🔽 in the Sort & Filter group on the Home tab

Shortcut Method

☐ Open the table or query in Datasheet View

☐ Click the **column heading list arrow** for the field you want to sort

☐ Click a sort option, such as Sort Smallest to Largest or Sort Newest to Oldest, then click **OK**

☐ To remove the sort, click **Clear filter from** *field*, where *field* is the name of the field, then click **OK**

Sort Records in Query Design View

Shortcut Method

☐ Open the query in Design View

☐ Click the **Sort cell** for the field you want to sort, click the **list arrow**, then click **Ascending** or **Descending**

Sort Records in a Form

Ribbon Method

☐ Open the form in Form View

☐ Click any value in the field you want to sort

☐ In the Sort & Filter group on the Home tab, click the **Ascending button** 🔼 or the **Descending button** 🔽

☐ To remove the sort, click the **Clear All Sorts button** 🔽 in the Sort & Filter group on the Home tab

Shortcut Method

☐ Open the form in Form View

☐ Click the **column heading list arrow** for the field you want to sort

☐ Click a sort option, such as Sort Smallest to Largest or Sort Newest to Oldest, then click **OK**

☐ To remove the sort, click **Clear filter from** *field*, where *field* is the name of the field, then click **OK**

Sort and Group Records in a Report

Ribbon Method

☐ Open the report in Layout View or Design View

☐ Click the **Group & Sort button** in the Grouping & Totals group on the Report Layout Tools Format tab or the Report Design Tools Design tab

☐ Select the appropriate options in the Group, Sort, and Total pane

Shortcut Method

☐ Open the report in Layout View or Design View

☐ Right-click the field you want to sort, then click a sort option, such as Sort A to Z

FILTER DATA

Use AutoFilter in a Table or Query Datasheet

Ribbon Method

☐ Open the table or query in Datasheet View

☐ Click a value in the field you want to filter

☐ Click the **Filter button** in the Sort & Filter group on the Home tab to display the AutoFilter menu

☐ Click a field value for which you want to filter, then click **OK**
   OR

☐ Click a field value for which you want to filter, point to *Data type* **Filters,** where *Data type* is the data type for the field, click a filter option, such as Equals, enter a value, then click **OK**

☐ To remove the filter, click the **column heading list arrow** for the field, click **Clear filter from** *field*, where *field* is the name of the field, then click **OK**

Shortcut Method

☐ Open the table or query in Datasheet View

☐ Click the **column heading list arrow** for the field you want to filter to display the AutoFilter menu

☐ Click a field value for which you want to filter, then click **OK**
   OR

☐ Click a field value for which you want to filter, point to *Data type* **Filters,** where *Data type* is the data type for the field, click a filter option, such as Equals, enter a value, then click **OK**

☐ To remove the filter, right-click the field, then click **Clear Filter from** *field*, where *field* is the name of the field

Filter Records Using Filter by Selection

Ribbon Method

☐ Open a table or query in Datasheet View or a form in Form View

☐ Click the field that contains criteria that you want to apply as a filter to the rest of the data

□ Click the **Selection button arrow** in the Sort & Filter group on the Home tab, click a filter option, enter filter criteria, then click **OK**, if necessary

□ To remove the filter, click the field, then click the **Toggle Filter button** in the Sort & Filter group on the Home tab

Shortcut Method

□ Open a table or query in Datasheet View or a form in Form View

□ Right-click the field that contains criteria that you want to apply as a filter, then click a filter option for the current value

OR

□ Point to *Data type* **Filters**, where *Data type* is the data type for the field, click a filter option, such as Equals, enter a value, then click **OK**

□ To remove the filter, right-click the field, then click **Clear Filter from** *field*, where *field* is the name of the field

Filter Records Using Filter by Form

Ribbon Method

□ Open a table or query in Datasheet View or a form in Form View

□ Click the field that contains criteria that you want to apply as a filter to the rest of the data

□ Click the **Selection button arrow** in the Sort & Filter group on the Home tab, then click **Filter by Form**

□ Click the cell that contains the value that you want all records in the filter results to contain, then type the criteria using Table AC-13 as a reference, or click the cell by which to filter, click the **list arrow**, then click the value by which to filter

□ To filter by additional criteria, click the **Or tab**, then enter additional criteria

□ Click the **Toggle Filter button** in the Sort & Filter group on the Home tab

Table AC-13 Comparison Operators

Operator	Description	Expression	Meaning
<	Less than	<"Cassidy"	Names from A through Cassidy, but not Cassidy
<=	Less than or equal to	<="Delaney"	Names from A through, and including, Delaney
>	Greater than	>450	Numbers greater than 450
>=	Greater than or equal to	>=450	Numbers greater than or equal to 450
<>	Not equal to	<>"Malone"	Any name except for Malone
OR	Needs to meet 1 of 2 criteria	"Murphy" OR "Malone"	Only names Murphy and Malone
AND	Needs to meet both of 2 criteria	>="Cassidy" AND <="Murphy"	All names between and including Cassidy and Murphy

Create and Apply Advanced Filters

Ribbon Method

- □ Open a table or query in Datasheet View or a form in Form View
- □ Click the field that contains criteria that you want to apply as a filter to the rest of the data
- □ Click the **Advanced button arrow** in the Sort & Filter group on the Home tab, then click **Advanced Filter/Sort**
- □ Double-click each field you want in the filter to add it to the filter design grid
- □ Click the **Criteria cell** for each field, then type the criteria you want each record in the filter results to meet, using Table AC-13 as a reference
- □ Click the **Sort cell** for each field, click the **list arrow**, then click **Ascending** or **Descending** as appropriate
- □ Click the **Toggle Filter button** in the Sort & Filter group on the Home tab

Filter Records in a Report

Shortcut Method

- □ Open the report in Layout View or Design View
- □ Click a field value for which you want to filter, then click **OK**
  OR
- □ Click a field value for which you want to filter, point to *Data type* **Filters**, where *Data type* is the data type for the field, click a filter option, such as Equals, enter a value, then click **OK**
- □ To remove the filter, right-click the field, then click **Clear Filter from** *field*, where *field* is the name of the field

CREATE AND MODIFY CHARTS

Create a Chart in a Form or Report

Ribbon Method

- □ Open the form or report in Design View
- □ Click the **Insert Chart button** 📊 in the Controls group on the Report Design Tools Design tab
- □ Click where you want to place the chart
- □ Follow the instructions in the Chart Wizard dialog boxes, then click **Finish**

Change the Format of a Chart

Shortcut Method

- □ In Design View, open a form or report that contains a chart
- □ Double-click the chart to open Microsoft Graph, then use the Microsoft Graph tools to change the format of the chart

Change the Chart Type

Shortcut Method

- [ ] In Design View, open a form or report that contains a chart
- [ ] Double-click the chart to open Microsoft Graph, click **Chart** on the menu bar, click **Chart Type**, click a different chart type and subtype, if necessary, then click **OK**

EXPORT DATA FROM ACCESS

Export Data from a Table or Query

Ribbon Method

- [ ] Open a table or query in Datasheet View
- [ ] Click the **External Data tab**, then click a button in the Export group
- [ ] In the Export dialog box, enter the path to the destination file or click **Browse** to navigate to the destination file
- [ ] Click the **File format list arrow**, then click a file format, if necessary
- [ ] Specify any export options
- [ ] Click **OK**, then click **Close**

Save and Run an Export

Ribbon Method

- [ ] Follow the steps in bullets 2–5 in Export Data from a Table or Query Ribbon Method above
- [ ] Click **OK**
- [ ] Click the **Save export steps check box**, enter the name of the export, if necessary, then click **Save Export**
- [ ] To run a saved export, click the **Saved Exports button** in the Export group on the External Data tab
- [ ] In the Manage Data Tasks dialog box, click a saved export, then click **Run**

SAVE DATABASE OBJECTS AS OTHER FILE TYPES

Save an Object as a PDF or XPS File

Ribbon Method

- [ ] In the Navigation Pane, click the object you want to export
- [ ] Click the **Office Button** , then point to **Save As**
- [ ] If necessary, click **Find add-ins for other file formats**, then follow the instructions to download and install the PDF or XPS add-in from Microsoft

  OR

- [ ] Click **PDF** or **XPS**
- [ ] In the File name list box, type or select a name for the file, and in the Save as type list, click **XPS Document** or **PDF Document**

☐ Specify an optimize option (Standard or Minimum size) and other options, then click **OK**

☐ In the Publish as PDF or XPS dialog box, click **Publish**

PRINT DATABASE OBJECTS

Print a Database Object

Ribbon Method

☐ Open the object you want to print

☐ Click the **Office Button** 🏢, then point to **Print**

☐ To select a printer, number of copies, and other options, click **Print**, select options, then click **OK** in the Print dialog box

OR

☐ To print the object with the default printer and settings, click **Quick Print**

Print Selected Records

Ribbon Method

☐ Open the object that contains the data you want to print, then select the record(s) you want to print

☐ Click the **Office Button** 🏢, point to **Print**, then click **Print**

☐ In the Print dialog box, click the **Selected Record(s) option button**, then click **OK**

ACCESS OBJECTIVE 6: MANAGING AND MAINTAINING DATABASES

PERFORM ROUTINE DATABASE OPERATIONS

Open a Database in Shared or Exclusive Mode

Ribbon Method

- □ Click the **Office Button** , then click **Open**
- □ Navigate to the database you want to open, then click the database to select it
- □ To open a database in shared mode, click **Open**

  OR

- □ To open a database in exclusive mode, click the **Open button arrow**, then click **Open Exclusive** (so that no other users can open the database) or **Open Exclusive Read-Only** (so that others can still open the database, but only in read-only mode)

Back Up a Database

Ribbon Method

- □ Save and close all objects in the database
- □ Click the **Office Button** , point to **Manage**, then click **Back Up Database**
- □ In the Save As dialog box, specify the name and location of the backup copy, then click **Save**

Compact a Database

Ribbon Method

- □ Save and close all objects in the database
- □ Click the **Office Button** , point to **Manage**, then click **Compact and Repair Database**

  OR

- □ Click the **Office Button** , click **Access Options**, click **Current Database**, click the **Compact on Close check box**, click **OK**, then close the database

Save a Database in an Earlier Format

Ribbon Method

- □ Save and close all objects in the database
- □ Click the **Office Button** , point to **Save As**, then click **Access 2002 - 2003 Database** or click **Access 2000 Database**

MANAGE DATABASES

Use a Password to Encrypt a Database

Ribbon Method

- □ Open the database in exclusive mode
- □ Save and close all objects in the database
- □ Click the **Database Tools tab**, then click the **Encrypt with Password button**
- □ In the Set Database Password dialog box, type the password, type it again to verify the password, then click **OK**

Turn on Error Checking

Ribbon Method

- □ Save and close all objects in the database
- □ Click the **Office Button** , then click **Access Options**
- □ Click **Object Designers**
- □ In the Error checking section, click the **Enable error checking check box**, if necessary, to select it
- □ Click **OK**

Display or Close the Navigation Pane

Ribbon Method

- □ Click the **Office Button** , then click **Access Options**
- □ Click **Current Database**
- □ To make sure the Navigation Pane is displayed when you open the database, click the **Display Navigation Pane check box**, if necessary, to select it

  OR

- □ To hide the Navigation Pane when you open the database, click the **Display Navigation Pane check box**, if necessary, to remove the check mark

Display a Specified Form at Startup

Ribbon Method

- □ Click the **Office Button** , then click **Access Options**
- □ Click **Current Database**
- □ In the Application Options section, click the **Display Form list arrow**, then click the form you want to open at startup
- □ Click **OK**

Create a Custom Property for a Database

Ribbon Method

- □ Open the database for which you want to create a custom property

Access

□ Click the **Office Button** 🔵, point to **Manage**, then click **Database Properties**

□ In the Properties dialog box, click the **Custom tab**

□ In the Name text box, enter or select a name for the property

□ Click the **Type list arrow**, then select a data type, if necessary

□ Enter or select the remaining values and options, depending on the data type

□ Click **OK**

Show Object Dependencies

Ribbon Method

□ In the Navigation Pane, click an object to select it or double-click it to open it

□ Click the **Database Tools tab**, then click the **Object Dependencies button**

□ In the Object Dependencies pane, click the **Objects that depend on me option button** or click the **Objects that I depend on option button**

□ Expand objects in the Object Dependencies pane as necessary to view dependencies

Use the Database Documenter

Ribbon Method

□ Click the **Database Tools tab**, then click the **Database Documenter button**

□ In the Documenter dialog box, click a tab corresponding to the objects you want to document; click the **All Object Types tab** to document all objects

□ Click **check boxes** to select the objects you want to document, or click the **Select All button** to select all the objects on the tab

□ Click **OK**

□ After Access generates an Object Definition report, click the **Print button** in the Print group on the Print Preview tab

Update Tables with the Linked Table Manager

Ribbon Method

□ Open the database that contains linked tables

□ Click the **Database Tools tab**, then click the **Linked Table Manager button** in the Database Tools tab

□ In the Linked Table Manager dialog box, click the **check box** for the table you want to update, then click **OK**

□ Click **OK**

MICROSOFT OFFICE POWERPOINT 2007 EXAM REFERENCE

Getting Started with PowerPoint 2007

The PowerPoint Microsoft Certified Application Specialist (MCAS) exam assumes a basic level of proficiency in PowerPoint. This section is intended to help you reference these basic skills while you are preparing to take the PowerPoint MCAS exam.

☐ Starting and exiting PowerPoint
☐ Viewing the PowerPoint window
☐ Using the Ribbon
☐ Changing views
☐ Using task panes
☐ Using keyboard KeyTips
☐ Creating, opening, and closing presentations
☐ Navigating in the PowerPoint window
☐ Saving presentations
☐ Getting Help

START AND EXIT POWERPOINT

Start PowerPoint

Mouse Method

☐ Click the **Start button** 🔵 on the Windows taskbar
☐ Point to **All Programs**
☐ Click **Microsoft Office**, then click **Microsoft Office PowerPoint 2007**

OR

☐ Double-click the **Microsoft PowerPoint program icon** 🔲 on the desktop

Exit PowerPoint

Ribbon Method

☐ Click the **Office button** 🔵, then click **Exit PowerPoint**

OR

☐ Click the **Close button** ❎ on the program window title bar

Shortcut Method

☐ Press **[Alt][F4]**

VIEW THE POWERPOINT WINDOW

Figure PPT-1

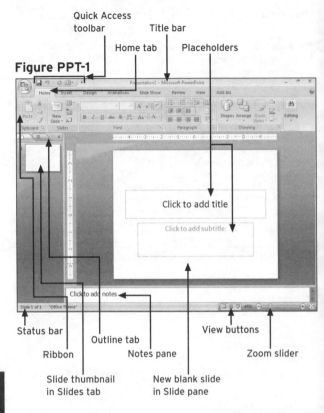

USE THE RIBBON

Display the Ribbon

Ribbon Method

☐ Click the **Customize Quick Access Toolbar button** ⚐ on the Quick Access toolbar, then click **Minimize the Ribbon** to remove the check mark and display the Ribbon

OR

☐ Double-click any tab

OR

☐ Right-click any tab, then click **Minimize the Ribbon** to deselect it

Shortcut Method

☐ Press **[Ctrl][F1]**

Hide the Ribbon

Ribbon Method

☐ Double-click the active tab

OR

☐ Right-click any tab, then click **Minimize the Ribbon**

Shortcut Method

☐ Press **[Ctrl][F1]**

CHANGE VIEWS

Ribbon Method

☐ Click the **View tab** on the Ribbon, then click the desired button in the Presentation Views group to switch to one of the following views: **Normal, Slide Sorter, Notes Page, Slide Show, Slide Master, Handout Master,** or **Notes Master**

Shortcut Method

☐ Click the **Normal button** 🔲, **Slide Sorter button** 🔡, or **Slide Show button** 🖵 on the

status bar to switch to Normal, Slide Sorter, or Slide Show view

OR

☐ Press and hold **[Shift]**, then click the **Normal button** 🔲 on the status bar to switch to Slide Master view

☐ Press and hold **[Shift]** then click the **Slide Sorter button** 🔡 on the status bar to switch to Handout Master view

USE TASK PANES

Display Task Panes

Ribbon Method

☐ See Table PPT-1 for a list of task panes and the Ribbon commands that open them

OR

☐ To open the Clip Art task pane, click the **Clip Art button** 🖼 in a content placeholder

Close Task Panes

Ribbon Method

☐ See Table PPT-1 for a list of task panes and the Ribbon commands that close them

PowerPoint

Shortcut Method

☐ Click the **Close button** ✕ on the task pane title bar

OR

☐ Click the **Task Pane Options button** ▼ on the task pane title bar, then click **Close**

Table PPT-1 Task Panes

Task pane	Click to open or close the task pane
Clip Art	**Clip Art button** in the Illustrations group on the Insert tab
Research	**Research button** in the Proofing group on the Review tab
Custom Animation	**Custom Animation button** in the Animations group on the Animations tab
Reuse Slides	**New Slide button arrow** in the Slides group on the Home tab, then click **Reuse Slides**
Selection and Visibility	**Arrange button** in the Drawing group on the Home tab, then click **Selection Pane** OR **Selection Pane button** in the Arrange group on the Drawing Tools Format tab

USE KEYBOARD KEYTIPS

Display KeyTips

☐ Press **[Alt]** to display the KeyTips for each command on the active tab on the Ribbon and on the Quick Access toolbar

☐ Press the letter or number shown in the KeyTip for a command to perform the command

☐ Press additional letters or numbers as needed to complete the command sequence

☐ If two letters appear, press each one in order

☐ For some commands, you have to click an option from a gallery or menu to complete the command sequence

☐ The KeyTips turn off automatically at the end of the command sequence

Hide KeyTips

☐ Press **[Alt]**

CREATE, OPEN, AND CLOSE PRESENTATIONS

Create a New Presentation

Ribbon Method

☐ Click the **Office button** 🔵, then click **New**
☐ Choose the appropriate options in the New Presentation dialog box

Shortcut Method

☐ Press **[Ctrl][N]**

Open an Existing Presentation

Ribbon Method

☐ Click the **Office button** 🔵, then click **Open**
☐ In the Open dialog box, navigate to the appropriate drive and folder
☐ Click the presentation file you want, then click **Open**

Shortcut Method

☐ Press **[Ctrl][O]**
☐ In the Open dialog box, navigate to the appropriate drive and folder
☐ Click the presentation file you want, then click **Open**

Close a Presentation

Ribbon Method

☐ Click the **Office button** 🔵, then click **Close**
☐ If prompted to save the presentation, click **Yes** or **No** as appropriate
  OR
☐ Click the **Close button** ✕ on the title bar
☐ If prompted to save the presentation, click **Yes** or **No** as appropriate

Shortcut Method

☐ Press **[Ctrl][W]** or **[Alt][F4]**
☐ If prompted to save the presentation, click **Yes** or **No** as appropriate

PowerPoint

NAVIGATE IN THE POWERPOINT WINDOW

Use Table PPT-2 as a reference to navigate in the PowerPoint window.

Table PPT-2 Keyboard Navigation Techniques

Press these keys	To move the insertion point
[Ctrl][Home] or **[Ctrl][End]**	To the beginning or end of the currently selected text box
[Home] or **[End]**	To the beginning or end of the line of text in a selected text box or text placeholder OR To the first or last slide on the Outline or Slides tab or in Slide Sorter view (if no object is selected on the slide)
[PgDn] or **[PgUp]**	Down or up one slide at a time
[Tab] or **[Shift][Tab]**	Between objects on a slide
[Ctrl][Right Arrow] or **[Ctrl][Left Arrow]**	One word to the right or left
[Ctrl][Enter]	To the next title or body text placeholder; if it is the last placeholder on a slide, a new slide with same layout will be inserted

SAVE PRESENTATIONS

Save an Existing Presentation with the Same File Name

Ribbon Method
☐ Click the **Save button** 🔲 on the Quick Access toolbar
   OR
☐ Click the **Office button** 🔵, then click **Save**

Shortcut Method
☐ Press **[Ctrl][S]**

Use Save As

Ribbon Method
☐ Click the **Office button** 🔵, then click **Save As**
☐ In the Save As dialog box, navigate to the drive and folder where you want to store the presentation
☐ Type an appropriate presentation name in the File name text box, then click **Save**

Shortcut Method

☐ Press **[F12]**

☐ Follow the steps in bullets 2–3 of the Use Save As Ribbon Method above

GET HELP

Ribbon Method

☐ Click the **Microsoft Office PowerPoint Help button** 🔘 on the Ribbon

☐ Use Table PPT-3 as a reference to select the most appropriate way to search for help in the PowerPoint Help window

Shortcut Method

☐ Press **[F1]**

☐ Use Table PPT-3 as a reference to select the most appropriate way to search for help in the PowerPoint Help window

Table PPT-3 PowerPoint Help Window Options

Option	To use
Search	Type a **keyword** in the Search box in the PowerPoint Help window, then click the **Search button**
Table of Contents	Click the **topic links** in the PowerPoint Help window as needed to find the information OR Click the **Show/Hide Table of Contents button** 🟢 or 🔲 on the PowerPoint Help toolbar to show the table of contents, then click a **topic** in the left pane of the window to display the information in the right pane

POWERPOINT EXAM REFERENCE

Objectives:

1. Creating and formatting presentations
2. Creating and formatting slide content
3. Working with visual content
4. Collaborating on and delivering presentations

POWERPOINT OBJECTIVE 1: CREATING AND FORMATTING PRESENTATIONS

CREATE PRESENTATIONS

Create a New Presentation from a Blank Presentation

Ribbon Method

☐ Click the **Office button** 🏢, then click **New**
☐ Click **Blank Presentation** under Blank and recent in the center pane of the New Presentation dialog box
☐ Click **Create**

Shortcut Method

☐ Press **[Ctrl][N]**

Create a New Presentation from a Template

Ribbon Method

☐ Click the **Office button** 🏢, then click **New**
☐ Click **Installed Templates** in the left pane of the New Presentation dialog box
☐ Click the appropriate template in the center pane of the New Presentation dialog box
☐ Click **Create**

OR

☐ Click the **Office button** 🏢, then click **New**
☐ Click **My templates** in the left pane of the New Presentation dialog box
☐ Click the appropriate template in the center pane of the New Presentation dialog box
☐ Click **OK**

PowerPoint

Create a New Presentation from an Existing Presentation

Ribbon Method

☐ Click the **Office button** 🗐, then click **New**
☐ Click **New from existing** in the left pane of the New Presentation dialog box
☐ Navigate to the existing presentation file you want to use in the New from Existing Presentation dialog box
☐ Click the presentation file, then click **Create New**

OR

☐ Click the **Office button** 🗐, then click **Open**
☐ Navigate to the existing presentation file you want to use in the Open dialog box
☐ Click the presentation file, then click the **Open list arrow**
☐ Click **Open as Copy**

Create a New Presentation from a Microsoft Office Word 2007 Outline

Ribbon Method

☐ Click the **Office button** 🗐, then click **New**
☐ Click **Blank Presentation** under Blank and recent in the center pane of the New Presentation dialog box
☐ Click **Create**
☐ Click the **New Slide arrow** in the Slides group on the Home tab, then click **Slides from Outline**
☐ Navigate to the existing document or outline file you want to use in the Insert Outline dialog box, then click **Insert**

OR

☐ Click the **Office button** 🗐, then click **Open**
☐ Click the **All PowerPoint Presentations list arrow**, then click **All Outlines**
☐ Navigate to the existing document or outline file you want to use in the Open dialog box, then click **Open**

Shortcut Method

☐ Press **[Ctrl][N]**
☐ Follow the steps in bullets 4–5 of the first Create a New Presentation from a Microsoft Office Word 2007 Outline Ribbon Method above

OR

☐ Press **[Ctrl][O]**
☐ Follow the steps in bullets 2–3 of the second Create a New Presentation from a Microsoft Office Word 2007 Outline Ribbon Method above

PowerPoint

CUSTOMIZE SLIDE MASTERS

Switch to Slide Master View

Ribbon Method
□ Click the **View tab** on the Ribbon, then click the **Slide Master button** in the Presentation Views group

Shortcut Method
□ Press and hold **[Shift]**, then click the **Normal button** on the status bar

Apply Themes to Slide Masters

Ribbon Method
□ Switch to Slide Master view
□ Click the **Themes button** in the Edit Theme group on the Slide Master tab, then click a theme in the gallery

Format the Slide Master Background

Ribbon Method
□ Switch to Slide Master view
□ Click the **Slide Master thumbnail** in the left pane
□ Click the **Background Styles button** in the Background group on the Slide Master tab
□ Click **Format Background**
□ Adjust the **options** for Fill or Picture in the Format Background dialog box as desired
□ Click **Apply to All**, then click **Close**

OR

□ Switch to Slide Master view
□ Click the **Slide Master thumbnail** in the left pane
□ Click the **Launcher** in the Background group on the Slide Master tab
□ Adjust the **options** for Fill or Picture in the Format Background dialog box as desired
□ Click **Apply to All**, then click **Close**

Add Background Graphics to a Slide Master

Ribbon Method
□ Switch to Slide Master view
□ Click the **Background Styles button** in the Background group on the Slide Master tab
□ Click **Format Background**
□ Click **Fill** in the Format Background dialog box, then click the **Picture or texture fill option button**
□ Under Insert from, click the **File button** or the **Clip Art button**
□ Select the graphic file in the Insert Picture dialog box and then click **Insert**, or click the clip art image in the Select Picture dialog box and then click **OK**
□ Click **Apply to All**, then click **Close**

Shortcut Method

☐ In Normal or Slide Master view, right-click a blank area of the slide in the Slide pane, then click **Format Background**
☐ Follow the steps in bullets 4–7 of the Add Background Graphics to a Slide Master Ribbon Method above

Apply Quick Styles to the Slide Background

Ribbon Method

☐ Switch to Slide Master view
☐ Click the **Slide Master thumbnail** in the left pane
☐ Click the **Background Styles button** in the Background group on the Slide Master tab
☐ Click a **Background style** in the gallery

    OR

☐ Switch to Slide Master view
☐ Click the **Background Styles button** in the Background group on the Slide Master tab
☐ Right-click a **Background style** in the gallery
☐ Click **Apply to All Layouts**

Change the Theme Font for All Slides in the Presentation

Ribbon Method

☐ In Normal view, click the **Design tab** on the Ribbon
☐ Click the **Fonts button** in the Themes group to open the theme fonts gallery
☐ Click a theme font in the gallery

    OR

☐ In Slide Master view, click the **Slide Master thumbnail** for the theme you want to change in the left pane
☐ Click the **Fonts button** in the Edit Theme group on the Slide Master tab
☐ Click a theme font in the gallery

ADD ELEMENTS TO SLIDE MASTERS

Add Slide Numbers to Slide Masters

Ribbon Method

☐ In Normal view, click the **Insert tab** on the Ribbon
☐ Click the **Slide Number** button in the Text group
☐ On the Slide tab in the Header and Footer dialog box, click the **Slide number check box**
☐ Click **Apply to All**

    OR

☐ In Slide Master view, click the **Slide Master thumbnail** or a **layout thumbnail** in the left pane
☐ Click the **text box** or **placeholder** on the slide or layout master where you want the slide number to appear
☐ Click the **Insert tab** on the Ribbon, then click the **Slide Number button** in the Text group

Add Footers to Slide Masters

Ribbon Method

- [ ] In Normal view, click the **Insert tab** on the Ribbon
- [ ] Click the **Header & Footer button** in the Text group
- [ ] On the Slide tab of the Header and Footer dialog box, click the **Footer check box**
- [ ] Type the footer text in the Footer text box
- [ ] Click **Apply to All**

  OR

- [ ] Switch to Slide Master view
- [ ] Click the **layout thumbnail** in the left pane to which you want to add a footer
- [ ] Click the **Footers check box** in the Master Layout group on the Slide Master tab to insert a check mark
- [ ] Type the footer text in the Footer placeholder on the slide in the Slide pane

Add Headers to Slide Masters

Ribbon Method

- [ ] Follow the instructions above to add a footer placeholder to a specific layout master
- [ ] In Slide Master view, click the **Slide Master thumbnail** or the **layout thumbnail** in the left pane on which you want to create a header
- [ ] Click and drag the **Footer placeholder** to the top of the slide to create a header
- [ ] Type the header text in the Footer placeholder to create the header

Add Placeholders to Slide Masters

Ribbon Method

- [ ] Switch to Slide Master view
- [ ] Click a **layout thumbnail** in the left pane
- [ ] Click the **Insert Placeholder button arrow** in the Master Layout group
- [ ] Click a placeholder type from the list
- [ ] Drag $+$ to draw the placeholder on the slide in the Slide pane

Add Graphic Elements to Slide Masters

Ribbon Method

- [ ] Switch to Slide Master view
- [ ] Click the **Slide Master thumbnail** or **layout thumbnail** in the left pane
- [ ] Click the **Insert tab** on the Ribbon, then click the appropriate button in the Illustrations group for the graphic element that you want to insert
- [ ] See Table PPT-4 for instructions on inserting different graphic elements

Table PPT-4 Inserting Graphic Elements

Graphic element	Examples	To insert
Shape	Lines, Rectangles, Basic Shapes, Block Arrows, Equation Shapes, Flowchart symbols, Stars and Banners, Callouts, and Action Buttons	Click the desired **shape** in the Shapes gallery, then drag ╋ to draw the shape in the slide pane
SmartArt	Graphic diagrams and charts of the following types: List, Process, Cycle, Hierarchy, Relationship, Matrix, and Pyramid	Click the desired **SmartArt graphic** in the Choose a SmartArt graphic dialog box, click **OK**, type text in the Text placeholders, then format the graphics as needed
Picture	Graphic image and picture files that are stored on a computer	Click the desired **image file** in the Insert Picture dialog box, then click **Insert**
Clip Art	Graphics such as drawn images or photographs from the Clip Organizer or Microsoft Office Online	Search for the desired clip art using a keyword search in the Clip Art task pane, then click the desired **image**
Chart	Column, Line, Pie, Bar, Area, XY (Scatter), Stock, Surface, Doughnut, Bubble, and Radar	Click the desired **chart** in the Insert Chart dialog box, then click **OK**

Add Date and Time to Slide Masters

Ribbon Method

☐ In Normal view or Slide Master view, click the **Insert tab**, then click the **Date & Time button** in the Text group
☐ On the Slide tab in the Header and Footer dialog box, click the **Date & time check box** to insert a check mark
☐ Click **Apply to All**

OR

☐ In Slide Master view, click the **Slide Master thumbnail** or a **layout thumbnail** in the left pane
☐ Click the location within the text box or placeholder on the slide in the Slide pane where you want the date and time to appear
☐ Click the **Insert tab**, then click the **Date & Time button** in the Text group
☐ In the Date and Time dialog box, click the desired date format, then click **OK**

PowerPoint

Set Date and Time to Update Automatically

Ribbon Method

- ☐ In Normal view or Slide Master view, click the **Insert tab**, then click the **Date & Time button** in the Text group
- ☐ On the Slide tab in the Header and Footer dialog box, click the **Date & time check box**
- ☐ Click the **Update automatically option button**
- ☐ Click the **Date list arrow** to change the date display format if necessary
- ☐ Click **Apply to All**

OR

- ☐ If you are in Normal view, click the location within the text box or placeholder on the slide where you want the date and time to appear
- ☐ If you are in Slide Master view, click the **Slide Master thumbnail** or a **layout thumbnail** in the left pane, then click the location within the text box or placeholder where you want the date and time to appear
- ☐ Click the **Insert tab** on the Ribbon, then click the **Date & Time button** in the Text group
- ☐ In the Date and Time dialog box, click the desired date format, click the **Update Automatically check box** to select it, then click **OK**

CREATE AND CHANGE PRESENTATION ELEMENTS

Change the Orientation of the Slides in the Presentation

Ribbon Method

- ☐ Click the **Design tab** on the Ribbon
- ☐ Click the **Slide Orientation button** in the Page Setup group
- ☐ Click **Landscape** or **Portrait**

Add or Change Transitions Between Selected Slides

Ribbon Method

- ☐ Click the **Animations tab** on the Ribbon
- ☐ Select the **slide** or **slides** to which you want to apply a transition
- ☐ Click a **transition effect** in the Transition to This Slide group, or click the **Transition to This Slide More button** ▼ to open the Transition gallery, then click a **transition effect** in the gallery

Add or Change Transitions Between All Slides in a Presentation

Ribbon Method

- ☐ Click a **slide**, then click the **Animations tab** on the Ribbon
- ☐ Click a **transition effect** in the Transition to This Slide group, or click the **Transition to This Slide More button** ▼ to open the Transition gallery, then click a **transition effect** in the gallery
- ☐ Click **Apply to All** in the Transition to This Slide group to apply the transition to all slides in the presentation

Remove Transitions Between Selected Slides

Ribbon Method
- [ ] Click the **Animations tab** on the Ribbon
- [ ] Select the **slide** or **slides** from which you want to remove the transitions
- [ ] Click the **No transition effect** in the Transition to This Slide group

Remove Transitions from All Slides in a Presentation

Ribbon Method
- [ ] Click the **Animations tab** on the Ribbon
- [ ] Click a **slide**, then click **No transition effect** in the Transition to This Slide group
- [ ] Click **Apply to All** in the Transition to This Slide group

Set Slide Size

Ribbon Method
- [ ] Click the **Design tab** on the Ribbon
- [ ] Click the **Page Setup button** in the Page Setup group
- [ ] In the Page Setup dialog box, click the **Slides sized for list arrow**
- [ ] Select a slide size

ARRANGE SLIDES

Insert a New Slide

Ribbon Method
- [ ] Click the **New Slide button** in the Slides group on the Home tab on the Ribbon to insert a slide with the same layout as the selected slide

  OR
- [ ] Click the **New Slide button arrow** in the Slides group on the Home tab to open the layout gallery
- [ ] Click a layout in the gallery to insert a new slide with the selected layout

Shortcut Method
- [ ] Right-click the **selected slide thumbnail** in the Slides tab
- [ ] Click **New Slide** on the shortcut menu to insert a slide with the same layout as the selected slide

Duplicate a Slide

Ribbon Method
- [ ] Select the **slide** or **slides** to be duplicated
- [ ] Click the **New Slide button arrow** in the Slides group on the Home tab on the Ribbon to open the layout gallery
- [ ] Click **Duplicate Selected Slides**

PowerPoint

Shortcut Method

☐ Right-click the **selected slide thumbnail** in the Slides tab
☐ Click **Duplicate Slide** on the shortcut menu

Delete Slides

Ribbon Method

☐ Select the **slide** or **slides** you want to delete
☐ Click the **Delete Slide button** in the Slides group on the Home tab

Shortcut Method

☐ Select the **slide** or **slides** you want to delete
☐ Right-click the **selected slide thumbnails** in the Slides tab, then click **Delete Slide** on the shortcut menu

OR

☐ Select the **slide** or **slides** you want to delete
☐ Press **[Delete]**

Use Slide Sorter View to Organize Slides

Ribbon Method

☐ In Slide Sorter view, select the **slide** or **slides** to be moved
☐ Drag the **selected slide thumbnails** in the Slide Sorter window to reposition them within the presentation

Cut and Paste Slides in Normal View

Ribbon Method

☐ In Normal view, select the **slide thumbnail(s)** in the Slides tab that you want to cut and paste
☐ Click the **Cut button** in the Clipboard group on the Home tab
☐ Click after the slide thumbnail in the Slides tab where you want to insert the slide(s)
☐ Click the **Paste button** in the Clipboard group on the Home tab

Shortcut Method

☐ In Normal view, select the **slide thumbnail(s)** in the Slides tab that you want to cut and paste
☐ Right-click the selected slide thumbnail(s), then click **Cut** on the shortcut menu
☐ Click after the slide thumbnail in the Slides pane where you want to insert the slide(s)
☐ Right click, then click **Paste** on the shortcut menu

OR

☐ In Normal view, select the **slide thumbnail(s)** in the Slides tab that you want to cut and paste
☐ Press **[Ctrl][X]**
☐ Click after the slide thumbnail in the Slides tab where you want to insert the slide(s)
☐ Press **[Ctrl][V]**

Reposition Slides in Normal View

Shortcut Method

☐ In Normal view, select the **slide thumbnail(s)** in the Slides tab that you want to reposition

☐ With the mouse pointer over the selected slide(s), press and hold the **left mouse button**, then drag the pointer to the new location in the Slides tab where you want the selected slides to be positioned

POWERPOINT OBJECTIVE 2: CREATING AND FORMATTING SLIDE CONTENT

INSERT, DELETE, AND FORMAT TEXT BOXES

Insert a Text Box

Ribbon Method

☐ Select the **slide** on which you want to insert a text box
☐ Click the **Insert tab** on the Ribbon, then click the **Text Box button** in the Text group
☐ Outside any current placeholders on the slide, click to create a text box that does not wrap the text within a shape, or drag to draw a text box that is a particular width so that the text wraps within the text box
☐ Type the desired **text**

OR

☐ Select the **slide** on which you want to insert a text box
☐ Click the **Shapes button** in the Drawing group on the Home tab
☐ Click the **Text Box button** in the Shapes Gallery
☐ Follow the steps in bullets 3–4 of the Insert a Text Box Ribbon Method above

Insert a Text Placeholder

Ribbon Method

☐ Click the **Layout button** in the Slides group on the Home tab, then click any **Text or Content layout**

Delete a Text Box

Ribbon Method

☐ Select the **text box**, then click the **Cut button** in the Clipboard group on the Home tab on the Ribbon

Shortcut Method

☐ Select the **text box**, then press **[Delete]**

OR

☐ Right-click the **text box**, then click **Cut**

Size Text Boxes

Ribbon Method

☐ Select the **text box**
☐ Click the **Drawing Tools Format tab**
☐ Click the **Shape Width text box** in the Size group and type in a new width value, or click the up and down arrows to adjust the Shape Width value
☐ Click the **Shape Height text box** in the Size group and type in a new height value, or click the up and down arrows to adjust the Shape Height value

OR

- ☐ Select the **text box**
- ☐ Click the **Drawing Tools Format tab**
- ☐ Click the **Launcher** in the Size group
- ☐ Click the **Size tab** in the Size and Position dialog box
- ☐ Adjust the Size and Scale settings as desired

Shortcut Method

- ☐ Select the **text box**, then drag any of the **sizing handles** to resize the text box as needed

    OR

- ☐ Select the **text box**, then right-click the **text box**
- ☐ Click **Size and Position** on the shortcut menu
- ☐ Adjust the Height and Width values in the Size and Position dialog box as desired

Format Text Box Fills

Ribbon Method

- ☐ Select the **text box**
- ☐ Click the **Drawing Tools Format tab**
- ☐ Click the **Shape Fill button** in the Shape Styles group
- ☐ Click a **color** in the Theme Colors, Standard Colors, or Recent Colors group, or click any one of the Picture, Gradient, or Texture options to format the text box fill

    OR

- ☐ Select the **text box**
- ☐ Click the **Drawing Tools Format tab**, then click the **Launcher** in the Shape Styles group
- ☐ Click **Fill** in the left pane in the Format Shape dialog box, then adjust the options as desired to format the text box fill
- ☐ Click **Close**

Shortcut Method

- ☐ Select the **text box**
- ☐ Right-click the **text box**, then click **Format Shape** on the shortcut menu
- ☐ Click **Fill** in the left pane of the Format Shape dialog box, then adjust the options as desired to format the text box fill
- ☐ Click **Close**

Format Text Box Borders

Ribbon Method

- ☐ Select the **text box**
- ☐ Click the **Drawing Tools Format tab**
- ☐ Click the **Shape Outline button** in the Shape Styles group
- ☐ Click a **color** in the Theme Colors or Standard Colors group, or click any one of the Weight or Dashes options to format the text box border

PowerPoint

OR
- [ ] Select the **text box**
- [ ] Click the **Drawing Tools Format tab**, then click the **Launcher** 🔲 in the Shape Styles group
- [ ] Click **Line Color** in the left pane of the Format Shape dialog box, then adjust the options as desired
- [ ] Click **Line Style** in the left pane, then adjust the options as desired
- [ ] Click **Close**

Shortcut Method

- [ ] Right-click the **text box**
- [ ] Click **Format Shape** on the shortcut menu
- [ ] Click **Line Color** in the Format Shape dialog box, then adjust the options as desired
- [ ] Click **Line Style** in the Format Shape dialog box, then adjust the options as desired
- [ ] Click **Close**

Format Text Box Effects

Ribbon Method

- [ ] Select the **text box**
- [ ] Click the **Drawing Tools Format tab** or click the **Home tab**
- [ ] Click the **Shape Effects button** in the Shape Styles group on the Format tab or in the Drawing group on the Home tab
- [ ] Point to an effect category, then click an effect in the gallery

Shortcut Method

- [ ] Right-click the **text box**
- [ ] Click **Format Shape** on the shortcut menu
- [ ] Adjust the options as desired in the Shadow, 3-D Format, and 3-D Rotation sections of the Format Text Effects dialog box
- [ ] Click **Close**

Format Text Box Fill, Border, and Effects Using Quick Styles

Ribbon Method

- [ ] Select the **text box**
- [ ] Click the **Quick Styles button** in the Drawing group on the Home tab
- [ ] Click a **Quick Style** in the gallery

OR
- [ ] Select the **text box**
- [ ] Click the **Drawing Tools Format tab**
- [ ] Click the **Shape Styles More button** 🔽 in the Shape Styles group
- [ ] Click a **shape style** in the gallery

Set Text Direction

Ribbon Method

- ☐ Select the **text box**
- ☐ Click the **Text Direction button** ⬛ in the Paragraph group on the Home tab
- ☐ Click a **text direction option** in the gallery

Shortcut Method

- ☐ Select the **text box**
- ☐ Right-click the **text box**, then click **Format Shape**
- ☐ Click **Text Box** in the left pane in the Format Shape dialog box
- ☐ Click the **Text direction list arrow** in the Text layout section
- ☐ Click a **text direction option**
- ☐ Click **Close**

Align Text Vertically

Ribbon Method

- ☐ Select the **text box**
- ☐ Click the **Align Text button** ⬛ in the Paragraph group on the Home tab on the Ribbon
- ☐ Click an alignment option

  OR

- ☐ Select the **text box**
- ☐ Click the **Align Text button** ⬛ in the Paragraph group, then click **More Options**
- ☐ In the Format Text Effects dialog box, click the **Vertical alignment list arrow** in the Text layout section, then click an alignment

Shortcut Method

- ☐ Select the **text box**
- ☐ Right-click the **text box**, then click **Format Shape** on the shortcut menu
- ☐ Click **Text Box** in the left pane of the Format Shape dialog box
- ☐ Click the **Vertical alignment list arrow** in the Text layout section, then click an alignment option
- ☐ Click **Close**

Set Margins for Text Boxes

Ribbon Method

- ☐ Select the **text box**
- ☐ Click the **Drawing Tools Format tab**, then click the **Launcher** ⬛ in the Shape Styles group
- ☐ Click **Text Box** in the left pane of the Format Shape dialog box
- ☐ Adjust the values in the Left, Right, Top, and Bottom text boxes in the Internal margin section
- ☐ Click **Close**

Shortcut Method

- ☐ Right-click the **text box**, then click **Format Shape** on the shortcut menu
- ☐ Follow the steps in bullets 3–5 of the Set Margins for Text Boxes Ribbon Method above

PowerPoint

Create Columns in Text Boxes

Ribbon Method

☐ Select the **text box**
☐ Click the **Columns button** ▦▾ in the Paragraph group on the Home tab
☐ Click an **option** on the list

Shortcut Method

☐ Right-click the **text box**, then click **Format Shape** on the shortcut menu
☐ Click **Text Box** in the left pane of the Format Shape dialog box
☐ Click the **Columns button** in the Internal margin section
☐ Adjust the value in the Number text box in the Columns dialog box to the number of columns desired
☐ Adjust the value in the Spacing text box to the desired spacing between the columns
☐ Click **OK**, then click **Close**

MOVE, COPY, AND FORMAT TEXT

Move Text Using Drag and Drop

Ribbon Method

☐ Select the **text**, then place the pointer on the selected text
☐ Drag the **text** to another location within the text box or outside the text box to create a new text box with the moved text

Copy and Paste Text

Ribbon Method

☐ Select the **text**
☐ Click the **Copy button** ▣ in the Clipboard group on the Home tab
☐ Click in the new location in the presentation where you want to copy the text
☐ Click the **Paste button** ▣ in the Clipboard group on the Home tab

Shortcut Method

☐ Select the **text**
☐ Right-click the **selected text**, then click **Copy** on the shortcut menu
☐ Click in the new location in the presentation where you want to copy the text
☐ Right-click the **selected text**, then click **Paste** on the shortcut menu
   OR
☐ Select the **text**
☐ Press **[Ctrl][C]**
☐ Click in the new location in the presentation where you want to copy the text
☐ Press **[Ctrl][V]**

Cut and Paste to Move Text

Ribbon Method

- ☐ Select the **text**
- ☐ Click the **Cut button** 🔏 in the Clipboard group on the Home tab
- ☐ Click in the new location in the presentation where you want to move the text
- ☐ Click the **Paste button** 📋 in the Clipboard group on the Home tab

Shortcut Method

- ☐ Select the **text**
- ☐ Right-click the **selected text**, then click **Cut** on the shortcut menu
- ☐ Click in the new location in the presentation where you want to move the text
- ☐ Right-click the **selected text**, then click **Paste** on the shortcut menu

OR

- ☐ Select the text
- ☐ Press **[Ctrl][X]**
- ☐ Click in the new location in the presentation where you want to move the text
- ☐ Press **[Ctrl][V]**

Use Paste Special to Paste Text and Objects

Ribbon Method

- ☐ Select the appropriate **slide**
- ☐ Select the **text** or **object**
- ☐ Click the **Cut button** 🔏 or **Copy button** 📄 in the Clipboard group on the Home tab
- ☐ Click in the new location in the presentation where you want to paste the text or object
- ☐ Click the **Paste button arrow** in the Clipboard group on the Home tab
- ☐ Click **Paste Special**
- ☐ Select the appropriate **Paste Special options** in the Paste Special dialog box
- ☐ Click **OK**

Shortcut Method

- ☐ Select the appropriate **slide**
- ☐ Select the **text** or **object**
- ☐ Right-click the selected text or object, then click **Cut** or **Copy** on the shortcut menu
- ☐ Follow the steps in bullets 4–8 of the Use Paste Special to Paste Text and Objects Ribbon Method above

OR

- ☐ Select the **text** or **object**
- ☐ Press **[Ctrl][X]** to cut or **[Ctrl][C]** to cut or copy the selected text or object
- ☐ Press **[Ctrl][Alt][V]** to open the Paste Special dialog box
- ☐ Select the appropriate **Paste Special options** in the Paste Special dialog box
- ☐ Click **OK**

PowerPoint

Apply Quick Styles to Text

Ribbon Method

□ Select the **text**
□ Click the **Drawing Tools Format tab** on the Ribbon
□ Click a **WordArt style** in the WordArt Styles group to apply a style, or click the **WordArt Styles More button** ⬇ in the WordArt Styles group, then click a **style** from the gallery

Change Text Size

Ribbon Method

□ Select the **text**
□ Click the **Increase Font Size button** A˘ or **Decrease Font Size button** A˘ in the Font group on the Home tab
OR
□ Click the **Font Size list arrow** in the Font group on the Home tab, then click a number to change the font size, or adjust the value in the Font Size text box in the Font group

Shortcut Method

□ Select the **text**
□ Press **[Ctrl][ ]]** (right bracket) to increase font size
□ Press **[Ctrl][[ ]** (left bracket) to decrease font size

Change the Font Type

Ribbon Method

□ Select the **text**
□ Click the **Font list arrow** in the Font group on the Home tab, then click a font from the list
OR
□ Select the **text**
□ Click the **Launcher** ⬜ in the Font group on the Home tab
□ Click the **Font list arrow** in the Font dialog box, then click a font from the list
□ Click **OK**

Shortcut Method

□ Right-click the **text**, click the **Font list arrow** on the Mini Toolbar, then click a font from the list

Change Text Color

Ribbon Method

□ Select the **text**
□ Click the **Font Color button** A ▾ in the Font group on the Home tab, then click a font **color** from the palette or click **More Colors** to open the Colors dialog box, click a **color**, then click **OK**

Shortcut Method

□ Right-click the text, then click the **Font Color button** $\boxed{\text{A}}$ on the Mini Toolbar
□ Click a font **color** from the palette, or click **More Colors** to open the Colors dialog box, click a **color**, then click **OK**

Apply Bold, Italic, Underline, and Shadow Formatting to Text

□ Select the appropriate **text**
□ Use the appropriate button or keyboard shortcut listed in Table PPT-5 to format text as desired

Table PPT-5 Text Formatting Buttons and Keyboard Shortcuts

Formatting effect	Button (in Font group on Home tab or on Mini Toolbar)	Keyboard shortcut
Bold	$\boxed{\text{B}}$	[Ctrl][B]
Italic	$\boxed{I}$	[Ctrl][I]
Underline	$\boxed{\underline{\text{u}}}$	[Ctrl][U]
Shadow	$\boxed{\text{S}}$	

Use the Format Painter to Copy Attributes of Objects or Text

Ribbon Method

□ Select the **text** or **object** with the attributes that you want to copy
□ Click the **Format Painter button** $\boxed{\checkmark}$ in the Clipboard group on the Home tab
□ Select the **text** or **object** to which you want to copy the formatting

Shortcut Method

□ Select the **text** or **object** with the attributes that you want to copy
□ Right-click the **text** or **object**, then click the **Format Painter button** $\boxed{\checkmark}$ on the Mini Toolbar
□ Select the **text** or **object** to which you want to copy the formatting

Create a Bulleted List

Ribbon Method

□ Click in the text box or placeholder where you want a new bulleted list to appear
□ Click the **Bullets button** $\boxed{\equiv}$ in the Paragraph group on the Home tab, or click the **Bullets list arrow** $\boxed{\equiv \cdot}$ in the Paragraph group, then click a **bulleted list style** in the gallery

PowerPoint

Shortcut Method

☐ Click in the text box or placeholder where you want a new bulleted list to appear
☐ Right-click the **selection**, point to **Bullets** on the shortcut menu, then click a **bulleted list style** in the gallery

Convert Text to a Bulleted List

Ribbon Method

☐ Select the **text** you want to be a bulleted list, or select the **text box** you want to contain a bulleted list
☐ Click the **Home tab** on the Ribbon, then click the **Bullets button** in the Paragraph group, or click the **Bullets list arrow** in the Paragraph group, then click a **bulleted list style** in the gallery

Shortcut Method

☐ Select the **text** you want to be a bulleted list, or select the **text box** you want to contain a numbered list
☐ Right-click the **selection**, point to **Bullets** on the shortcut menu, then click a **bulleted list style** in the gallery

Create a Numbered List

Ribbon Method

☐ Click in the text box or placeholder where you want a new numbered list to appear
☐ Click the **Numbering button** in the Paragraph group on the Home tab, or click the **Numbering list arrow** in the Paragraph group, then click a **numbering style** in the gallery
☐ Type the first item in the numbered list, press **[Enter]**, then type the second item in the list, and so on until all desired numbered items have been created

Shortcut Method

☐ Click in the text box or placeholder where you want a new numbered list to appear
☐ Right-click the **selection**, point to **Numbering** on the shortcut menu, then click the desired **numbering style** in the gallery
☐ Type the text for the first item, press **[Enter]**, type the text for the second item, and so on until all desired numbered list items have been created

Convert Text to a Numbered List

Ribbon Method

☐ Select the text you want to be a numbered list, or select the text box you want to contain a numbered list
☐ Click the **Home tab** on the Ribbon, then click the **Numbering button** in the Paragraph group, or click the **Numbering list arrow**, then click a **numbering style** in the gallery

Shortcut Method

- ☐ Select the **text** you want to be a numbered list, or select the **text box** you want to contain a numbered list
- ☐ Right-click the selection, point to **Numbering** on the shortcut menu, then click a **numbering style** in the gallery

Format Bullets in a List

Ribbon Method

- ☐ Select the **text**, or select the **text box** or **placeholder** to format all the bullets in the list
- ☐ Click the **Home tab** on the Ribbon, click the **Bullets list arrow** ⫶☰ ▾ in the Paragraph group, then click **Bullets and Numbering**
- ☐ Click a **bullet style** on the Bulleted tab in the Bullets and Numbering dialog box to change the bullet style
- ☐ Adjust the value in the Size text box to change the bullet size
- ☐ Click the **Color button** 🖋 ▾, then click a **color** to change the bullet color
- ☐ Click the **Picture button**, select a **picture** in the Picture Bullet dialog box, then click **OK** to create a picture bullet
- ☐ Click **OK** in the Bullets and Numbering dialog box

Shortcut Method

- ☐ Select the **text**, or select the **text box** or **placeholder** to format all the bullets in the list
- ☐ Right-click the selection, point to **Bullets** on the shortcut menu, then click **Bullets and Numbering**
- ☐ Follow the steps in bullets 3–7 of the Format Bullets in a List Ribbon Method above

Format Numbered Lists

Ribbon Method

- ☐ Select the **text**, or select the **text box** or **placeholder** to format all the numbers in the list
- ☐ Click the **Home tab** on the Ribbon, click the **Numbering list arrow** ⫶☰ ▾ in the Paragraph group, then click **Bullets and Numbering**
- ☐ Click a **numbering style** on the Numbered tab in the Bullets and Numbering dialog box to change the numbering style
- ☐ Adjust the value in the Size text box to change the number size
- ☐ Click the **Color button** 🖋 ▾, then click a **color** to change the number color
- ☐ Click **OK**

Shortcut Method

- ☐ Select the **text**, or select the **text box** or **placeholder** to format all the numbers in the list
- ☐ Right-click the selection, point to **Numbering** on the shortcut menu, then click **Bullets and Numbering**
- ☐ Follow the steps from the third bullet above in the Ribbon Method

Promote and Demote Bullets and Numbering

Ribbon Method

- ☐ Select the appropriate item(s) in the bulleted or numbered list
- ☐ Click the **Home tab** on the Ribbon, then click the **Increase List Level button** 📧 in the Paragraph group to demote the list item(s)
- ☐ Click the **Decrease List Level button** 📧 in the Paragraph group to promote the list item(s)

Shortcut Method

- ☐ Select the appropriate item(s) in the bulleted or numbered list
- ☐ Press **[Tab]** to demote the list item(s)
- ☐ Press **[Shift][Tab]** to promote the list item(s)

    OR

- ☐ Select the appropriate **slide**
- ☐ In the Outline tab, select the appropriate list item(s), then right-click the selection
- ☐ Click **Promote** on the shortcut menu to promote the list item(s)
- ☐ Click **Demote** on the shortcut menu to demote the list item(s)

Align Paragraph Text Horizontally

- ☐ Select the **text**
- ☐ Use the appropriate button command or keyboard shortcut listed in Table PPT-6 to align the text as desired

Table PPT-6 Text Alignment Buttons and Keyboard Shortcuts

Alignment	Button (in Paragraph group on Home tab or on Mini Toolbar)	Keyboard shortcut
Left	📧	[Ctrl][L]
Center	📧	[Ctrl][E]
Right	📧	[Ctrl][R]
Justify	📧	

    OR

- ☐ Select the **text**
- ☐ Click the **Home tab** on the Ribbon, click the **Launcher** 🔲 in the Paragraph group
- ☐ In the General section of the Paragraph dialog box, click the **Alignment list arrow**, then click an **alignment option**
- ☐ Click **OK**

Change Line Spacing in Paragraphs

Ribbon Method

- ☐ Select the **text**
- ☐ Click the **Line Spacing button** 📧 in the Paragraph group on the Home tab, then click the line spacing you want **(1.0, 1.5, 2.0, 2.5, or 3.0)** on the list

PowerPoint

OR

- [ ] Select the **text**
- [ ] Click the **Line Spacing button** 🔲 in the Paragraph group on the Home tab, then click **Line Spacing Options**
- [ ] On the Indents and Spacing tab of the Paragraph dialog box, adjust the values in the Before text box and After text box as desired
- [ ] Click the **Line Spacing list arrow**, select the desired spacing option, then adjust the number in the **At text box** as necessary
- [ ] Click **OK**

Shortcut Method

- [ ] Select the **text**, right-click the **text**, then click **Paragraph** on the short-cut menu
- [ ] Follow the steps in bullets 3–5 of the second Change Line Spacing in Paragraphs Ribbon Method above

Change Indentation in Paragraphs

Ribbon Method

- [ ] Select the **text**
- [ ] Click the **View tab** on the Ribbon, then click the **Ruler check box** in the Show/Hide group to display the Ruler
- [ ] Drag the **indent markers** 🔲 on the Ruler to adjust the position of the text on the line

Shortcut Method

- [ ] Select the **text**
- [ ] Right-click the **text** in the text box, then click **Paragraph** on the short-cut menu
- [ ] In the Paragraph dialog box, click the **Before text arrows** in the Indentation section
- [ ] Click the **Special list arrow**, then select an option if desired
- [ ] Click **OK**

Insert WordArt

Ribbon Method

- [ ] Select the appropriate **slide**
- [ ] Click the **Insert tab** on the Ribbon, then click the **WordArt button** in the Text group
- [ ] In the WordArt gallery, click the appropriate **WordArt style**
- [ ] In the inserted WordArt text box, type the **text** you want to create as WordArt
- [ ] Drag the **WordArt object** to the appropriate location on the slide

Format WordArt Text

Ribbon Method

- [ ] Select the existing WordArt object
- [ ] Click a **WordArt style** in the WordArt Styles group on the Drawing Tools Format tab, or click the **Text Fill**, **Text Outline**, or **Text Effects button** in the WordArt Styles group and select an appropriate formatting style

PowerPoint

OR

☐ Select the existing WordArt object
☐ Click the **Launcher** 🖾 in the WordArt Styles group on the Drawing Tools Format tab
☐ Adjust the options as desired in the Text Fill, Text Outline, Outline Style, Shadow, 3-D Format, 3-D Rotation, and Text Box sections of the Format Text Effects dialog box
☐ Click **Close**

Shortcut Method

☐ Right-click the existing WordArt object, then click **Format Text Effects** on the shortcut menu
☐ Follow the steps in bullets 3–4 of the second Format WordArt Text Ribbon Method above

Apply Quick Styles to WordArt

Ribbon Method

☐ Select the existing WordArt object
☐ Click a **WordArt style** in the WordArt Styles group on the Drawing Tools Format tab, or click the **WordArt Style More button** 🖃, then select an appropriate Quick Style from the gallery

OR

☐ Select the existing WordArt object
☐ Click the **Home tab** on the Ribbon, click the **Quick Styles** button in the Drawing group, then select an appropriate Quick Style from the gallery

Change WordArt Shape

Ribbon Method

☐ Select the existing WordArt object
☐ Click a **Shape style** in the Shape Styles group on the Drawing Tools Format tab, or click the **Shape Styles More button** 🖃, then click an appropriate shape style in the gallery

OR

☐ Select the existing WordArt object
☐ Click the **Shape Fill button, Shape Outline button**, or **Shape Effects button** in the Drawing group on the Home tab or in the Shape Styles group on the Drawing Tools Format tab
☐ Select the desired shape fill, outline, and effects options to format the WordArt shape

Change WordArt Text Shape

Ribbon Method

☐ Select the existing WordArt object
☐ Click the **Text Effects button** in the WordArt Styles group on the Drawing Tools Format tab
☐ Point to **Transform**, then click an appropriate style from the Follow Path or Warp group

ADD AND LINK EXISTING CONTENT TO PRESENTATIONS

Reuse Slides from an Existing Presentation

Ribbon Method

- □ Select the appropriate **slide**
- □ Click the **New Slide button arrow** in the Slides group on the Home tab
- □ Click **Reuse Slides** to open up the Reuse Slides task pane
- □ Click the **Browse button** and open an existing presentation file or slide library, click the **Open a Slide Library link** and select a library, or click the link to any files in the Open list
- □ Click the **Keep source formatting check box** in the Reuse Slides task pane if you want to retain the formatting from the original presentation
- □ In the All slides list, click each **slide thumbnail** that you want to use in the existing presentation

Apply Current Slide Masters to Content

Ribbon Method

- □ Select the appropriate **slide** or **slides**
- □ Click the **Layout button** in the Slides group on the Home tab
- □ In the Layout gallery, scroll to the theme section for the slide master you want to apply
- □ Click the appropriate layout

Shortcut Method

- □ Select the appropriate **slide** or **slides**
- □ Right-click the **selected slides**, point to **Layout** on the shortcut menu, then click the layout that has the theme you want to apply

Copy Objects within Presentations

Ribbon Method

- □ Select the **object(s)** you want to copy
- □ Click the **Copy button** 🖺 in the Clipboard group on the Home tab
- □ Click the **slide** in which you want to paste the object(s)
- □ Click the **Paste button** in the Clipboard group on the Home tab

Shortcut Method

- □ Select the **object(s)** you want to copy
- □ Right-click the **selection**, then click **Copy** on the shortcut menu, or press **[Ctrl][C]** to copy the elements to the clipboard
- □ Click the **slide** in which you want to paste the object(s)
- □ Right-click the **slide**, then click **Paste** in the shortcut menu, or press **[Ctrl][V]** to paste the object(s)

PowerPoint

Copy Elements Between Presentations

Ribbon Method

- ☐ Open the presentation that has the slide(s) or object(s) you want to copy
- ☐ Select the **slides** or **object(s)** you want to copy
- ☐ Click the **Home tab** on the Ribbon, then click the **Copy button** 🗐 in the Clipboard group on the Home tab
- ☐ Open the presentation into which you want to copy the slide(s) or object(s)
- ☐ Click the location in the presentation where you want to paste the copied slide(s) or object(s)
- ☐ Click the **Paste button** in the Clipboard group on the Home tab

Shortcut Method

- ☐ Open the presentation that has the slide(s) or object(s) you want to copy
- ☐ Select the **slides** or **object(s)** you want to copy
- ☐ Right-click the selection, then click **Copy** on the shortcut menu, or press **[Ctrl][C]**
- ☐ Open the presentation into which you want to copy the slide(s) or object(s)
- ☐ Click the location in the presentation where you want to paste the copied slide(s) or object(s)
- ☐ Right-click the location, then click **Paste** in the shortcut menu, or press **[Ctrl][V]**

Insert Hyperlinks

Ribbon Method

- ☐ Select the **object** or **text** to which you want to apply the hyperlink
- ☐ Click the **Insert tab** on the Ribbon, then click the **Hyperlink button** in the Links group
- ☐ In the Insert Hyperlink dialog box, make the appropriate selections using Table PPT-7 as a reference, then click **OK**

Shortcut Method

- ☐ Select the **object** or **text** to which you want to apply the hyperlink
- ☐ Right-click the selection, then click **Hyperlink**, or press **[Ctrl][K]**
- ☐ In the Insert Hyperlink dialog box, make the appropriate selections using Table PPT-7 as a reference, then click **OK**

Table PPT-7 Inserting Hyperlinks Using the Insert Hyperlink Dialog Box

To link to	Do this
Another place in the document	Click **Place in Document**, select a location in the Select a place in this document list, then click **OK**
Another document	Click **Existing File or Web Page**, navigate to the appropriate drive and folder, click the filename in the list, then click **OK**
A new document	Click **Create New Document**, name the document, verify the drive and folder, choose to edit it now or later, then click **OK**
A Web page	Click **Existing File or Web Page**, click the **Address text box**, type the **URL**, then click **OK** (*Note:* Make sure you are connected to the Internet to successfully follow this link)
An e-mail address	Click **E-mail Address**, type the address and any other text to display, then click **OK**

Insert a Movie on a Slide

Ribbon Method

- ☐ Click the **Insert tab** on the Ribbon, click the **Movie button arrow** in the Media Clips group, then click **Movie from File**
- ☐ In the Insert Movie dialog box, navigate to the appropriate drive and folder, click the movie file you want, then click **OK**
- ☐ In the message box, click **Automatically** or **When Clicked** to determine how the movie will play
- ☐ Drag the **movie icon** to the appropriate location on the slide
- ☐ Click the **Movie Tools Options tab** on the Ribbon to set the Movie options, preview the movie, and change the size of the movie

  OR

- ☐ Click the **Insert tab** on the Ribbon, click the **Movie button arrow** in the Media Clips group, then click **Movie from Clip Organizer**
- ☐ In the Clip Art task pane, type an appropriate **keyword** in the Search for text box, click **Go**, then click the movie file you want
- ☐ Drag the **movie thumbnail** to the appropriate location on the slide

Insert a Sound on a Slide

Ribbon Method

- ☐ Click the **Insert tab** on the Ribbon, click the **Sound button arrow** in the Media Clips group, then click **Sound from File**
- ☐ In the Insert Sound dialog box, navigate to the appropriate drive and folder, click the sound file you want, then click **OK**
- ☐ In the message box, click **Automatically** or **When Clicked** to determine how the sound will play
- ☐ Drag the **sound icon** to the appropriate location on the slide

PowerPoint

OR

☐ Click the **Insert tab** on the Ribbon, click the **Sound button arrow** in the Media Clips group, then click **Sound from Clip Organizer**
☐ In the Clip Art task pane, type an appropriate **keyword** in the Search for text box, click **Go**, then click the sound file you want
☐ Drag the **sound icon** to the appropriate location on the slide

APPLY, CUSTOMIZE, MODIFY, AND REMOVE ANIMATIONS

Apply Built-in Animations to Text or an Object

Ribbon Method

☐ Select the **text** or **object** to be animated
☐ Click the **Animations tab** on the Ribbon, then click the **Animate list arrow** in the Animations group
☐ To animate text, click **All At Once** or **By 1st Level Paragraphs** under Fade, Wipe, or Fly In; to animate an object, click **Fade**, **Wipe**, or **Fly In**

Remove Animations from Text or an Object

Ribbon Method

☐ Select the **animated text** or **object**
☐ Click the **Animations tab** on the Ribbon, click the **Animate list arrow** in the Animations group, then click **No Animation**

OR

☐ Select the **animated text** or **object**
☐ Click the **Animations tab** on the Ribbon, then click the **Custom Animation button** in the Animations group
☐ In the Custom Animations task pane, click the **Remove button** to remove all of the animations from the text or object, or click the specific **animation(s)** to be removed, then click the **Remove button**

Change Existing Animations

Ribbon Method

☐ Select the **animated object** or **text**
☐ Click the **Animations tab** on the Ribbon, click the **Animate list arrow** in the Animations group, then click a different animation option

OR

☐ Select the **animated text** or **object**
☐ Click the **Animations tab** on the Ribbon, then click the **Custom Animation button** in the Animations group
☐ In the Custom Animation task pane, click the **animation** that you want to change
☐ Click the **Change button** in the task pane, then select the desired animation options

PowerPoint

Create Custom Animations

Ribbon Method
☐ Select the **object** or **text** to be animated
☐ Click the **Animations tab** on the Ribbon, then click the **Custom Animation button** in the Animations group
☐ In the Custom Animation task pane, click the **Add Effect button**, point to **Entrance**, **Emphasis**, **Exit**, or **Motion Paths** to open a menu of effects, then select one of the effects
☐ With the animation selected in the Custom Animation task pane, click the **list arrows** under the Modify line at the top of the task pane, then click the appropriate options to modify the animation
☐ Select an **animation**, then click the **Reorder buttons** near the bottom of the task pane to adjust the animation's place among the order of the animations on the slide

Insert Entrance Effects

Ribbon Method
☐ Select the **object** or **text** to be animated
☐ Click the **Animations tab** on the Ribbon, then click the **Custom Animation button** in the Animations group
☐ Click the **Add Effect button** in the Custom Animation task pane, point to **Entrance**, then click an effect

Insert Emphasis Effects

Ribbon Method
☐ Select the **object** or **text** to be animated
☐ Click the **Animations tab** on the Ribbon, then click the **Custom Animation button** in the Animations group
☐ Click the **Add Effect button** in the Custom Animation task pane, point to **Emphasis**, then click an effect

Insert Exit Effects

Ribbon Method
☐ Select the **object** or **text** to be animated
☐ Click the **Animations tab** on the Ribbon, then click the **Custom Animation button** in the Animations group
☐ Click the **Add Effect button** in the Custom Animation task pane, point to **Exit**, then click an effect

Change Effect Speeds

Ribbon Method
☐ Select the **animated object** or **text**
☐ Click the **Animations tab** on the Ribbon, then click the **Custom Animation button** in the Animations group
☐ If necessary, click the **animation effect** to change in the Custom Animation task pane
☐ Click the **Speed list arrow** in the Custom Animation task pane, then select a speed option

PowerPoint

OR

- [ ] Select the **animated object** or **text**
- [ ] Click the **Animations tab** on the Ribbon, then click the **Custom Animation button** in the Animations group
- [ ] If necessary, click the **animation effect** to change in the Custom Animation task pane
- [ ] Right-click the **animation effect** or click the **animation effect arrow**, then click **Effect Options**
- [ ] Click the **Timing tab** in the effect dialog box, click the **Speed list arrow**, then click a **speed**
- [ ] Click **OK**

Change Start Settings

Ribbon Method

- [ ] Select the **animated object** or **text**
- [ ] Click the **Animations tab** on the Ribbon, then click the **Custom Animation button**
- [ ] If necessary, click the **animation effect** to change in the Custom Animation task pane
- [ ] Click the **Start list arrow** in the Custom Animation task pane, then select a **Start option**

OR

- [ ] Select the **animated object** or **text**
- [ ] Click the **Animations tab** on the Ribbon, then click the **Custom Animation button**
- [ ] If necessary, click the **animation effect** to change in the Custom Animation task pane
- [ ] Right-click the **animation effect** or click the **animation effect arrow**, then click a **Start option** on the menu

POWERPOINT OBJECTIVE 3: WORKING WITH VISUAL CONTENT

CREATE SMARTART GRAPHICS

Insert a SmartArt Graphic on a Slide

Ribbon Method

☐ Click the **Insert tab** on the Ribbon, then click the **SmartArt Graphic button** in the Illustrations group
☐ In the Choose a SmartArt Graphic dialog box, click the appropriate **SmartArt category** in the left pane, click the desired **SmartArt graphic** in the center pane, then click **OK**
☐ Enter and modify the text and format of the graphic as desired
OR
☐ Select the appropriate **slide** containing a content placeholder
☐ Click the **Insert SmartArt Graphic button** 🖼 on the content placeholder
☐ Follow the steps in bullets 2–3 above

Create SmartArt Graphic Diagrams from Bullet Points

Ribbon Method

☐ Select the **bulleted text**
☐ Click the **Home tab** on the Ribbon, then click the **Convert to SmartArt button** 🖼 in the Paragraph group
☐ Click a **SmartArt graphic** in the gallery

Shortcut Method

☐ Select the **bulleted text**
☐ Right-click the **selected bulleted text**, then point to **Convert to SmartArt** on the shortcut menu to open the SmartArt gallery
☐ Click a **SmartArt graphic** in the gallery

MODIFY SMARTART DIAGRAMS

Add Text to SmartArt Diagrams

Ribbon Method

☐ Select the **SmartArt graphic**
☐ Click each **Text placeholder**, then type the **text**
OR
☐ Select the **SmartArt Graphic**
☐ Click the **SmartArt Tools Design tab** on the Ribbon, then click the **Text Pane button** in the Create Graphic group, or click the **Text Pane Control button** on the left side of the SmartArt Graphic selection box

□ In the Text Pane, type text in the appropriate locations, then press **[Enter]** to insert a new bullet if desired

Shortcut Method

□ Right-click the **SmartArt graphic** on the slide, then click **Show Text Pane** on the shortcut menu
□ In the Text Pane, type text in the appropriate locations, then press **[Enter]** to insert a new bullet if desired

Change Theme Colors in SmartArt Diagrams

Ribbon Method

□ Select the **SmartArt graphic**
□ Click the **SmartArt Tools Design tab** on the Ribbon, click the **Change Colors button** in the SmartArt Styles group, then click a set of theme colors in the gallery

Add Effects Using Quick Styles to SmartArt Graphics

Ribbon Method

□ Select the **SmartArt Graphic**
□ Click the **SmartArt Tools Design tab** on the Ribbon, then click a **Quick Style** in the SmartArt Styles group or click the **SmartArt Styles More button** ⬇, then click a **Quick Style** in the gallery

OR

□ Select the **SmartArt graphic**, then select a **shape** or **shapes** in the graphic
□ Click the **SmartArt Tools Format tab** on the Ribbon, then click a **Quick Style** in the Shape Styles group or click the **Shape Styles More button**, then click a **Quick Style** in the gallery

OR

□ Select the **SmartArt Graphic**, a **shape** or **shapes** within the graphic, or **text** within the graphic
□ Click the **SmartArt Tools Format tab** on the Ribbon, then click a **Quick Style** in the WordArt Styles group or click the **WordArt Styles More button**, then click a **Quick Style** in the gallery

Change the Layout of SmartArt Graphics

Ribbon Method

□ Select the **SmartArt graphic**
□ Click the **SmartArt Tools Design tab**, then click a **Quick Style** in the Layouts group or click the **Layouts More button** ⬇, then click a new **layout** in the gallery

Shortcut Method

□ Right-click the **SmartArt Graphic**
□ Click **Change Layout** on the shortcut menu
□ In the Choose a SmartArt Graphic dialog box, click the desired new **layout** in the center pane, then click **OK**

Change the Orientation of Shapes or Objects in SmartArt Graphics

Ribbon Method

□ Select the **SmartArt Graphic**
□ Click the shape or object in the SmartArt graphic, then drag the **rotation handle** on the object

OR

□ Select the **SmartArt Graphic**
□ Click the **SmartArt Tools Format tab** on the Ribbon, click the **Shape Effects button** in the Shape Styles group, point to **3-D Rotation**, then click the **desired rotation** in the gallery

OR

□ Select the **SmartArt Graphic**
□ Click **SmartArt Tools Format tab** on the Ribbon, click the **Change Shape button** in the Shapes group, then select a new shape with a different orientation

Add Shapes to a SmartArt Graphic

Ribbon Method

□ Select the **SmartArt Graphic**
□ Click the **SmartArt Tools Design tab** on the Ribbon, then click a **shape or object** in the SmartArt Graphic
□ Click the **Add Shape button** in the Create Graphic group on the Ribbon, or click the **Add Shape button arrow**, then click **Add Shape After**, **Add Shape Before**, **Add Shape Above**, **Add Shape Below**, or **Add Assistant** according to the type of SmartArt graphic and desired location for the new shape

Shortcut Method

□ Right-click the **SmartArt Graphic shape** on the slide, then point to **Add Shape**
□ Click **Add Shape After**, **Add Shape Before**, **Add Shape Above**, **Add Shape Below**, or **Add Assistant** according to the type of SmartArt graphic and desired location for the new shape

Remove Shapes from a SmartArt Graphic

Ribbon Method

□ Select the **SmartArt graphic**
□ Click the **Text Pane button** in the Create Graphic group on the Ribbon or click the **Text Pane Control button** on the SmartArt graphic
□ Select the text in the Text Pane that you want to delete, then press **[Delete]** twice

Shortcut Method

□ Select the **SmartArt Graphic**
□ Select the **shape** that you want to delete, then press **[Delete]**

PowerPoint

Change SmartArt Graphic Type

Ribbon Method

- [ ] Select the **SmartArt graphic**
- [ ] Click the **SmartArt Tools Design tab**
- [ ] Click the **Layouts More button** 📄 in the Layouts group, then click **More Layouts**
- [ ] In the Choose a SmartArt Graphic dialog box, click a **SmartArt category** in the left pane, click the desired new **layout** in the center pane, then click **OK**

Shortcut Method

- [ ] Right-click the **SmartArt graphic** on the slide
- [ ] Click **Change Layout** on the shortcut menu
- [ ] In the Choose a SmartArt Graphic dialog box, click a **SmartArt category** in the left pane, click the desired new **layout** in the center pane, then click **OK**

INSERT ILLUSTRATIONS, PICTURES, AND SHAPES

Insert Pictures from a File

Ribbon Method

- [ ] Click the **Insert tab** on the Ribbon, then click the **Picture button** in the Illustrations group
- [ ] Locate and then click the **graphic file** in the Insert Picture dialog box
- [ ] Click **Insert**

Shortcut Method

- [ ] Select the appropriate **slide** containing a content placeholder
- [ ] Click the **Insert Picture from File button** 🖼 on the content placeholder
- [ ] Locate and then click the **graphic file** in the Insert Picture dialog box
- [ ] Click **Insert**

Insert Clip Art

Ribbon Method

- [ ] Click the **Insert tab** on the Ribbon
- [ ] Click the **Clip Art button** in the Illustrations group
- [ ] In the Clip Art task pane, type a **keyword** in the Search for text box, click the **Results should be list arrow**, click the **Clip Art check box** to insert a check mark, click **Go**, then click the **clip art** you want

Shortcut Method

- [ ] Select the appropriate **slide** containing a content placeholder
- [ ] Click the **Clip Art button** 🖼 in the content placeholder
- [ ] In the Clip Art task pane, type a **keyword** in the Search for text box, click the **Results should be list arrow**, click the **Clip Art check box** to insert a check mark, click **Go**, then click the **clip art** you want

Insert a Drawn Shape

Ribbon Method

☐ Click a **Shape** in the Shapes gallery in the Drawing group on the Home tab, or click the **Shapes button** in the Drawing group on the Home tab on the Ribbon, then click a **shape** in the gallery

☐ Position ✛ where you want the shape to appear, then drag to create the shape and release the mouse button, or click to insert the shape in the default size

Add Text to Shapes

Ribbon Method

☐ Click the **shape** on the slide, then begin typing

OR

☐ Click a **Shape** in the Shapes gallery in the Drawing group on the Home tab, or click the **Shapes button** in the Drawing group on the Home tab on the Ribbon, then click a **shape** in the gallery

☐ Position ✛ where you want the shape to appear, then drag to create the shape and release the mouse button, or click to insert the shape in the default size

☐ Type the **text**

OR

☐ Click the **Insert tab** on the Ribbon, click the **Shapes button** in the Illustrations group, then click a **shape** in the gallery

☐ Position ✛ where you want the shape to appear, then drag to create the shape or click to insert the shape in the default size

☐ Type the **text**

MODIFY ILLUSTRATIONS, PICTURES, AND SHAPES

Apply Quick Styles to Shapes and Pictures

Ribbon Method

☐ Select the **shape** or **picture**
☐ Click the **Drawing Tools Format tab** on the Ribbon
☐ Click a **shape style** in the Shape Styles group, or click the **Shape Styles More button** ▼ in the Shape Styles group, then click a **shape style** in the gallery

OR

☐ Select the **shape** or **picture** on the slide
☐ Click the **Home tab** on the Ribbon, then click the **Quick Styles button** in the Drawing group
☐ Click a **style** from the gallery

PowerPoint

Apply Fills to Shapes or Illustrations

Ribbon Method

☐ Select the **shape** or **illustration**
☐ Click the **Shape Fill button arrow** in the Shape Styles group on the Drawing Tools Format tab or in the Drawing group on the Home tab
☐ Click a **color** in the Theme Colors, Standard Colors, or Recent Colors group, or click any one of the Picture, Gradient, or Texture options to format the shape fill

OR

☐ Select the **shape** or **picture**
☐ Click the **Home tab** on the Ribbon, then click the **Quick Styles button** in the Drawing group
☐ Click a **style** from the gallery

Shortcut Method

☐ Select the **shape** or **picture**
☐ Right-click the **shape** or **picture**, then click the **Fill Color list arrow** 🎨▾ on the Mini Toolbar
☐ Click a **color** in the Theme Colors, Standard Colors, or Recent Colors group, or click any one of the Picture, Gradient, or Texture options to format the shape fill

Remove Borders from Shapes

Ribbon Method

☐ Select the **shape**
☐ Click the **Shape Outline button arrow** in the Shape Styles group on the Drawing Tools Format tab or in the Drawing group on the **Home tab**
☐ Click **No Outline** in the palette

Shortcut Method

☐ Right-click the **shape**, then click the **Outline Color list arrow** ✏️▾ on the Mini Toolbar to open the palette
☐ Click **No Outline**

Recolor Pictures

Ribbon Method

☐ Select the **picture**
☐ Click the **Picture Tools Format tab** on the Ribbon, then click the **Recolor button** in the Adjust group
☐ Click a **color mode** or **variation** (Dark and Light)

OR

☐ Select the **picture**
☐ Click the **Picture Tools Format tab** on the Ribbon, then click the **Launcher** 🔲 in the Shape Styles group
☐ In the Format Picture dialog box, click **Picture** in the left pane, then click a **color mode** or **variation** (Dark and Light)

Remove Backgrounds from Pictures by Setting a Transparent Color

Ribbon Method

☐ Select the **picture**
☐ Click the **Picture Tools Format tab** on the Ribbon, then click the **Recolor button** in the Adjust group
☐ Click **Set Transparent Color**, then click the **Set Transparent Color pointer** 🖑 on the color in the picture you want to be transparent

Modify the Brightness and Contrast of an Illustration or Picture

Ribbon Method

☐ Select the **illustration** or **picture**
☐ Click the **Picture Tools Format tab** on the Ribbon, then click the **Contrast button** in the Adjust group
☐ Select a **percentage** from the gallery (+40% to -40%), or click **Picture Correction Options**, then drag the **Brightness** and **Contrast sliders** in the Picture section of the Format Picture dialog box as desired to adjust the picture

Shortcut Method

☐ Right-click the **picture** on the slide, then click **Format Picture**
☐ Drag the **Brightness** and **Contrast sliders** in the Picture section of the Format Picture dialog box as desired to adjust the picture

---

ARRANGE, ORDER, AND ROTATE ILLUSTRATIONS AND OTHER OBJECTS

Adjust the Size of an Illustration, Picture, or Other Object

Ribbon Method

☐ Select the **illustration**, **picture**, or **object**
☐ Click the **Picture Tools Format tab** or the **Drawing Tools Format tab** on the Ribbon
☐ Click the **Shape Width text box** in the Size group and type a number, or click the up and down arrows to adjust the width
☐ Click the **Shape Height text box** in the Size group and type a number, or click the up and down arrows to adjust the height

OR

☐ Select the **illustration**, **picture**, or **object**
☐ Click the **Picture Tools Format tab** or the **Drawing Tools Format tab** on the Ribbon, click the **Launcher** 🔲 in the Size group
☐ Adjust the **settings** in the Size and Position dialog box to the desired size
☐ Click **Close**

PowerPoint

Shortcut Method

☐ Select the **illustration**, **picture**, or **object**
☐ Drag the **sizing handles** to resize the illustration, picture, or object

Adjust the Scale of an Illustration, Picture, or Other Object

Ribbon Method

☐ Select the **illustration**, **picture**, or **object**
☐ Click the **Picture Tools Format tab** or the **Drawing Tools Format tab** on the Ribbon
☐ Click the **Launcher** 🖼 in the Size group
☐ In the Size and Position dialog box, click the **Lock aspect ratio check box** if you want the illustration, picture, or object to maintain aspect ratio when changing size
☐ Adjust the **settings** for Height and Width in the Scale section of the Size and Position dialog box to set the scale as desired
☐ Click **Close**

Shortcut Method

☐ Select the **illustration**, **picture**, or **object**
☐ Drag the **sizing handles** to rescale the illustration, picture, or object
OR
☐ Right-click the **illustration**, **picture**, or **object**, then click **Size and Position**
☐ Click the **Lock aspect ratio check box** in the Size and Position dialog box if you want the illustration, picture, or object to maintain aspect ratio when changing size
☐ Click **Close**
☐ Drag the **sizing handles** to scale the illustration, picture, or object

Adjust Rotation for an Illustration, Picture, or Other Object

Ribbon Method

☐ Select the **illustration**, **picture**, or **object**
☐ Click the **Picture Tools Format tab** or the **Drawing Tools Format tab** on the Ribbon
☐ Click the **Rotate button** in the Arrange group, then click **Rotate Right 90°**, **Rotate Left 90°**, **Flip Horizontal**, or **Flip Vertical**, or click **More Rotation Options** and adjust the value in the Rotation text box, then click **Close**

Shortcut Method

☐ Select the **illustration**, **picture**, or **object**
☐ Drag the green **rotation handle** to rotate the illustration, picture, or object

Change the Order (Bring to Front and Send to Back) for Illustrations and Other Objects

Ribbon Method

- [ ] Select a **slide** that has at least two objects
- [ ] Select the **illustration**, **picture**, or **object** that you want to reorder
- [ ] Click the **Picture Tools Format tab** or the **Drawing Tools Format tab** on the Ribbon
- [ ] Click the **Bring to Front button** in the Arrange group or click the **Send to Back button** in the Arrange group; or, if there are more than two objects on the slide, click the **Bring to Front list arrow** and click **Bring to Front** or **Bring Forward**, or click the **Send to Back list arrow**, then click **Send to Back** or **Send Backward**

Shortcut Method

- [ ] Select a **slide** that has at least two objects
- [ ] Right-click the **illustration**, **picture**, or **object** that you want to reorder
- [ ] Point to **Bring to Front**, then click **Bring to Front** or **Bring Forward**; or point to **Send to Back**, then click **Send to Back** or **Send Backward**

Group Objects

Ribbon Method

- [ ] Press and hold **[Ctrl]**, then click the **illustrations**, **pictures**, or **objects** to be grouped
- [ ] Click the **Picture Tools Format tab** or the **Drawing Tools Format tab** on the Ribbon
- [ ] Click the **Group button** in the Arrange group, then click **Group**

Shortcut Method

- [ ] Press and hold **[Ctrl]**, then click the **illustrations**, **pictures**, or **objects** to be grouped
- [ ] Right-click the **selection**
- [ ] Point to **Group**, then click **Group**

Ungroup Objects

Ribbon Method

- [ ] Select the **grouped object**
- [ ] Click the **Picture Tools Format tab** or the **Drawing Tools Format tab** on the Ribbon
- [ ] Click the **Group button** in the Arrange group, then click **Ungroup**

Shortcut Method

- [ ] Select the **grouped object**
- [ ] Right-click the **selection**, point to **Group**, then click **Ungroup**

PowerPoint

Align Objects

Ribbon Method

- ☐ Press and hold **[Ctrl]**, then select the **illustrations**, **pictures**, or **objects** to be aligned
- ☐ Click the **Picture Tools Format tab** or the **Drawing Tools Format tab** on the Ribbon
- ☐ Click the **Align button** in the Arrange group
- ☐ Click the desired option: **Align Left**, **Align Center**, **Align Right**, **Align Top**, **Align Middle**, **Align Bottom**, **Distribute Horizontally**, or **Distribute Vertically**

Use Gridlines and Guides to Arrange Objects

Ribbon Method

- ☐ Press and hold **[Ctrl]**, then click the **illustrations**, **pictures**, or **objects** to be arranged
- ☐ Click the **Picture Tools Format tab** or the **Drawing Tools Format tab** on the Ribbon
- ☐ Click the **Align button** in the Arrange group, then click **View Gridlines**, or click the **View tab** on the Ribbon, then click the **Gridlines check box** in the Show/Hide group
- ☐ Drag the **selection** using the gridlines as desired

  OR

- ☐ Press and hold **[Ctrl]**, then click the **illustrations**, **pictures**, or **objects** to be arranged
- ☐ Click the **Picture Tools Format tab** or the **Drawing Tools Format tab** on the Ribbon
- ☐ Click the **Align button** in the Arrange group, then click **Grid Settings** to open the Grid and Guides dialog box
- ☐ In the Grids and Guides dialog box, click the **Display grid on screen check box**
- ☐ Click the **Display drawing guides on screen check box**
- ☐ Click the **Snap objects to other objects check box** if desired
- ☐ Click **OK**
- ☐ Drag the **selection** using the grid, guides, and snap to feature as needed

Shortcut Method

- ☐ Press and hold **[Ctrl]**, then click the **illustrations**, **pictures**, or **objects** to be arranged
- ☐ Right-click any blank area of any slide, then click **Grids and Guides** to open the Grids and Guides dialog box
- ☐ Follow the steps in bullets 4–8 of the second Use Gridlines and Guides to Arrange Objects Ribbon Method above

  OR

- ☐ Press and hold **[Ctrl]**, then click the **illustrations**, **pictures**, or **objects** to be arranged
- ☐ Press **[Shift][F9]** to show or hide the grid
- ☐ Press **[Alt][F9]** to show or hide the drawing guide
- ☐ Drag the **selection** using the gridlines and guides as desired

INSERT AND MODIFY CHARTS

Insert a Chart on a Slide

Ribbon Method

☐ Click the **Insert tab** on the Ribbon, then click the **Chart button** in the Illustrations group
☐ In the left pane of the Insert Chart dialog box, click the **chart type**, click the **thumbnail** for the desired chart in the center pane, then click **OK**
☐ The screen splits into two windows: A PowerPoint window on the left with the sample chart on the slide, and an Excel window on the right with sample data in the worksheet
☐ Replace the sample data in the Excel worksheet with the labels and values for your chart
☐ Close the Chart in the Microsoft Office Excel window

Shortcut Method

☐ Select the appropriate **slide** containing a content placeholder
☐ Click the **Insert Chart button** 📊 in the content placeholder
☐ Follow the instructions in bullets 2–5 in the Insert a Chart on a Slide Ribbon Method above

Change the Chart Type

Ribbon Method

☐ Select the **chart**
☐ Click the **Chart Tools Design tab** on the Ribbon, then click the **Change Chart Type button** in the Type group
☐ In the left pane of the Change Chart Type dialog box, click the new **chart type**, click the **thumbnail** for the new chart in the center pane, then click **OK**

Shortcut Method

☐ Right-click the **chart**
☐ Click **Change Chart Type** in the shortcut menu
☐ In the left pane of the Change Chart Type dialog box, click the new **chart type**, click the **thumbnail** for the new chart type in the center pane, then click **OK**

Format Fill and Other Chart Effects

Ribbon Method

☐ Select the **chart**
☐ Click the **Chart Tools Design tab** on the Ribbon, then click a **Chart Style button** in the Chart Styles group to apply a Quick Style
OR
☐ Select the **chart**
☐ Click the **Chart Tools Format tab** on the Ribbon, then click the desired formatting buttons in the Chart Styles group and/or the WordArt Styles group to apply formatting to the chart elements

OR

☐ Select the **chart**

☐ Click the series or feature you want to format, click the **Home tab** on the Ribbon, then click the **Shape Fill**, **Shape Outline**, **Shape Effects**, or **Quick Styles** buttons as needed to format the chart

Shortcut Method

☐ Right-click the **chart feature** on the slide

☐ Click **Format Legend**, **Format Data Series**, **Format Axis**, or **Format Gridlines** (depending on what feature you want to format) in the shortcut menu to open the Format dialog box for that feature

☐ In the left pane of the dialog box, click the **format** you want to apply, adjust the options as desired in appropriate sections of the dialog box, then click **OK**

Add a Chart Legend

Ribbon Method

☐ Select the **chart**

☐ Click the **Chart Tools Layout tab** on the Ribbon, then click the **Legend button** in the Labels group

☐ Click a **legend style** from the gallery, or click **More Legend Options** to open the Format Legend dialog box and create a custom legend for the chart

Add a Chart Title

Ribbon Method

☐ Select the **chart**

☐ Click the **Chart Tools Layout tab** on the Ribbon, then click the **Chart Title button** in the Labels group

☐ Click a **chart title style** from the gallery, or click **More Title Options** to open the Format Chart Title dialog box and create a custom title for the chart

INSERT AND MODIFY TABLES

Insert a Table in a Slide

Ribbon Method

☐ Click the **Insert tab** on the Ribbon, then click the **Table button** in the Tables group

☐ Drag in the grid to create the desired number of columns and rows for the table

OR

☐ Click the **Insert tab** on the Ribbon, click the **Table button** in the Tables group, then click **Insert Table**

☐ In the Insert Table dialog box, adjust the values in the Number of columns text box and the Number of rows text box to create the desired table, then click **OK**

PowerPoint

OR
- ☐ Click the **Insert tab** on the Ribbon, click the **Table button** in Tables group, then click **Draw Table**
- ☐ Drag ✐ on the slide to draw the lines for the columns and rows in the table

Shortcut Method
- ☐ Select the appropriate **slide** containing a content placeholder
- ☐ Click the **Insert Table button** ▦ in the content placeholder
- ☐ In the Insert Table dialog box, adjust the values in the Number of columns text box and the Number of rows text box to create the desired table, then click **OK**

Apply Quick Styles to a Table

Ribbon Method
- ☐ Select the **table**
- ☐ Click the **Table Tools Design tab** on the Ribbon
- ☐ Click the **Table Styles More button** in the Table Styles group, then click a **Quick Style** in the gallery, or click the **Quick Styles button** in the WordArt Styles group, then click a **style** from the gallery to format the table text

Change Alignment and Orientation of Table Text

Ribbon Method
- ☐ Select the **table**
- ☐ Click the **Table Tools Layout tab** on the Ribbon, then click the appropriate alignment button in the Alignment group to change the alignment
- ☐ Click the **Text direction button** in the Alignment group, then click an option from the menu to change the text orientation; or click **More Options** to open the Format Text Effects dialog box and change the Text box layout and features

Add Images to Tables

Ribbon Method
- ☐ Select the **table**
- ☐ Click the **Table Tools Design tab** on the Ribbon, then click the **Shading button** in the Table Styles group
- ☐ Click **Picture** to open the Insert Picture dialog box, navigate to and click the **picture file**, then click **Insert**

PowerPoint

POWERPOINT OBJECTIVE 4: COLLABORATING ON AND DELIVERING PRESENTATIONS

REVIEW PRESENTATIONS

Insert a Comment

Ribbon Method

☐ Select the appropriate **slide** or **object** to which the comment applies
☐ Click the **Review tab** on the Ribbon, click the **New Comment button** in the Comments group, then type in the comment balloon that opens

Shortcut Method

☐ Right-click an existing **comment thumbnail**, then click **Insert Comment** on the shortcut menu
☐ Type in the comment balloon that opens

Review Comments

Ribbon Method

☐ If the comments are not visible, click the **Review tab** on the Ribbon, then click the **Show Markup button** in the Comments group
☐ Click the **Next** and **Previous buttons** in the Comments group as needed, then click each **comment thumbnail** on the slides to review the comments

Modify a Comment

Ribbon Method

☐ Select a **comment thumbnail**
☐ Click the **Review tab** on the Ribbon, then click **Edit Comment** in the Comments group to open the comment for editing
☐ Use standard text editing techniques to modify the comment

Shortcut Method

☐ Right-click a **comment thumbnail**, then click **Edit Comment** on the shortcut menu to open the comment for editing
☐ Use standard text editing techniques to modify the comment

Delete a Comment

Ribbon Method

☐ Select a **comment thumbnail**
☐ Click the **Review tab** on the Ribbon, then click the **Delete Comment button** in the Comments group
OR
☐ Click the **Review tab** on the Ribbon, click the **Delete Comment arrow** in the Comments group, then click **Delete All Markup on the Current Slide** or **Delete All Markup in this Presentation** to delete the desired comments

PowerPoint

Shortcut Method
☐ Right-click the **comment thumbnail**, then click **Delete Comment** on the shortcut menu to delete the current comment

Show and Hide Markup

Ribbon Method
☐ Click the **Review tab** on the Ribbon, then click the **Show Markup button** to show comments, or to hide comments if they are showing

PROTECT PRESENTATIONS

Add a Digital Signature to Presentations

Ribbon Method
☐ Click the **Office button** , point to **Prepare**, then click **Add a Digital Signature**
☐ Type the reason in the Purpose for signing this document section in the **Sign text box**, then click **Sign**

Set Passwords on Presentations

Ribbon Method
☐ Click the **Office button** , point to **Prepare**, then click **Encrypt Document**
☐ In the Encrypt Document dialog box, type a case-sensitive **password** in the Password text box (Warning: you must remember your password exactly in order to be able to access the presentation again once it is password-protected)
☐ Click **OK**
☐ Reenter the case-sensitive **password** in the Reenter password text box in the Confirm Password dialog box
☐ Click **OK**

SECURE AND SHARE PRESENTATIONS

Identify Presentation Features Not Supported by Previous Versions

Ribbon Method
☐ Click the **Office button** , point to **Prepare**, then click **Run Compatibility Checker**
☐ In the Microsoft Office PowerPoint Compatibility Checker dialog box read any notes in the Summary section, review the number of occurrences, click **Help** as needed, then click **OK**

PowerPoint

Remove Inappropriate Information Using Document Inspector

Ribbon Method

- [ ] Click the **Office button** 🔘, point to **Prepare**, then click **Inspect Document**
- [ ] Click **Yes** to save the presentation if there are changes that have not been saved
- [ ] In the Document Inspector dialog box, click the **check boxes** as desired to check for the following information: Comments and Annotations, Document Properties and Personal Information, Custom XML data, Invisible On-Slide Content, Off-Slide Content, and Presentation Notes
- [ ] Click **Inspect**
- [ ] Review the results in the Document Inspector dialog box, click **Remove** or **Remove All** as desired to remove any unwanted information
- [ ] Click **Reinspect**, then click **Inspect** to verify that the information has been removed
- [ ] When all the inspection results meet your approval, click **Close**

Restrict Permissions to a Document Using Information Rights Management (IRM)

Note: To complete IRM on your computer. You must have the Windows Rights Management Services Client Software installed. You must connect to the server and download the license and permissions.

Ribbon Method

- [ ] Click the **Office button** 🔘, point to **Prepare**, point to **Restrict Permission**, then click **Do Not Distribute**
- [ ] Click **Restrict permission to this document check box**, then assign the desired levels (**Read**, **Change**, and **Full Control**) to each user
- [ ] Change the **options** in the dialog box as desired, then click **OK**

Mark Presentations as Final

- [ ] Click the **Office button** 🔘, point to **Prepare**, then click **Mark as Final**
- [ ] Click **OK**, then click **OK**

Compress Images

Ribbon Method

- [ ] Click the **picture** that you want to compress, click the **Picture Tools Format tab**, then click the **Compress Pictures button** in the Adjust group
- [ ] Click the **Apply to selected pictures only check box** to compress only the selected picture, or click **Options**, then click the **Automatically perform basic compression on save check box** in the Compression options section of the Compression Settings dialog box

Save Presentations as Appropriate File Types

Ribbon Method

- □ Click the **Office button** 🏵, point to **Save As**, then click **Other Formats**
- □ Click the **Save as type list arrow** in the Save As dialog box, then click the appropriate file type
- □ Locate the drive and folder, name the file, then click **Save**

Save Files in .PPSX Format So They Open as a Slide Show

Ribbon Method

- □ Click the **Office button** 🏵, point to **Save As**, then click **PowerPoint Show** to open the Save As dialog box with PowerPoint Show (*.ppsx) selected
- □ Click **Save**

Save Presentations for Web Viewing (HTML Format)

Ribbon Method

- □ Click the **Office button** 🏵, point to **Save As**, then click **Other Formats** to open the Save As dialog box
- □ Click the **Save as type list arrow**, then click **Web Page** or **Single File Web Page**
- □ Click **Change Title**, then type a title for the Web page to help identify the Web site, if desired
- □ Click **Publish** to open the Publish as Web page dialog box
- □ Select the **slides** to publish in the Publish what? section, then change the other **options** for the Web page in the dialog box as desired
- □ Click **OK**, then click **Publish**

Save Slides as Graphic Images

Ribbon Method

- □ Click the **Office button** 🏵, point to **Save As**, then click **Other Formats**
- □ Click the **Save as type list arrow** in the Save As dialog box, then click the graphic file format you want
- □ Click **Save**
- □ In the Message box, click **Every Slide** to save each slide in the presentation as a graphic file, or click **Current Slide Only** to save only the selected slide as a graphic file

PREPARE PRINTED MATERIALS

Add Headers, Footers, and Page Numbers to Handout Masters

Ribbon Method

☐ Click the **View tab** on the Ribbon, then click the **Handout Master button** in the Presentation Views group to open Handout Master view

☐ Verify that check marks are in the **Header**, **Footer**, and **Page Number check boxes** in the Placeholders group on the Handout Master tab on the Ribbon

☐ Click the **Header placeholder** on the handout master, then type the desired text

☐ Click the **Footer placeholder** on the handout master, then type the desired text

☐ Click the **Close Master View button** in the Close group

OR

☐ Click the **View tab** on the Ribbon, then click the **Handout Master button** in the Presentation Views group to open the Handout Master view

☐ Click the **Insert tab** on the Ribbon, then click the **Header & Footer button** in the Text group to open the Header and Footer dialog box while in Handout Master view

☐ Click the **Header check box**, then type a header in the **Header here text box**

☐ Click the **Page number check box** to insert a check mark

☐ Click the **Footer check box**, then type a footer in the **Footer here text box**

☐ Click **Apply to All**

☐ Click the **Handout Master tab** on the Ribbon, then click the **Close Master View button** in the Close group

OR

☐ Click the **Insert tab** on the Ribbon, then click the **Header & Footer button** in the Text group

☐ Click the **Notes and Handouts tab** in the Header and Footer dialog box

☐ Follow the steps in bullets 3-7 in the second Add Headers, Footers, and Page Numbers to Handout Masters Ribbon Method above

Apply Quick Styles to Handout Masters

Ribbon Method

☐ Click the **View tab** on the Ribbon, then click the **Handout Master button** in the Presentation Views group to open Handout Master view

☐ Click an **object** on the handout master to which you want to apply the Quick Style

☐ Click the **Picture Tools Format tab** or click the **Drawing Tools Format Tab** on the Ribbon, then click a **Quick Style**, or click the **More button** to open a style gallery and click a **Quick Style** in the gallery

☐ Click the **Handout Master tab** on the Ribbon, then click the **Close Master View button** in the Close group

PowerPoint

Print a Presentation as Slides

Ribbon Method

☐ Click the **Office button** , point to **Print**, then click **Print**
☐ In the Print dialog box, click the **Print what list arrow**, then click **Slides**
☐ Specify other options in the dialog box as desired
☐ Click **Preview**, specify any additional **options** on the Print Preview tab, then click **Print** in the Print group
☐ Click **OK**

Shortcut Method

☐ Press **[Ctrl][P]**
☐ Follow the steps in bullets 2–5 in the Print a Presentation as Slides Ribbon Method above

Print a Presentation as Handouts

Ribbon Method

☐ Click the **Office button** , point to **Print**, then click **Print**
☐ In the Print dialog box, click the **Print what list arrow**, click **Handouts**, click the **Slides per page list arrow** in the Handouts area, then click the appropriate **number of handouts**
☐ Specify other options in the dialog box as desired
☐ Click **Preview**, specify other options as desired on the Print Preview tab, then click **Print** in the Print group
☐ Click **OK**

Shortcut Method

☐ Press **[Ctrl][P]**
☐ Follow the steps in bullets 2–5 in the Print a Presentation as Handouts Ribbon Method above

Print a Presentation as Outlines

Ribbon Method

☐ Click the **Office button** , point to **Print**, then click **Print**
☐ In the Print dialog box, click the **Print what list arrow**, click **Outline View**, then specify other options in the dialog box as desired
☐ Click **Preview**, specify other options as desired on the Print Preview tab, then click **Print** in the Print group
☐ Click **OK**

Shortcut Method

☐ Press **[Ctrl][P]**
☐ Follow the steps in bullets 2–4 in the Print a Presentation as Outlines Ribbon Method above

Print Presentation Notes

Ribbon Method

☐ Click the **Office button** , point to **Print**, then click **Print**
☐ In the Print dialog box, click the **Print what list arrow**, click **Notes Pages**, then specify other options in the dialog box as desired

☐ Click **Preview**, specify other options as desired on the Print Preview tab, then click **Print** in the Print group
☐ Click **OK**

Shortcut Method

☐ Press **[Ctrl][P]**
☐ Follow the steps in bullets 2–4 in the Print Presentation Notes Ribbon Method above

---

PREPARE FOR AND REHEARSE PRESENTATION DELIVERY

Set Up a Slide Show

Ribbon Method

☐ Click the **Slide Show tab** on the Ribbon, then click the **Set Up Slide Show button** in the Set Up group
☐ Specify the desired **options** in the Set Up Show dialog box, using Table PPT-8 as a guide
☐ Click **OK**

Table PPT-8 Set Up Show Dialog box

Section	Options
Show type	Choose whether show will be delivered by a speaker or browsed by an individual in a window or at a kiosk
Show options	Select whether to loop continuously, whether to show with or without narration or animation, and pen color
Performance	Set resolution options and graphics acceleration options
Show slides	Specify whether to show all or selected slides
Advance slides	Choose to proceed through slides manually or using timings
Multiple monitors	Set show to run on one or multiple monitors using Presenter view to use thumbnails to select slides, preview text, see Speaker notes in larger format, and run other programs that you don't want the audience to see during the presentation

Hide Specific Slides

Ribbon Method

☐ Click the **Slide Show tab** on the Ribbon
☐ Select the **slides** you want to hide
☐ Click the **Hide Slide button** in the Set Up group

Shortcut Method

☐ Select the **slides** you want to hide
☐ Right-click the **selected slides**, then click **Hide Slide** on the shortcut menu

Create Custom Slide Shows

Ribbon Method

☐ Click the **Slide Show tab** on the Ribbon, click the **Custom Slide Show button** in the Set Up group, then click **Custom Shows**
☐ In the Custom Shows dialog box, click **New**
☐ In the Define Custom Show dialog box, click the **Slide show name text box**, then type the name of the slide show
☐ To add a slide to the show, click the **slide** you want to include in the slide show in the Slides in presentation section, then click **Add**
☐ To remove a slide from a show, click the **slide** in the Slides in custom show section, then click **Remove**
☐ To change the order of slides by selecting a slide or slides, click the **Move Up button** 🔼 or the **Move Down button** 🔽
☐ Click **OK**, then click **Close** in the Custom Shows dialog box

Edit a Custom Show

Ribbon Method

☐ Click the **Slide Show tab** on the Ribbon, then click the **Custom Slide Show button** in the Set Up group
☐ In the Custom Shows dialog box, click the appropriate **slide show**, then click **Edit**
☐ To add a slide to the show, click the **slide** you want to include in the slide show in the Slides in presentation section, then click **Add**
☐ To remove a slide from a show, click the **slide** in the Slides in custom show section, then click **Remove**
☐ To change the order of slides by selecting a slide or slides, click the **Move Up button** 🔼 or the **Move Down button** 🔽
☐ Click **OK**, then click **Close** in the Custom Shows dialog box

Rehearse and Time the Delivery of a Presentation

Ribbon Method

☐ Click the **Slide Show tab** on the Ribbon, then click the **Rehearse Timings button** in the Set Up group
☐ The slide show begins to run, and the Rehearsal toolbar opens and times the slide
☐ Advance through the presentation, clicking the **Next button** ➡ when sufficient time has passed for each slide
☐ Click the **Repeat button** 🔁 to repeat a slide
☐ Click the **Pause button** ⏸ to pause the presentation and stop the clock
☐ Once all the slides have been rehearsed, click **Yes** in the message box that appears to keep the new slide timings, or click **No** to use other timings or try again

PowerPoint

Start a Slide Show

Ribbon Method

☐ Click the **Slide Show tab** on the Ribbon, then click the **From Beginning button** in the Start Slide Show group to begin from the first slide

OR

☐ Click the **Slide Show tab** on the Ribbon, then click the **From Current Slide button** in the Start Slide Show group to begin from the current slide

Shortcut Method

☐ Select the **slide** from which you want to begin the show, then click the **Slide Show button** 🖳 on the status bar

Use a Pen or Highlighter to Annotate a Presentation

Shortcut Method

☐ View the **presentation** in Slide Show view, then right-click the **slide** you want to annotate
☐ Point to **Pointer Options** on the shortcut menu, then click the appropriate **arrow**, **pen**, or **highlighter option** on the submenu
☐ Drag on the slide to create the annotation you want, then release the mouse button
☐ Make appropriate annotations as you advance through all the slides in the presentation, then click **Keep** or **Discard** in the message box that appears asking if you want to keep your annotations

Menu Method

☐ View the **presentation** in Slide Show view, then move the pointer to the lower left corner of the screen
☐ Click the **Pen Options button** 🖉 on the Slide Show menu, then click the appropriate **arrow**, **pen**, or **highlighter option** on the submenu
☐ Drag on the slide to create the annotation you want, then release the mouse button
☐ Make appropriate annotations as you advance through all the slides in the presentation, then click **Keep** or **Discard** in the message box that appears asking if you want to keep your annotations

Navigate to Specific Slides

Shortcut Method

☐ View the presentation in Slide Show view, then right-click the **slide**
☐ Click the appropriate navigation **option** on the shortcut menu

OR

☐ View the presentation in Slide Show view
☐ Navigate through the presentation, using Table PPT-9 as a reference

Table PPT-9 Keyboard Navigation During a Slide Show

Press	Effect on the slide show
[N] [Enter] [PgDn] or [Spacebar]	Start the next animation or advance to the next slide
[P] [PgUp] or [Backspace]	Start the previous animation or return to the previous slide
[*Number*][Enter]	Go to specified slide number
[Esc] [Ctrl][Break] or [-] (hyphen)	End slide show
[Home] or [1][Enter]	Return to first slide
[End]	Go to last slide
[Tab]	Go to first or next hyperlink on a slide
[Shift][Tab]	Go to last or previous hyperlink on a slide

Package Presentations for a CD

Ribbon Method

☐ Insert a blank CD in the appropriate drive on your computer
☐ Click the **Office button** 🪟, point to **Publish**, then click **Package for CD**
☐ In the Package for CD dialog box, type an appropriate **name** in the Name the CD text box
☐ Click **Copy to Folder** or **Copy to CD**
☐ Make the desired selections in the Copy to Folder or Copy to CD dialog box, close the Copy to Folder or Copy to CD dialog box, then click **Close** in the Package for CD dialog box

PowerPoint

MICROSOFT OFFICE OUTLOOK 2007
EXAM REFERENCE
Getting Started with Outlook 2007

The Outlook Microsoft Certified Application Specialist (MCAS) exam assumes a basic level of proficiency in Outlook. This section is intended to help you reference these basic skills while you are preparing to take the Outlook MCAS exam.

☐ Starting and exiting Outlook
☐ Setting up an Outlook profile
☐ Using toolbars
☐ Using the Ribbon
☐ Using keyboard KeyTips
☐ Opening Outlook tools
☐ Viewing Outlook tools
☐ Getting Help

START AND EXIT OUTLOOK

Start Outlook

Button Method
☐ Click the **Start button** 🌐 on the Windows taskbar
☐ Point to **All Programs**
☐ Click **Microsoft Office**, then click **Microsoft Office Outlook 2007**
OR
☐ Double-click the **Microsoft Office Outlook program icon** 🔘 on the desktop
OR
☐ Click the **Microsoft Office Outlook 2007 icon** on the Quick Launch Toolbar

Exit Outlook

Menu Method
☐ Click **File** on the menu bar, then click **Exit**

Button Method
☐ Click the **Close button** ☒ on the Outlook program window title bar

Shortcut Method
☐ Press **[Alt][F4]**

Refresh the Inbox

Menu Method

☐ Click **Tools** on the menu bar, point to **Send/Receive**, then click the appropriate option

Button Method

☐ In the Inbox folder, click the **Send/Receive button** on the Standard toolbar

Shortcut Method

☐ Press **[F9]** to send and receive all messages in Outlook

SET UP AN OUTLOOK PROFILE

Button Method

☐ Click the **Start button** 🌐 on the Windows taskbar, then click **Control Panel**
☐ In the Control Panel window, make sure you are in Vista View, click **User Accounts and Family Safety**, then click **Mail**
☐ In the Mail Setup - Outlook dialog box, click **Show Profiles**
☐ In the Mail dialog box, click **Add**
☐ In the New Profile dialog box, type a name for the profile in the Profile Name text box, then click **OK**
☐ Navigate through the Add E-mail Account Wizard, making selections and specifying settings as appropriate to create the profile, then click **Finish**
☐ Click **OK** in the Mail dialog box

USE TOOLBARS

Note: The main Outlook program window uses toolbars and menus. The Mail, Contact, Appointment/Calendar, Task, and Journal Entry windows use the Ribbon.

Display Toolbars

Menu Method

☐ Click **View** on the menu bar, point to **Toolbars**, then click the toolbar you want to display

OR

☐ Right-click any toolbar, then click the toolbar you want to display on the shortcut menu

Customize Toolbars

Menu Method

☐ Click **Tools** on the menu bar, then click **Customize**

Outlook

OR

☐ Click **View** on the menu bar, point to **Toolbars**, then click **Customize**
   OR
☐ Right-click any toolbar, then click **Customize** on the shortcut menu
☐ In the Customize dialog box, select the appropriate options, then click **Close**

Button Method

☐ Click the **Toolbar Options button** ⬚ on the toolbar you want to customize
☐ Point to **Add or Remove Buttons**, then click **Customize**
☐ In the Customize dialog box, select the appropriate options, then click **Close**

Reposition Toolbars

Mouse Method

☐ Position the pointer over the **Toolbar Move handle** at the left end of any docked toolbar
   OR
☐ Position the pointer over the title bar of any floating toolbar
☐ When the pointer changes to ✥, press and hold the mouse button
☐ Drag the toolbar to a blank area of the window or to a different location, then release the mouse button

USE THE RIBBON

Note: The Ribbon is available from within the Mail, Contact, Appointment/Calendar, Task, and Journal Entry windows. The main Outlook program window uses toolbars and menus.

Display the Ribbon

Ribbon Method

☐ Double-click any tab

Shortcut Method

☐ Right-click any tab, then click **Minimize the Ribbon** to deselect it
   OR
☐ Click the Quick Access toolbar arrow, then click **Minimize the Ribbon**

Hide the Ribbon

Ribbon Method

☐ Double-click the active tab

Shortcut Method

☐ Right-click any tab, then click **Minimize the Ribbon** to select it

Work with the Ribbon

Ribbon Method

□ Click a tab on the Ribbon, click a **button** or a **button list arrow** in any group, then click a command or gallery option, if necessary

OR

□ Click a **dialog box launcher** 🔲 to open a dialog box or a pane offering more options

Customize the Quick Access Toolbar

Ribbon Method

□ Right-click any Quick Access toolbar button
□ To hide that button, click **Remove from Quick Access Toolbar**
□ To add or remove a button, click **Customize Quick Access Toolbar**, click a command in the left or right column, then click **Add** or **Remove**

Reposition the Quick Access Toolbar

Ribbon Method

□ Right-click any Quick Access toolbar button
□ Click **Show Quick Access Toolbar Below the Ribbon**

USE KEYBOARD KEYTIPS

Display Keyboard KeyTips

Shortcut Method

□ Press **[Alt]** to display the KeyTips for each command on the active tab on the Ribbon and on the Quick Access toolbar
□ Press the letter or number shown in the KeyTip for the specific active tab on the Ribbon
□ Press additional letters or numbers as needed to complete the command sequence
□ If two letters appear, press each one in order
□ For some commands, you will find that you have to click an option from a gallery or menu to complete the command sequence
□ The KeyTips turn off automatically at the end of the command sequence

Hide KeyTips

Shortcut Method

□ Press **[Alt]** to hide the KeyTips for each Ribbon command

OPEN OUTLOOK TOOLS

Menu Method

□ Click **Go** on the menu bar, then click the appropriate item, using Table OL-1 as a reference

Button Method

□ Click the appropriate button in the Navigation Pane, using Table OL-1 as a reference

Shortcut Method

□ Press the appropriate keyboard combination, using Table OL-1 as a reference

Table OL-1 Common Outlook Navigation Options

Command on the Go menu	Navigation Pane button	Keyboard combination	Description
Mail		[Ctrl][1]	View new e-mail messages, create new e-mail messages, and move messages to folders
Calendar		[Ctrl][2]	View, create, and manage appointments
Contacts		[Ctrl][3]	Create, view, and edit contacts
Tasks		[Ctrl][4]	Schedule and assign tasks
Notes		[Ctrl][5]	Create and edit notes
Folder List		[Ctrl][6]	View the contents of a folder or create a new folder
Shortcuts		[Ctrl][7]	View and manage shortcuts to folders in Outlook
Journal		[Ctrl][8]	Create and edit Journal entries

Outlook

VIEW OUTLOOK TOOLS

View the Inbox Folder

Note: You can use the Inbox folder to send, receive, and read mail, as well as read and respond to any tasks or meeting requests. See Figure OL-1.

Figure OL-1   The Inbox Window

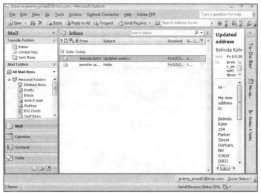

View the Calendar Window

Note: You can use the Calendar to create appointments and events, organize meetings, view group schedules, and manage another user's Calendar. You can view the Calendar by day, week, or month. See Figure OL-2.

Figure OL-2   The Calendar Window

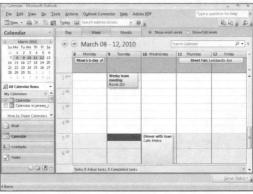

Outlook

View the Contacts Window

Note: You can use the Contacts window to store e-mail addresses, addresses, phone numbers, and any other information that relates to your contacts, such as birthdays, children's names, or spouse's names. See Figure OL-3.

Figure OL-3   The Contacts Window

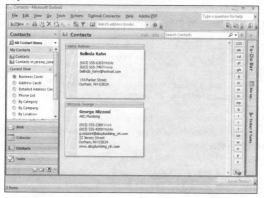

View the Tasks Window

Note: The Tasks window contains a list of all tasks you have created for yourself or others, or that others have assigned for you to do. You can use the tasks list to update the status of your projects, set a task as recurring, delegate tasks, and mark tasks as completed. See Figure OL-4.

Figure OL-4   The Tasks Window

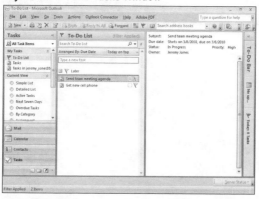

Outlook

GET HELP

Menu Method

☐ Click **Help** on the menu bar, then click **Microsoft Office Outlook Help**
☐ Use Table OL-2 as a reference to select the most appropriate way to search for help using the Outlook Help task pane

Button Method

☐ Click the **Microsoft Office Outlook Help button** 🔘 on the Standard toolbar
☐ Use Table OL-2 as a reference to select the most appropriate way to search for help using the Outlook Help task pane

OR

☐ Click the **Type a question for help box** on the menu bar
☐ Type a question or keywords relating to an Outlook topic, then press **[Enter]**
☐ View the results of the keyword search in the Search Results task pane, then click a topic title in the task pane to view the topic in a new window

Shortcut Method

☐ Press **[F1]**
☐ Use Table OL-2 as a reference to select the most appropriate way to search for help using the Outlook Help task pane

Table OL-2 Outlook Help Task Pane Options

Option	To use
Browse Outlook Help	Click the link for the topic you want to explore further, then click the topic you want and read the results in the task pane
Search	Type a keyword in the Search text box, click the Search All button, then click the hyperlinked text to read more in the Microsoft Office Outlook Help Window

OUTLOOK EXAM REFERENCE

Note: To complete many of the tasks in this book you must address, type, and send your message.

Objectives:

1. Managing messaging
2. Managing scheduling
3. Managing tasks
4. Managing contacts and personal contact information
5. Organizing information

OUTLOOK OBJECTIVE 1: MANAGING MESSAGING

CREATE AND SEND AN E-MAIL MESSAGE

Send and Address E-mail Messages

Menu Method

☐ Click **File** on the menu bar, point to **New**, then click **Mail Message**
☐ In the Untitled Message window, type the e-mail address(es) for the recipient(s) or the name of a distribution list in the To and Cc boxes, separating each e-mail address with a semicolon (;), or to select recipient names from the Address Book, click the **To button** or the **Cc button** to open the Select Names dialog box, click in the appropriate text box, select the appropriate name(s) using Table OL-3 as a reference, then click **OK**
☐ In the Subject text box, type an appropriate subject for the message
☐ In the message body, type the message
☐ Click the **Send button**

Button Method

☐ Click the **New list arrow** on the Standard toolbar, then click **Mail Message** (*Note*: The button may differ based on current view)
☐ Follow the steps in bullets 2–5 of the Send and Address E-mail Messages Menu Method above

Shortcut Method

☐ Press **[Ctrl][Shift][M]**
☐ Follow the steps in bullets 2–5 of the Send and Address E-mail Messages Menu Method above

Outlook

Table OL-3 Message Addressing Options

Option	Sends
To	The primary recipient of the message
Carbon Copy (Cc)	A copy of the message, usually to people who do not need to respond
Blind Carbon Copy (Bcc)	A copy of the message to recipients whose names and addresses are not visible to the To and Cc recipients
Distribution list	A collection of contacts assigned a group name

Reply to or Forward an E-mail Message

Ribbon Method

- ☐ Open the mail message to which you want to respond
- ☐ In the Respond group on the Message tab, click one of the menu options described in Table OL-4
- ☐ Type the message in the message body, then add any additional recipients as appropriate
- ☐ Click the **Send button**

Shortcut Method

- ☐ Open the mail message to which you want to respond
- ☐ Press one of the keyboard combinations listed in Table OL-4, as appropriate
- ☐ Follow the steps in bullets 3–4 in the Reply to or Forward an E-mail Message Ribbon Method above

Table OL-4 E-mail Message Response Options

Command in the Response group	Button	Keyboard combination	Action
Reply		[Ctrl][R]	To send a message that includes the original text and your comments directly to the original sender
Reply to All	Reply to All	[Ctrl][Shift][R]	To send a message that includes the original message and your comments directly to the sender and all recipients of the original message
Forward		[Ctrl][F]	To send a message that includes the original message and your comments directly to the recipient(s) of your choosing, but not to the sender

Outlook

Send a Message Again

Ribbon Method

☐ Open the Sent Items folder
☐ Open the mail message that you want to resend
☐ Use Table OL-4 to choose the appropriate response button or keyboard shortcut

Forward a Message with an Attachment

Ribbon Method

☐ Open the mail message that has the attachment you want to forward
☐ Click the **Forward button** 🔄 in the Response group of the Message tab
☐ The attachment(s) associated with the message appear in the Attached text box
☐ To remove an attachment, right-click it, then press **[Delete]**

CREATE AND MANAGE YOUR SIGNATURE AND AUTOMATED MESSAGES

Include a Signature

Menu Method

☐ Click **Tools** on the menu bar, then click **Options**
☐ In the Options dialog box, click the **Mail Format tab**
☐ Under Signatures, click **Signatures**
☐ In the Signatures and Stationery dialog box, click **New**
☐ In the New Signature dialog box, type the signature name, then click **OK**
☐ In the Edit signature section of the Signatures and Stationery dialog box, type and format the signature text or click the **Business Card button**, select any other appropriate options under the Choose default signature section, then click **OK**
☐ Click **OK** in the Options dialog box

Modify an E-mail Signature

Menu Method

☐ Click **Tools** on the menu bar, then click **Options**
☐ In the Options dialog box, click the **Mail Format tab**, then click **Signatures**
☐ In the Signatures and Stationery dialog box, select a signature from the Select signature to edit list
☐ In the Edit signature section, make the appropriate changes, then click **OK** in the Signatures and Stationery dialog box
☐ Click **OK** in the Options dialog box

Outlook

Create E-mail Signatures for Multiple Accounts

Menu Method

- [ ] Click **Tools** on the menu bar, then click **Options**
- [ ] In the Options dialog box, click the **Mail Format tab**, then click **Signatures**
- [ ] In the Signatures and Stationery dialog box, click **New**
- [ ] In the New Signature dialog box, type a name, then click **OK**
- [ ] Repeat for additional signatures, then click **OK** in the Signatures and Stationery dialog box

Create an E-mail Template for Out-of-Office Messages

Menu Method

- [ ] Click **File** on the menu bar, point to **New**, then click **Mail Message**
- [ ] Click the **Options tab**, then click the **Plain Text button** in the Format group
- [ ] Type the message to use as your automated reply
- [ ] Click the **Office Button** 🟠, then click **Save As**
- [ ] In the Save As dialog box, click the **Save as type list arrow**, then click **Outlook Template (*.oft)**
- [ ] Type a name for the template in the File name text box, then click **Save**

Set Out-of-Office Message Options

Note: In order to use the Out-of-Office Assistant, you must be using Microsoft Exchange Server 2007. If you have a different version of Microsoft Exchange, your steps will vary. If you are using another server program, you will not be able to use the Out-of-Office Assistant.

Menu Method

- [ ] Click **Tools** on the menu bar, then click **Out-of-Office Assistant**
- [ ] In the Out-of-Office Assistant dialog box, click **Send Out of Office auto-replies**
- [ ] In the Send Out of Office auto-replies dialog box, use the tabs to select options such as expiration date, send only to your contacts, and other options, then click **OK**
- [ ] Click **OK** in the Out-of-Office Assistant dialog box

MANAGE E-MAIL MESSAGE ATTACHMENTS

Attach a File to a Message

Ribbon Method

- [ ] Open a new e-mail message
- [ ] Click the **Attach File button** 📎 in the Include group on the Message tab
- [ ] In the Insert File dialog box, navigate to the appropriate drive and folder, click the file you want to attach, then click **Insert**

Outlook

OR

☐ Open a new e-mail message
☐ Click the **Insert tab**, then click the **Attach File button** 📎 in the Include group
☐ In the Insert File dialog box, navigate to the appropriate drive and folder, click the file you want to attach, then click **Insert**

Attach a Calendar to a Message

Ribbon Method

☐ Open a new e-mail message
☐ Click the **Calendar button** 📅 in the Include group on the Message tab
☐ In the Insert Calendar dialog box, navigate to the appropriate drive and folder, click the file you want to attach, then click **Insert**

OR

☐ Open a new e-mail message, then click in the message area
☐ Click the **Insert tab**, then click the **Calendar button** 📅 in the Include group
☐ In the Send a Calendar via E-mail dialog box, select the calendar, date range, and other options, then click **OK**

Compress a Graphic Attachment

Ribbon Method

☐ Open a new e-mail message, then click in the message area
☐ Click the **Insert tab**, then click the **Picture button** 🖼 in the Illustrations group
☐ In the Insert Picture dialog box, navigate to the appropriate drive and folder, click the file you want to attach, then click **Insert**
☐ Click the **Compress Pictures button** in the Adjust group on the Format tab
☐ Choose the appropriate options in the Compress Pictures dialog box, then click **OK**

Preview an Attachment

Ribbon Method

☐ Open the message that has the attachment
☐ Click the icon for the attachment, then click the **Preview file button**
☐ Click **OK**, if necessary
☐ Click the **Message button** to return to the message

Save an Attachment to a Specific Folder or Drive

Menu Method

☐ Open the message that has the attachment
☐ Right-click the icon for the attachment, then click **Save As** from the shortcut menu
☐ In the Save As dialog box, navigate to the drive and folder where you want to save the file, then click **OK**

Outlook

Open an Attachment

Menu Method

☐ Open the message that has the attachment
☐ Right-click the icon for the attachment, then click **Open** from the short-cut menu
☐ If you are familiar with the source of the attachment and want to view it, click **OK** in the Opening Mail Attachment warning box
☐ The file opens in its native format

CONFIGURE E-MAIL MESSAGE SENSITIVITY AND IMPORTANCE SETTINGS

Set Message Sensitivity Options

Ribbon Method

☐ Open a new e-mail message
☐ Click the **dialog box launcher** in the Options group on the Message tab
☐ In the Message Options dialog box, click the **Sensitivity list arrow**, click the appropriate option, then click **Close**

Set Message Importance Options

Ribbon Method

☐ Open a new e-mail message
☐ Click the **High Importance button** or the **Low Importance button** in the Options group on the Message tab
  OR
☐ Click the **Follow-Up button** and select the appropriate option
  OR
☐ Open a new e-mail message
☐ Click the **dialog box launcher** in the Options group on the Message tab
☐ In the Message Options dialog box, select the appropriate options in the Message settings section, then click **Close**

Forward a Flagged Message

Ribbon Method

☐ In the Inbox folder, open the message with flag that you want to forward
☐ Click the **dialog box launcher** in the Options group on the Message tab
☐ In the Message Options dialog box, change the importance level to **Low** or **Normal**, then click **Close**

CONFIGURE E-MAIL MESSAGE SECURITY SETTINGS

Set Security Options for a New Message

Ribbon Method

☐ Open a new e-mail message
☐ Click the **dialog box launcher** in the Options group on the Message tab
☐ In the Message Options dialog box, click the **Security Settings button**
☐ In the Security Properties dialog box, select the appropriate options, then click **Close**
☐ Click **Close** in the Message Options dialog box

Include a Digital Signature

Menu Method

☐ Click **Tools** on the menu bar, then click **Trust Center**
☐ In the Trust Center dialog box, click **E-mail Security**
☐ Under Encrypt E-mail, click the **Add digital signatures to outgoing messages check box** to select it, then click **OK**

Set Permissions for Messages

Ribbon Method

Note: In order to set message permissions you must configure your computer to use Information Rights Management.

☐ Open a new e-mail message
☐ Click the **Office Button**, then click **Permission**

   OR

☐ Click the **Permission button** in the Options group on the Message tab

Use Encryption on a Single Message

Ribbon Method

☐ Open a new e-mail message
☐ Click the **dialog box launcher** in the Options group on the Message tab
☐ In the Message Options dialog box, click **Security Settings**
☐ In the Security Settings dialog box, click the **Encrypt message contents and attachments check box**, then click **OK**
☐ Click **Close** in the Message Options dialog box

Use Encryption on All Messages

Menu Method

☐ Click **Tools** on the menu bar, then click **Trust Center**
☐ In the Trust Center dialog box, click **E-mail Security**
☐ Click the **Encrypt contents and attachments for outgoing messages check box** in the Encrypted e-mail section, then click **OK**

Outlook

CONFIGURE E-MAIL MESSAGE DELIVERY OPTIONS

Set Delivery Options

Ribbon Method

- ☐ Open a new e-mail message
- ☐ Click the **dialog box launcher** in the Options group on the Message tab
- ☐ In the Message Options dialog box, select the appropriate options in the Delivery options section, then click **Close**

Insert or Delete a Flag

Ribbon Method

- ☐ Open the message window for the message you want to flag
- ☐ Click the **Follow Up button** 🏳 in the Options group on the Message tab, then click the appropriate flag color

  OR

- ☐ Click **Add Reminder**, then in the Flag for Follow Up dialog box, select the appropriate action, due date, and flag color, then click **OK**

Send a Message at a Later Time

Ribbon Method

- ☐ Open a new e-mail message
- ☐ Click the **dialog box launcher** in the Options group on the Message tab
- ☐ In the Message Options dialog box, click the **Do not deliver before check box**, enter the date, then click **Close**

  OR

- ☐ Open a new e-mail message
- ☐ Click the **Delay Delivery button** 🖼 in the More Options group on the **Options tab**
- ☐ In the Message Options dialog box, click the **Do not deliver before check box**, enter the date, then click **Close**

Use Receipts

Ribbon Method

- ☐ Open a new e-mail message
- ☐ Click the **dialog box launcher** in the Options group on the Message tab
- ☐ In the Message Options dialog box, click the **Request a delivery receipt check box** and/or the **Request a read receipt check box**, then click **Close**

  OR

- ☐ Open a new e-mail message
- ☐ Click the **Options tab**, then click the appropriate receipt check box in the Tracking group

Create an E-mail Poll

Ribbon Method

- ☐ Open a new e-mail message
- ☐ Click the **dialog box launcher** in the Options group on the Message tab
- ☐ In the Message Options dialog box, click the **Use voting buttons check box**, then click the appropriate voting options or type custom voting options, separating each with a semi-colon (;)
- ☐ Click the **Have replies sent to check box**, type or select an e-mail address, then click **Close**

   OR

- ☐ Open a new e-mail message
- ☐ Click the **Options tab**, click the **Use Voting Buttons button** 🔲 in the Tracking group, then click the appropriate option from the menu

---

VIEW E-MAIL MESSAGES

Show, Hide, or Move the Reading Pane

Menu Method

- ☐ Click **View** on the menu bar, point to **Reading Pane**, then click **Right** or **Bottom** to display or move the Reading Pane
- ☐ Position the pointer over the left or top of the Reading Pane, then drag using ◀▶ or 🔼 to change the view
- ☐ Click **View** on the menu bar, point to **Reading Pane**, then click **Off**

Preview a Message with the Reading Pane

Menu Method

- ☐ Click the message you want to open in the Inbox folder to view it in the Reading Pane
- ☐ To open the message, click **File** on the menu bar, point to **Open**, then click **Selected Items**

Shortcut Method

- ☐ Click the message you want to open in the Inbox folder to view it in the Reading Pane
- ☐ To open the message, press **[Ctrl][O]**

Mouse Method

- ☐ Click the message you want to open in the Inbox folder to view it in the Reading Pane
- ☐ To open the message, double-click it

Automatically Preview Messages

Menu Method

- ☐ Click **View** on the menu bar, then click **AutoPreview**

OUTLOOK OBJECTIVE 2: MANAGING SCHEDULING

CREATE APPOINTMENTS, MEETINGS, AND EVENTS

Add Appointments to the Calendar

Menu Method

☐ Click **File** on the menu bar, point to **New**, then click **Appointment**
☐ In the Untitled - Appointment window, click the **Maximize button**, click the **Appointment tab** if necessary, then enter the subject, location, start and end time, and other appropriate information for the appointment
☐ Click the **Save & Close button** 🔲 in the Actions group

Button Method

☐ Click the **New list arrow** on the Standard toolbar, then click **Appointment**
☐ Follow the steps in bullets 2–3 in the Add Appointments to the Calendar Menu Method above

Shortcut Method

☐ Press **[Ctrl][Shift][A]**
☐ Follow the steps in bullets 2–3 in the Add Appointments to the Calendar Menu Method above

Schedule a Meeting and Invite Attendees

Menu Method

☐ Click **File** on the menu bar, point to **New**, then click **Meeting Request**
☐ In the Untitled - Meeting window, click the **Maximize button**, then click the **Meeting tab**, if necessary
☐ Click the **To text box**, then enter recipient names or type the e-mail addresses of the meeting attendees, separating each with a semicolon (;), or to select recipient names from the Address Book, click the **To button**, then in the Select Attendees and Resources dialog box select the attendees and resources from the Name list box, click the appropriate button for each name (Required, Optional, Resources), then click **OK**
☐ Enter the subject, location, start and end time, and other appropriate information, then click the **Send button**

Button Method

☐ Click the **New list arrow** on the Standard toolbar, then click **Meeting Request**
☐ Follow the steps in bullets 2–4 in the Schedule a Meeting and Invite Attendees Menu Method above

Shortcut Method

☐ Press **[Ctrl][Shift][Q]**
☐ Follow the steps in bullets 2–4 in the Schedule a Meeting and Invite Attendees Menu Method above

Add a Recurring Calendar Item

Ribbon Method

- ☐ Open a new meeting request or appointment window
- ☐ Click the **Recurrence button** ☑ in the Options group
- ☐ In the Appointment Recurrence dialog box, make the appropriate selections, then click **OK**

Shortcut Method

- ☐ Open a new meeting request or appointment window
- ☐ Press **[Ctrl][G]**
- ☐ In the Appointment Recurrence dialog box, make the appropriate selections, then click **OK**

Add a Calendar Item from a Message or a Task

Ribbon Method

- ☐ Open the message or task from which you want to create an appointment
- ☐ Click the **Follow Up button** ☑ in the Options group on the Message tab or on the Task tab
- ☐ Click one of the flag options, or click **Add Reminder** to open the custom dialog box, make the appropriate selections, then click **OK**

Set a Private Appointment

Menu Method

- ☐ Open a new calendar item
- ☐ Enter the subject, location, and other appropriate information
- ☐ Click the **Private button** in the Options group, then click the **Save & Close button** ☑ in the Actions group

SEND MEETING REQUESTS

Invite Attendees

Menu Method

- ☐ Open a new meeting request
- ☐ Enter the subject, location, and other appropriate information
- ☐ Click the **Scheduling button** ☑ in the Show group on the **Meeting tab**
- ☐ Click **Add Others**, then click **Add from Address Book**
- ☐ In the Select Attendees and Resources dialog box, click the **Name only option button** to select it, if necessary
- ☐ Enter the name of a person or resource that you want to invite to the meeting in the **Search text box**
- ☐ Select the name from Name box, click the **Required, Optional,** or **Resources buttons**, then click **OK**
- ☐ Click the **Send button**

Determine Availability of Attendees

Menu Method

☐ Open a new meeting request
☐ Enter the subject, location, and other appropriate information
☐ Click the **Scheduling button** 🔲 in the Show group on the **Meeting tab**
☐ Add attendees, then view the free/busy grid to determine a time when all attendees are free
☐ Choose a time in the Suggested Times pane, then click the **Send button**

Create a Group Schedule

Menu Method

☐ In the Calendar window, click **Actions** on the menu bar, then click **View Group Schedules**
☐ In the Group Schedules dialog box, click **New**
☐ Type the group name in the Create New Group Schedule dialog box, then click **OK**
☐ Select members and other options in the *group name* dialog box, then click **Save and Close**

Use a Group Schedule

Menu Method

☐ In the Calendar window, click **Actions** on the menu bar, then click **View Group Schedules**
☐ In the Group Schedules dialog box, click the *group name*, then click **Open**
☐ View the information and make changes in the *group name* dialog box, then click **Save and Close**

Track Responses to Meeting Requests

Menu Method

☐ Click **Tools** on the menu bar, then click **Options**
☐ In the Options dialog box, click **E-mail Options**
☐ In the E-mail Options dialog box, click **Tracking Options**
☐ Select the appropriate options in the Tracking Options dialog box, then click **OK**
☐ Click **OK** in the E-mail Options dialog box, then click **OK** in the Options dialog box

Schedule Resources for Meetings

Note: In order to schedule a resource, the resource must have its own mailbox and be included in your Contacts folder.

Menu Method

☐ In the Calendar window, click **Actions** on the menu bar, then click **Plan a Meeting**
☐ In the Plan a Meeting dialog box, click **Add Others**, then click **Add from Address Book**
☐ In the Select Attendees and Resources dialog box, click the **Name only option button** to select it, if necessary

☐ Enter the name of the resource that you want to use at the meeting in the **Search text box**
☐ Click the name of the resource in the Name box, then click **Resources**
☐ Repeat the previous bullet for each resource you want, then click **OK**
☐ If the Microsoft Office Internet Free/Busy dialog box opens, click **Cancel**
☐ In the Plan a Meeting dialog box, click **Make Meeting**
☐ In the Untitled – Meeting window, click the **Maximize button**, enter the appropriate information, then click the **Send button**
☐ Click **Close** in the Plan a Meeting dialog box

UPDATE, CANCEL, AND RESPOND TO MEETING REQUESTS

Respond to a Meeting Request

Button Method

☐ In the Inbox, open the meeting request to which you want to respond
☐ Click the appropriate button on the Ribbon, using Table OL-5 as a reference
☐ In the message box, click the appropriate response option, then click **OK**

Table OL-5 Meeting Request Options

Buttons	Button name	Used to
✓	Accept	Accept the meeting and add it to your calendar
?	Tentative	Tentatively accept the meeting and add it to your calendar
✕	Decline	Decline the meeting and move the request to your Deleted Items folder

Update a Meeting

Ribbon Method

☐ In the Inbox, open the meeting request which you want to update
☐ Make the changes to the meeting request, then click the **Send Update button**

Suggest a New Meeting Time

Ribbon Method

☐ In the Inbox, open the meeting request to which you want to respond
☐ Click the **Propose New Time button** 🔲 in the Respond group
☐ In the Propose New Time dialog box, select a new time, then click **Propose Time**
☐ In the New Time Proposed message window, type a note if necessary, then click the **Send button**

Outlook

Accept a Proposed Meeting Time

Ribbon Method

□ In the Inbox, open a meeting request
□ Click the **Accept New Time button** ✓ in the Respond group on the Message tab, then click the **Send button**

Cancel a Meeting Request

Ribbon Method

□ In the Inbox, open the meeting request which you want to cancel
□ Click **Cancel Meeting** in the Actions group
□ If a message box opens, click the appropriate option, then click **OK**

Change the Meeting Time and Send an Update to All Attendees

Ribbon Method

□ In the Inbox, open the meeting request for which you want to change the time
□ Make changes to the start or end time, then click the **Send Update button**

Add or Delete Attendees

Ribbon Method

□ In the Inbox, open the meeting request to which you want to add attendees
□ Click **Add or Remove Attendees** in the Attendees group on the Meeting tab
□ In the Select Attendees and Resources dialog box make the appropriate changes, then click **OK**
□ Click the **Send Update button**

Change a Single Instance of a Recurrence

Ribbon Method

□ In the Calendar window, open the recurring meeting you want to modify
□ In the Open Recurring Item dialog box, click the **Open this occurrence option button**, then click **OK**
□ Maximize the Meeting window, then make the appropriate changes to the meeting request
□ Click the **Send Update button**

Send Updates to New Attendees

Ribbon Method

□ In the Inbox, open the meeting request which you want to update
□ Click **Add or Remove Attendees** in the Attendees group on the Meeting or Recurring Meeting tab
□ In the Select Attendees and Resources dialog box, make the appropriate changes, then click **OK**
□ Delete all names from the To box except for the new attendee(s), then click **Send Update**

Cancel Meetings

Ribbon Method

- ☐ In the Inbox, open the appointment which you want to cancel
- ☐ Click the **Cancel Meeting button** 🖳 in the Actions group on the Meeting or Recurring Meeting tab
- ☐ Click the **Send Cancellation button**

CUSTOMIZE CALENDAR SETTINGS

Set the Work Week, Time Zone, and Holiday Options

Menu Method

- ☐ In the Calendar window, click **Tools** on the menu bar, then click **Options**
- ☐ In the Options dialog box, click the **Preferences tab** if necessary, then click **Calendar Options**
- ☐ Make the appropriate selections in the Calendar Options dialog box using Table OL-6 as a reference, then click **OK**
- ☐ Click **OK** in the Options dialog box

Table OL-6 Calendar Options Dialog Box

Dialog box section	Used to
Calendar work week	Set work days and hours
Calendar options	Add holidays, change background color, change meeting request options
Advanced options	Select different calendar or time zone, schedule resources

SHARE YOUR CALENDAR WITH OTHERS

Set Free/Busy Options

Menu Method

- ☐ Click **Tools** on the menu bar, then click **Options**
- ☐ In the Options dialog box, click the **Preferences tab** if necessary, then click **Calendar Options**
- ☐ Click **Free/Busy Options** in the Calendar Options dialog box
- ☐ Make the appropriate selections in the Free/Busy Options dialog box, then click **OK**
- ☐ Click **OK** in the Calendar Options dialog box, then click **OK** in the Options dialog box

Share Your Calendar with Other Users

Note: In order to view your calendar, users must have a Microsoft Passport account or be on your network.

Task Pane Method

☐ In the Calendar window, maximize the Navigation Pane if necessary
☐ Click **Share My Calendar** in the Navigation Pane
☐ In the Sharing dialog box, select the Calendar to share, then click **Add**
☐ In the Add Users dialog box, select an address, click **Add User**, repeat until all contacts are selected, then click **OK**
☐ Choose the appropriate options in the Sharing Permissions dialog box, then click **OK**
☐ Click **OK** in the Sharing dialog box

Send a Calendar in an E-mail Message

Task Pane Method

☐ In the Calendar window, maximize the Navigation Pane, if necessary
☐ Click **Send a Calendar via E-mail** in the Navigation Pane
☐ In the Send a Calendar via E-mail dialog box, select the calendar to share, select a date range, select a details option using Table OL-7 as a reference, then click **OK**
☐ Select addresses, type a note in the message box, then click the **Send button**

Table OL-7 Calendar Sharing Detail Options

Option	Shows
Availability only	Shows time as Free, Busy, Out-of-the-Office, or Tentative
Limited details	Includes the availability and subject of calendar items
Full details	Includes the availability, subject and details of calendar items

Publish a Calendar Online

Task Pane Method

☐ In the Calendar window, maximize the Navigation Pane, if necessary
☐ Click **Publish My Calendar** in the Navigation Pane
☐ Navigate through the Microsoft Office Online Registration wizard, if necessary
☐ In the Publish Calendar to Microsoft Office Online dialog box, select the appropriate options, then click **OK**

VIEW OTHER CALENDARS

View a Shared Calendar

Task Pane Method

☐ In the Calendar window, maximize the Navigation Pane, if necessary
☐ Click **Open a Shared Calendar** in the Navigation Pane
☐ In the Open a Shared Calendar dialog box, select the user name for the calendar you wish to view, then click **OK**

Outlook

Subscribe to an Online Calendar

Task Pane Method

☐ Locate the Web site for the calendar to which you want to subscribe (www.*calendar_name*.ics)
☐ Click the link for the calendar, then click **Yes** if asked to verify the validity of the calendar
☐ In the Add this Internet Calendar to Outlook and subscribe to updates message box, click **OK**
☐ To open a calendar to which you have subscribed, click the **Internet Calendar Subscription button** in the Navigation Pane

View Multiple Calendars

Button Method

☐ In the Calendar window, open two or more shared calendars
☐ Click the **View in Overlay button** 🔲 at the top of the far-right calendar
☐ Click 🔲 again to view in Side-by-Side mode

OUTLOOK OBJECTIVE 3: MANAGING TASKS

CREATE, MODIFY, AND MARK TASKS AS COMPLETE

Create a Task

Menu Method

□ Click **File** on the menu bar, point to **New**, then click **Task**
□ In the Untitled – Task window, click the **Maximize button**, then enter or select the appropriate information for the subject, dates, priority level, reminder dates and times, and any other appropriate information
□ Click the **Save & Close button** 🖫 in the Actions group

Button Method

□ Click the **New list arrow** on the Standard toolbar, then click **Task**
□ Follow the steps in bullets 2–3 in the Create a Task Menu Method above

Shortcut Method

□ Press **[Ctrl][Shift][K]**
□ Follow the steps in bullets 2–3 in the Create a Task Menu Method

Create a Recurring Task

Menu Method

□ Open a new task window or a current task you want to recur
□ Click the **Recurrence button** 🔘 in the Options group on the Task tab
□ Select the appropriate options for the range and pattern of recurrence in the Task Recurrence dialog box, then click **OK**
□ Click the **Save & Close button** 🖫 in the Actions group

Modify a Task

Button Method

□ In the Tasks window, open the task you want to modify
□ Make the appropriate modifications
□ Click the **Save & Close button** 🖫 in the Actions group on the Task tab

Create a Task from a Message

Ribbon Method

□ Open the message from which you want to create a task
□ Click the **Follow Up button** 🚩 in the Options group on the Task tab
□ Click one of the flag options, or click **Add Reminder** to open the custom dialog box, make the appropriate selections, then click **OK**

Change the Status of a Task

Ribbon Method

☐ Open the task whose status you want to update
☐ Make the appropriate updates using the **Status list arrow**, **Priority list arrow**, and **% Complete up and down arrows**
☐ Click the **Save & Close button** 🖫 in the Actions group on the Task tab

Make a Task Private

Ribbon Method

☐ Open the task whose status you want to make private
☐ Click the **Private button** in the Options group on the Task tab
☐ Click the **Save & Close button** 🖫 in the Actions group on the Task tab

ACCEPT, DECLINE, ASSIGN, UPDATE, AND RESPOND TO TASKS

Accept or Decline a Task

Button Method

☐ In the Inbox, open the message containing the task request
☐ Click the **Accept button** ✓ or the **Decline button** ✗ as appropriate, in the Manage Task group on the Task tab
☐ In the Accepting Tasks or the Declining Tasks dialog box, click the appropriate response option, then click **OK**
☐ If necessary, type an explanation in the message window
☐ Click the **Send button**

Assign a Task

Menu Method

☐ Click **File** on the menu bar, point to **New**, then click **Task Request**
☐ In the Untitled – Task window, click the **Maximize button**, type each recipient's name or e-mail address in the To text box separated by a semi-colon (;), or click the **To button**, select the appropriate recipient in the Select Task Recipient dialog box, then click **To**
☐ Repeat the previous bullet for each recipient, then click **OK**
☐ Select any other appropriate options, then click the **Send button**

Button Method

☐ Click the **New list arrow** on the Standard toolbar, then click **Task Request**
☐ Follow the steps in bullets 2–4 in the Assign a Task Menu Method above

Shortcut Method

☐ Press **[Ctrl][Shift][U]**
☐ Follow the steps in bullets 2–4 in the Assign a Task Menu Method above

Outlook

Reassign a Task

Menu Method

☐ Click the **Tasks button** 🗒 in the Navigation Pane to open the Tasks window, double-click the task you want to delegate in the Tasks list, then click the **Maximize button**
☐ Click the **Assign Task button** 🗒 in the Manage Task group on the Task tab
☐ Type each recipient's name in the To text box separated by a semicolon (;), or click the **To button**, select the appropriate person in the Select Task Recipient dialog box, then click **To**
☐ Repeat the previous bullet for each task recipient, then click **OK**
☐ If a message box appears, click **OK**

Send an Update on the Status of a Task

Ribbon Method

☐ Open the task whose status you want to update
☐ Make the appropriate updates using the **Status list arrow**, **Priority list arrow**, and **% Complete up and down arrows**
☐ To send an update to the contact who assigned the task, click the **Send Status Report button** 🗒 in the Manage Task group, address the message, then click the **Send button**
☐ Click the **Save & Close button** 🖫 in the Actions group on the Task tab

OUTLOOK OBJECTIVE 4: MANAGING CONTACTS AND PERSONAL CONTACT INFORMATION

CREATE AND MODIFY CONTACTS

Create a Contact

Menu Method

☐ Click **File** on the menu bar, point to **New**, then click **Contact**
☐ In the Untitled - Contact window, click the **Maximize button**, then enter the name, address, phone number, e-mail address, IM address, and other appropriate information for the person
☐ Click the **Save & Close button** 🖫 in the Actions group on the Contact tab

Button Method

☐ Click the **New list arrow** on the Standard toolbar, then click **Contact**
☐ Follow the steps in bullets 2–3 in the Create a Contact Menu Method above

Shortcut Method

☐ Press **[Ctrl][Shift][C]**
☐ Follow the steps in bullets 2–3 in the Create a Contact Menu Method above

Create a Contact Using Another Contact

Ribbon Method

☐ In the Contacts window, open the contact you want to use as a basis for a new contact
☐ Click the **Save & New list arrow** in the Actions group on the Contact tab, then click **New Contact from Same Company**
☐ Make the appropriate modifications to the new contact, then click the **Save & Close button** 🖫 in the Actions group on the Contact tab

Create a Contact from a Message

Menu Method

☐ Open the message that contains the contact you want to add
☐ Right-click the e-mail address or name of the contact you want to add, then click **Add to Outlook Contacts**
☐ Make any modifications in the Contact window, then click the **Save & Close button** 🖫 in the Actions group on the Contact tab

Create a Contact Using a Business Card

Ribbon Method

☐ Open the message that contains the business card
☐ Double-click the business card attachment to open it in a contact window
☐ Make the appropriate modifications to the new contact, then click the **Save & Close button** 🖫 in the Actions group on the Contact tab

Outlook

Modify a Contact

Ribbon Method

☐ In the Contacts window, double-click the contact you want to edit
☐ In the Contacts window, click the **Maximize button**, make the appropriate modifications, then click the **Save & Close button** 🖫 in the Actions group on the Contact tab

Attach an Item to a Contact

Ribbon Method

☐ Open the contact to which you want to add an item
☐ Click the **Insert tab**, then in the Include group, click the appropriate button to include a file, e-mail, 🖫 nature, or business card
☐ Click the **Contact tab**, then click the **Save & Close button** 🖫 in the Actions group on the Contact tab

Modify an Electronic Business Card

Ribbon Method

☐ Open the contact whose business card you want to edit
☐ Click the **Business Card button** in the Options group on the Contact tab
☐ In the Edit Business Card dialog box, add and delete fields, format the card, and make other appropriate modifications, then click **OK**
☐ Click the **Save & Close button** 🖫 in the Actions group on the Contact tab

Send an Electronic Business Card in an E-mail

Menu Method

☐ In the Contacts window, click the contact whose business card you want to forward
☐ Click **Actions** on the menu bar, then click **Send as Business Card**

Add a Signature Using a Business Card

Menu Method

☐ Click **Tools** on the menu bar, then click **Options**
☐ In the Options dialog box, click the **Mail Format tab**
☐ Under Signatures, click **Signatures**
☐ In the Signatures and Stationery dialog box, click **New**
☐ Click the **Business Card button**
☐ In the Insert Business Card dialog box, select the business card, then click **OK**
☐ In the Signatures and Stationery dialog box, click **OK**
☐ Click **Apply** in the Options dialog box, then click **OK**

Outlook

CREATE AND MODIFY DISTRIBUTION LISTS

Create a Distribution List

Menu Method
☐ Click **File** on the menu bar, point to **New**, then click **Distribution List**
☐ In the Untitled - Distribution List dialog box, type the name of the group in the Name text box, then click **Select Members**
☐ In the Select Members dialog box, click a name to select it, then click **Members** to add the contact to the group
☐ Repeat for each member, then click **OK**
☐ Click the **Save & Close button** 📓 in the Actions group on the Distribution List tab

Modify a Distribution List

Button Method
☐ In the Contacts window, double-click the distribution list you want to modify
☐ To add a new member, click the **Add New button** 📇 in the Members group on the Show tab, enter the contact information in the Add New Member dialog box, then click **OK**
☐ To delete a member, click the name in the member list, then on the Distribution tab, in the Actions group, click the **Delete button** ✕
☐ To edit a member's information, double-click the contact, make the modifications in the Contact window, then click the **Save & Close button** 📓 in the Actions group on the Distribution List tab
☐ Make any other appropriate changes to the group, then click 📓

Create Another Address Book

Menu Method
☐ Click **Tools** on the menu bar, then click **Account Settings**
☐ In the Account Settings dialog box, click the **Address Books tab**, then click the **New button**
☐ Use the Add New E-mail Accounts wizard to choose the appropriate options, then click **Finish**
☐ Close and restart Outlook in order to access your new address book

Import Addresses from a File

Menu Method
☐ Click **File** on the menu bar, then click **Import and Export**
☐ Follow the steps in the Import and Export wizard to select the data file and destination location, then click **Finish**

Outlook

OUTLOOK OBJECTIVE 5: ORGANIZING INFORMATION

ORGANIZE OFFICE OUTLOOK 2007 ITEMS BY COLOR

Customize the View

Menu Method
- ☐ Open the appropriate Outlook tool in the view you want to customize
- ☐ Click **View** on the menu bar, point to **Current View**, then click **Customize Current View**
- ☐ In the Customize View dialog box, click the appropriate button using Table OL-8 as a reference, then click **OK**
- ☐ Click **OK** in the Customize View dialog box

Table OL-8 Customize View Dialog Box Options

Click this button...	To open this dialog box...	To perform these tasks
Fields	Show Fields	Select fields to add, create a new field, or choose the order of the displayed fields
Group By	Group By	Select the order by which to group items, and whether to group in ascending or descending order
Sort	Sort	Select the items by which to sort, and whether to sort in ascending or descending order
Filter	Filter	Set filter criteria by searching for a certain word or words, specifying a sender, time, or importance level, specifying whether there is an attachment, specifying message size, or by setting advanced options
Other	Other Settings	Select fonts and size for the columns, and font settings for the row headers
Automatic Formatting	Automatic Formatting	Select rules (guidelines) and assign properties for formatting the view
Format Columns	Format Columns	Choose available fields, change column width, and specify alignment.

Organize Messages, Tasks, or Notes Using Categories

Menu Method
- ☐ In the appropriate folder, select the message(s), task(s), or note(s) to categorize
- ☐ Click **Edit** on the menu bar or right-click the selected message(s), point to **Categories**, then click the appropriate category

Organize Contacts Using Categories

Menu Method

☐ In the Contacts window, select the contact(s)
☐ Click **Tools** on the menu bar, then click **Organize**
☐ In the Ways to Organize Contacts pane, click **Using Categories**, if necessary
☐ Click the **Add contacts selected below to list arrow**, click the appropriate category, then click **Add**
☐ Click the Ways to Organize Contacts pane **Close button**

Button Method

☐ In the Contacts window, open the contact you want to categorize
☐ Click the **Categories button** 🖻 in the Options group on the Contact tab
☐ Click the appropriate category from the list, then click **OK**

Use Categories to Manage Calendar Items

Ribbon Method

☐ In the Calendar window, open the appointment you want to categorize
☐ Click the **Categories button** 🖻 in the Options group on the Appointment tab
☐ Click the appropriate category from the list, then click **OK**

Menu Method

☐ In the Calendar window, select the appropriate appointment(s)
☐ Click **Edit** on the menu bar or right-click the selected message(s), point to **Categories**, then click the appropriate category

Apply Automatic Formatting to Calendar Items

Menu Method

☐ In the Calendar window, click **Edit** on the menu bar, then click **Automatic Formatting**
☐ In the Automatic Formatting dialog box, click **Add**
☐ Type the condition name in the Name text box
☐ Click **Condition**, specify the conditions in the Filter dialog box using Table OL-9 as a reference, then click **OK**
☐ Click **OK** in the Automatic Formatting dialog box, then click **OK** in the Customize View dialog box

Table OL-9 Filter Dialog Box Tabs

Tab	Options
Appointments and Meetings	Set filter options by searching for a certain word or words in a particular field, or by specifying a sender or time
More Choices	Set additional filter options by specifying category or importance, whether there is an attachment, or message size
Advanced	Define and add new advanced filter criteria

Outlook

Use a Custom Color

Ribbon Method

☐ In the Calendar window, open the appointment you want to categorize
☐ Click the **Categories button** 🔲, in the Options group on the Appointments tab, then click **All Categories**
☐ In the Color Categories dialog box, click **New**
☐ In the Add New Category dialog box, choose a color, name, and keyboard shortcut for the new category, then click **OK**
☐ Click **OK** in the Color Categories dialog box

Menu Method

☐ In the Calendar window, select the appropriate appointment(s)
☐ Click **Edit** on the menu bar or right-click the selected message(s), point to **Categories**, then click the appropriate category

Track Activities for a Contact

Button Method

☐ In the Contacts window, open the contact
☐ Click the **Activities button** in the Show group on the Contact tab
☐ Click the **Show list arrow**, then click the appropriate item

Sort Items

Menu Method

☐ Open the appropriate Outlook tool in the view you want to sort
☐ Click **View** on the menu bar, point to **Current View**, then click **Customize Current View**
☐ In the Customize View dialog box, click **Sort**
☐ In the Sort dialog box, specify the appropriate sorting options, then click **OK**
☐ In the Customize View dialog box, click **OK**

CREATE AND MANAGE OFFICE OUTLOOK 2007 DATA FILES

Save a Message as a File

Menu Method

☐ In the Inbox folder, click the message you want to save as a file, or open the message you want to save as a file, then maximize the message window
☐ Click **File** on the menu bar, then click **Save As**
☐ In the Save As dialog box, navigate to the appropriate drive and folder, then type a name for the file in the File name text box
☐ Click the **Save as type list arrow**, click the appropriate file format using Table OL-10 as a reference, then click **Save**

Outlook

Table OL-10 Message File Formats

File format	Message can be opened in	Description	File extension
Text Only	Any text editor	Saves the text of a message to be opened and edited in a word processing program, but does not save all formatting	.txt
Outlook Template	Microsoft Outlook	Can be used to create other messages	.oft
Outlook Message Format	Microsoft Outlook	Saves the message intact	.msg
Outlook Message Format– Unicode	Microsoft Outlook	Saves the message in a format that supports multilingual data	.msg
HTML	Any browser	Can be displayed on the Web	.htm, .html
MHT	Any browser	Saves a message with multiple links or pages as one file with its additional resources intact	.mht

Create a Personal Folders File

Menu Method

☐ Click **File** on the menu bar, point to **New**, then click **Outlook Data File**
☐ In the New Outlook Data File dialog box, click the storage type, then click **OK**
☐ In the Create or Open Outlook Data File dialog box, navigate to the drive and folder where you want to store the file, type a name in the File name text box, then click **OK**

Work with Office Outlook 2007 Data Files

☐ Click **Tools** on the menu bar, then click **Options**
☐ In the Options dialog box, click the **Mail Setup tab**, if necessary, then click **Data Files**
☐ In the Account Settings dialog box, change the settings, remove or add an account, set the default, or choose other options, then click **Close**
☐ Click **OK** in the Options dialog box

Outlook

ORGANIZE MAIL FOLDERS

Create a Mail Folder

Menu Method

☐ Click **File** on the menu bar, point to **New**, then click **Folder**
☐ In the Create New Folder dialog box, type the folder name in the Name text box, specify the contents of the folder, choose a folder location, then click **OK**

Button Method

☐ Click the **New list arrow** on the Standard toolbar, then click **Folder**
☐ In the Create New Folder dialog box, type the folder name in the Name text box, specify the contents of the folder, choose a folder location, then click **OK**

Shortcut Method

☐ Press **[Ctrl][Shift][E]**
☐ In the Create New Folder dialog box, type the folder name in the Name text box, specify the contents of the folder, choose a folder location, then click **OK**

Move a Mail Folder

Mouse Method

☐ In the Inbox folder, drag the folder to the appropriate location in the Folder List pane using 🖑

Move Mail Between Folders

Menu Method

☐ In the Inbox folder, click the appropriate message(s)
☐ Click **Edit** on the menu bar, then click **Move to Folder**, or right-click the message you want to move, then click **Move to Folder**
☐ In the Move Items dialog box, click the appropriate folder, then click **OK**

Button Method

☐ In the Inbox folder, click the message(s) you want to move
☐ Click the **Move to Folder button** 🔲 on the Standard toolbar
☐ Click the appropriate folder on the menu, or click **Move to Folder**, then in the Move Items dialog box, click the appropriate folder, then click **OK**

Shortcut Method

☐ In the Inbox folder, click the appropriate message(s)
☐ Press **[Ctrl][Shift][V]**
☐ In the Move Items dialog box, click the appropriate folder, then click **OK**

Mouse Method

☐ In the Inbox folder, drag the message to the appropriate folder in the Folder List pane using 🖑

Archive Messages

Menu Method

- ☐ In the Inbox folder, click **File** on the menu bar, then click **Archive**
- ☐ In the Archive dialog box, click the **Archive this folder and all subfolders option button**, then click the appropriate folder in the folders list
- ☐ Click any other appropriate options, then click **OK**

Save Messages to a Specific Location

Menu Method

- ☐ Click **Tools** on the menu bar, then click **Options**
- ☐ In the Options dialog box, click the **Preferences tab**, then click **E-mail Options**
- ☐ In the E-mail Options dialog box, click the **Save copies of messages in Sent Items folder check box** to select it, if necessary, then click **Advanced E-mail Options**
- ☐ In the Advanced E-mail Options dialog box, make the appropriate selections or leave the defaults, then click **OK**
- ☐ Click **OK** in the E-mail Options dialog box, then click **OK** in the Options dialog box

Manually Empty the Deleted Mail Folder

Menu Method

- ☐ Click **Tools** on the menu bar or right-click the **Deleted Items folder** in the Mail Folders pane, then click **Empty "Deleted Items" Folder**

Shortcut Method

- ☐ Open the **Deleted Items folder**
- ☐ Select the item(s) to permanently delete, or press **[Ctrl][A]** to select all items
- ☐ Press **[Delete]**, then click **Yes** in the alert box

Automatically Empty the Deleted Mail Folder

- ☐ Click **Tools** on the menu bar, then click **Options**
- ☐ In the Options dialog box, click the **Other tab**
- ☐ Click the **Empty the Deleted Items folder upon exiting check box** to select it

  OR

- ☐ Click **Advanced Options**
- ☐ In the Advanced Options dialog box, click the **Warn before permanently deleting items check box**, then click **OK**
- ☐ Click **OK** in the Options dialog box

Delete a Folder and Its Contents

Menu Method

- ☐ In the Inbox folder, click the appropriate folder(s)
- ☐ Click **Edit** on the menu bar, then click **Delete**
- ☐ Click **Yes** in the Message box

Outlook

OR

☐ In the Inbox folder, right-click the appropriate folder(s), then click **Delete folder** from the shortcut menu

Button Method

☐ In the Inbox folder, click the appropriate folder(s)
☐ Click the **Delete button** ☒ on the Standard toolbar
☐ Click **Yes** in the Message box

Shortcut Method

☐ In the Inbox folder, click the appropriate folder(s)
☐ Press **[Ctrl][D]** or **[Delete]**
☐ Click **Yes** in the Message box

SET JUNK E-MAIL SETTINGS

Add Users to the Safe or Blocked Senders Lists

Menu Method

☐ In the Inbox, click the message that contains the user whose status you want to change
☐ Click **Actions** on the menu bar, point to **Junk E-mail**, then click the option using Table OL-11 as a reference

OR

☐ In the Inbox, click the message that contains the user whose status you want to change
☐ Click **Actions** on the menu bar, point to **Junk E-mail**, then click the **Junk E-mail Options**
☐ In the Junk E-mail Options dialog box, make the appropriate selections, then click **OK**

Ribbon Method

☐ Open the message from the sender whose status you want to change
☐ Using Table OL-11 as a reference, click the appropriate button in the Junk E-mail group on the Message tab

OR

☐ Click the **dialog box launcher** in the Junk E-mail group on the Message tab
☐ In the Junk E-mail Options dialog box, make the appropriate selections, then click **OK**

Outlook

Table OL-11 Junk E-mail Options

Use this option...	To do this...
Add Sender to Blocked Senders List	Automatically move messages from this sender to the Junk E-mail folder
Add Sender to Safe Senders List	Automatically move messages from this sender to the Inbox
Add Sender's domain (@*example*.com) to Safe Senders List	Automatically move messages from all senders who have the same domain to the Inbox
Add Recipient to Safe Recipients List	Used to ensure that messages from distribution groups you belong to go to your Inbox instead of the Junk E-mail folder

Empty the Junk E-mail Folder

☐ Right-click the **Junk E-mail folder** in the Mail Folders list
☐ Click **Empty Junk E-mail** from the shortcut menu

Move Items Out of the Junk E-mail Folder

Toolbar Method

☐ Open the **Junk E-mail folder** from the Mail Folders list
☐ Click the message you want to move
☐ Click the **Not Junk button** on the Standard toolbar
☐ In the Mark as Not Junk dialog box, click **OK**

Shortcut Method

☐ Open the **Junk E-mail folder** from the Mail Folders list
☐ Click the message you want to move
☐ Press **[Ctrl][Shift][J]**
☐ In the Mark as Not Junk dialog box, click **OK**

LOCATE OFFICE OUTLOOK 2007 ITEMS BY THE SEARCH FEATURE

Use Instant Search

Menu Method

☐ Click **Tools** on the menu bar, point to **Instant Search**, then click **Instant Search**
☐ On the Find bar, type appropriate search words in the Look for text box, click the **Show Instant Search Pane list arrow**, then click the appropriate option
☐ To remove the search, click the **Clear Search button** ⊠ on the Find bar

Outlook

Shortcut Method
□ Press **[Ctrl][E]**
□ On the Find bar, type appropriate search words in the Look for text box, click the **Show Instant Search Pane list arrow**, then click the appropriate option
□ To remove the search, click the **Clear Search button** ☒ on the Find bar

Search Message Folders in a Single Search

Menu Method
□ In the Inbox folder, click **File** on the menu bar, point to **New**, then click **Search Folder**
□ In the New Search Folder dialog box, choose the appropriate search folder, specify criteria such as person, task, size, status, or category, then click **OK**

Use a Custom Search Folder

Menu Method
□ In the Inbox folder, click **File** on the menu bar, point to **New**, then click **Search Folder**
□ In the New Search Folder dialog box, scroll to and click **Create a custom Search Folder**, then click **Choose**
□ In the Custom Search Folder dialog box, specify the criteria and folder(s), then click **OK**
□ Click **OK** in the New Search Folder dialog box

Button Method
□ In the Inbox folder, press **[Ctrl][Shift][P]**
□ Follow the steps in bullets 2–4 in the Use a Custom Search Folder Menu Method above

CREATE, MODIFY, AND REMOVE RULES TO MANAGE E-MAIL MESSAGES

Create a Rule for Moving Messages
□ In the Inbox folder, click **Tools** on the menu bar, then click **Rules**
□ In the Rules and Alerts dialog box, click the appropriate options to add, edit, forward, or delete a rule, then click **OK**

CUSTOMIZE YOUR OFFICE OUTLOOK 2007 EXPERIENCE

Change the Display of the To-Do Bar
□ To minimize the To-Do Bar, click the **Minimize the To-Do Bar button** ⟩⟩ on the To-Do Bar
□ To close the To-Do Bar, click the **Close To-Do Bar button** ☒ on the To-Do Bar
□ To maximize the To-Do Bar, click **Normal**

Outlook

Modify the To-Do Bar

☐ Click **View** on the menu bar, point to **To-Do Bar**, then click **Options**
☐ In the To-Do Bar Options dialog box, choose the appropriate options, then click **OK**

Change the Format of an E-mail Message

☐ Open a new e-mail message
☐ Click the **Options tab**, then in the Format group, click **HTML**, **Rich Text**, or **Plain Text**

Change the Default Format for All E-mail Messages

Menu Method

☐ Click **Tools** on the menu bar, then click **Options**
☐ In the Options dialog box, click the **Mail Format tab**
☐ In the Message format section, select the default message format
☐ In the Stationery and Fonts sections, click the **Stationery and Fonts button**
☐ In the Signatures and Stationery dialog box, select the default message fonts, then click **OK**
☐ Click **OK** in the Options dialog box

Make Outlook 2007 Available over the Web

Note: You must be using Microsoft Exchange Server in order to access this feature.

☐ Click **Tools** on the menu bar, then click **Account Settings**
☐ In the Account Settings dialog box, click the Exchange account, then click the **Change button**
☐ In the Exchange dialog box, click **More Settings**
☐ In the Exchange dialog box, click the **Connection tab**, then click the **Connect to Microsoft Exchange using HTTP check box** to select it
☐ Specify the proxy settings, URL, and other options, then click **OK**

Add and Delete Fields

Menu Method

☐ Open the appropriate Outlook tool in the view you want to customize
☐ Click **View** on the menu bar, point to **Current View**, then click **Customize Current View**
☐ In the Customize View dialog box, click **Fields**
☐ To add a field, click the field you want to add in the Available fields list, then click **Add**
☐ To delete a field, click the field you want to delete in the Show these fields in this order list, then click **Remove**
☐ Click **OK** in the Show Fields dialog box, then click **OK** in the Customize View dialog box

Outlook

INDEX